Joss Whedon's Big Damn Movie

Joss Whedon's Big Damn Movie

Essays on Serenity

Edited by FREDERICK BLICHERT

WORLDS OF WHEDON
Series Editor Sherry Ginn

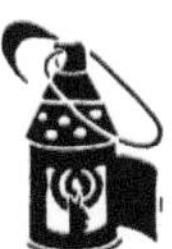

McFarland & Company, Inc., Publishers
Jefferson, North Carolina

Library of Congress Cataloguing-in-Publication Data

Names: Blichert, Frederick editor.
Title: Joss Whedon's big damn movie : essays on Serenity /
    edited by Frederick Blichert.
Description: Jefferson, North Carolina : McFarland & Company, Inc.,
    Publishers, 2018. | Series: Worlds of Whedon | Includes bibliographical
    references and index.
Identifiers: LCCN 2018001713 | ISBN 9781476671994
    (softcover : acid free paper) ∞
Subjects: LCSH: Serenity (Motion picture)
Classification: LCC PN1997.2.S465 J67 2018 | DDC 791.43/72—dc23
LC record available at https://lccn.loc.gov/2018001713

British Library cataloguing data are available

ISBN (print) 978-1-4766-7199-4
ISBN (ebook) 978-1-4766-3269-8

Front cover: Summer Glau as River Tam in the 2005 film *Serenity*
(Universal Pictures/Photofest)

Printed in the United States of America

McFarland & Company, Inc., Publishers
    Box 611, Jefferson, North Carolina 28640
        www.mcfarlandpub.com

Table of Contents

Introduction
Spotlight on Serenity

Frederick Blichert

I found myself in the very unenviable position of
having to reintroduce all of the characters, to be true
to everything that had happened before without repeating
it or contradicting it, and making it palatable to an
audience who has never seen the show.
—Joss Whedon [2005: 18]

Serenity was never going to be wholly new. It is not a standalone film, and it does not claim to be. Joss Whedon wrote and directed the feature film as a narrative conclusion to his FOX series *Firefly*, canceled mid-way though its first and only season. The film thus functions as a sequel or as a cinematic series finale—or both. It rather forcefully provides closure, where the series failed to wrap up much of anything, having been cut short quite abruptly. In fact, *Serenity* is largely composed of recycled content originally conceived for later episodes of *Firefly*. The film's plot "was supposed to take two years to develop and now takes a little under two hours" says Whedon (2005: 16).

Nevertheless, *Serenity* is hardly just more of the same. As Whedon has made clear, the series required a great many adjustments if it was going to succeed as a film. It had to be consistent with *Firefly* to keep existing fans onboard, but it also had to be accessible to new audiences. On some level, television has to do something similar from week to week—though perhaps less so with the decline of the traditional broadcasting model and the rise of binge-friendly platforms like Netflix. *Firefly* could always be appreciated by new viewers who happened upon it, with built-in repetition as well as recaps before every episode. But Whedon describes something else. A brief recap can bring new viewers up to date, but this cinematic outing was not about to begin with "previously on *Firefly*" just for the sake of narrative consistency or overall clarity. New tools had to be employed to achieve this balance of continuity and unity. The backstory is thus retold without any literal repetition of previously screened content. The characters are reintroduced without boring the fans. The plot continues without leaving anyone behind.

The format matters too. Whedon knew all too well that making the leap to the big screen would come with its own new set of opportunities and limitations. As his directorial feature debut, *Serenity* was a big risk and could have easily backfired, could have easily been seen as an ill-advised attempt to simply shift from one medium to another. Even if treated as an extended episode of *Firefly*, *Serenity* stands out as a particularly cinematic vision and a peculiarly repetitive and fast-paced outing for Whedon.

So while *Serenity* is a final chapter to *Firefly*, it is also something other than *Firefly*, and we must treat it as such. That is the aim of this book: to separate *Serenity* from *Firefly* and evaluate it on its own terms, as a single film. This is, no doubt, impossible to do without acknowledging *Firefly*, without situating *Serenity* in relation to *Firefly*. Rather than divorce the film from the series, the essays in this collection seek to explore the features of *Serenity* that mark it as something other than a straightforward continuation, whether by evaluating it separately, focusing on the film's own unique features, or confronting the disjunctions between the two texts head-on.

"They tried to kill us"

Firefly has a fairly straightforward premise, though its themes reflect a thoughtful engagement with politics and history and are often invitingly enigmatic. Projecting Civil War politics into space, the series follows Malcolm "Mal" Reynolds (Nathan Fillion), who fought against the unification of planets under the Alliance, a central government born out of a merger between China and the United States of America. Mal is joined by his crew, a rag-tag group of wanderers, as they eke out a living doing various odd jobs—some less legal than others. Together, they drift along through the 'verse aboard the Firefly-class ship Serenity, named after the final battle of the Unification War at Serenity Valley. Unlike most science fiction though, *Firefly* takes the concept of a "final frontier" to an extreme level, with its characters herding cattle, slinging pistols, and speaking like old timey lawmen in the West. Mal is a space cowboy in the most literal sense imaginable.

The major narrative throughline of the series concerns the Tam siblings: River (Summer Glau) and Simon (Sean Maher). In *Firefly*'s pilot, Simon comes aboard Serenity as a passenger, but the crew soon discovers that his mysterious cargo, a large crate, actually contains River, kept in stasis after being rescued from an Alliance facility where she was held and subjected to invasive experiments. As Mal and the crew continue to evade the Alliance and go about their regular business, they also take on the Tams as crew and help them unravel the mysteries of River's imprisonment and newfound psychic abilities.

Firefly was a fairly natural progression from Whedon's earlier television success with *Buffy the Vampire Slayer* (1997–2003), another self-reflexive series with a penchant for witty dialogue and genre bending. *Firefly*, like *Buffy*, had plenty to say about the real world through fanciful metaphors and analogies—as Jane Espenson, a writer for both series, puts it, "Joss is never about the stuff, but about the stuff behind the stuff" (2004: 1). *Firefly* certainly used its Old West/space setting to comment on all kinds of contemporary issues, all kinds of "stuff," from post-colonialism, to corporate and state control, to the ethics of sex work, to bigotry and intolerance, and more.

As has been well-documented and loudly opined, *Firefly* was canceled after only 11 episodes had aired, with 3 final episodes airing months later in the summer of 2003. FOX saw the series as a failure, one of many that had occupied the 8 p.m. Friday night time slot once reserved for *The X-Files* (1993–2002). *Firefly*, like many of its predecessors, failed to recapture the ratings magic of the supernatural police drama. Many have criticized FOX for its failure to properly support Whedon's series. For one, the episodes did not air in their intended order, with the exposition-heavy two-part pilot actually being broadcast *after* cancellation. Episodes were also periodically rescheduled to make room for the Major League Baseball postseason, also broadcast on FOX at the time (DeCandido 2004: 56).

Ginjer Buchanan argues that the series itself was difficult to market for FOX, as it deviated from many established genre conventions, and did itself no favors by so heavily employing Western tropes in an industry that had long ago declared the Western dead (2004: 53). FOX rather dubiously elected to treat *Firefly* as a wacky genre-bender, leaning on the series' comedic elements to attract audiences that likely did not know what they were in for (Pascale 2014: 215).

Even before its cancellation, fans were worried about low ratings and raised money to take out a full-page ad in *Variety*, seeking new viewers that might keep the series solvent. The ad was indeed a direct appeal to FOX to give *Firefly* another chance: "You Keep Flying, We'll Keep Watching," read the headline (Pascale 2014: 218). The ad failed to bring enough new viewers onboard, and fans were predictably unhappy to lose the series. Banding together, they organized letter-writing campaigns and petitions in the hopes of attracting other networks or film studios who might carry the *Firefly* torch, and they used "guerrilla marketing" to advertise the as-yet unproduced, unannounced, and unlikely continuation of their dreams (Hadlock et al. 2006).

It is not entirely clear how much these measures affected the studio. The popular narrative is one in which Universal could not help but see the project as a slam-dunk with a pre-sold fanbase, but Whedon has certainly troubled this notion, suggesting that the studio was "definitely going ahead" of its own accord, and that DVD sales of *Firefly* "definitely helped them just be comfortable with the decisions they were making," but that "they really had been supporting us for quite some time already" (Whedon, 2005: 17).

Regardless of how much of an impact fan activism had on *Serenity*'s eventual production, Whedon has often praised his fans and their devotion to the 'verse. In a recorded message to an early *Serenity* audience, his language is that of a shared and hard-won battle. "They tried to kill us," he says. "They did kill us. And here we are. We've done the impossible, and that makes us mighty" (qtd. in Abbott 2010: 227). The bond that *Firefly* fans had to *Serenity* ran deep, and its release was heralded as a major victory that bridged the gap between producer and consumer.

Serenity opens with a series of refreshers. We learn about the depletion of Earth's resources and the establishment of settlements, eventually unified after the war. We also learn that River was a prisoner of the Alliance, and we see her rescue. For the first time, we see her in custody and get to witness Simon's infiltration of the Alliance facility to rescue her. The scene both repeats information revealed in *Firefly* and presents us with perhaps the most glaring discontinuity between series and film: in *Firefly*'s pilot "Serenity" (20 December 2002), Simon describes paying members of an underground movement to rescue River for him, but here we see him getting his own hands dirty. While the film clearly concludes the series, it presents us with gaps like this that certainly invite a closer look at the relationship between these texts.

The film zeroes in on River, with the crew discovering that she has been conditioned to be a living weapon, a psychic with a subliminal trigger. The major revelation, though, is that the Alliance's reason for hunting her down has more to do with control of information, as she has learned their darkest secret: while attempting to pacify the population of the planet Miranda, the Alliance killed the bulk of its inhabitants, turning the rest into the enraged, cannibalistic Reavers first mentioned in *Firefly*. The series' boogeymen are here made flesh, represented as mindless zombies, driven by the pure rage that the Alliance had attempted to weed out of them. Mal and the crew's mission then becomes one of dissemination, of informing the entire 'verse of the Alliance's crime, both in the name of justice and to free the Tams from further pursuit.

On the level of form and style *Serenity* does break the mold established by *Firefly*. Director of photography Jack Green was tasked with making the whole thing look good in the widescreen 2.35:1 anamorphic format prescribed by Universal, which meant, among other things, foregoing some of the hand-held, documentary aesthetic of *Firefly*, except in a few select scenes (Goldman

2005: 12). Widescreen and the promise of a theatrical release also allow for far more wide shots and long takes than on the small screen. The interior of the ship *Serenity* for example, is first glimpsed in its entirety in one single, extended shot, lasting almost four-and-a-half minutes early on. Here, the camera follows Mal as he walks through every room, also reintroducing us to the central characters onboard. Or later a barroom brawl is shot with sparse editing and in wide shots allowing a clear view of the action and impressive stunts. The looser schedule and higher budget also allowed for more ambitious visual effects and a digital intermediary for smoother post production (10).

J.P. Telotte adds that the film's content marked a distinctly cinematic shift away from *Firefly*'s televised origins. He suggests that the film is "pointedly mindful of its medium, after a fashion that we do not typically see in most television series, but that has always marked some of the best cinematic [science fiction]" (2008: 68). He identifies the self-reflexive nature of *Serenity*'s engagement with screens and image-making and distribution processes as at least part of the reason for *Serenity*'s success as a cinematization of an earlier television series (68–9). Of course, Telotte also recognizes the rarity of such a success, of reviving a television series via cinema: "Few have managed it successfully, mainly because by the time a series has ended its broadcast life, audience interest has often also run its course" (79). But *Firefly*'s audience has certainly never suffered from a lack of interest.

'Verse Studies

A great deal of *Firefly*/*Serenity* scholarship already exists, including essay collections like *Investigating* Firefly *and* Serenity (I.B. Taurus), and Firefly *Revisited* (Rowman & Littlefield), as well as a special issue of the Whedon studies journal *Slayage* devoted entirely to the 'verse. Whedon's work more generally is prone to receiving much scholarly attention, particularly through *Slayage* and the efforts of the Whedon Studies Association.

A great deal of this work focuses on *Firefly* primarily or exclusively, or else treats *Serenity* as an extension of the show. This methodology is entirely valid and has generated some great and insightful work. Indeed, *Serenity* does build on and off of *Firefly*, and the intersections between these texts represent the fundamental characteristics of *Firefly* and *Serenity* as parts of a whole. This book thus provides a unique platform for scholarship that narrows down the focus to the film, exploring the ways in which *Serenity* departs from its televised predecessor.

While this book seeks to stand out in this regard, it would be unfair to state that no one has considered *Serenity* on its own terms. Many have, and their work, much of it excellent, can be found scattered in different collections, in the pages of *Slayage*, and in various other journals. Nevertheless, relatively few publications have focused specifically on *Serenity*, with *Firefly* often standing at the forefront of critical and scholarly consideration. The essays collected here all seek to shed light on the film and further have been selected to compliment one another and offer a broader engagement with *Serenity* that will hopefully prove useful and instructive to scholars and fans alike.

Big Damn Essays

London Brickley looks at *Serenity*'s Reavers as symbols of the film's own cannibalistic use of *Firefly*'s corpse to sustain itself. Brickley explores the nature of the Reavers' monstrosity while considering the adaptation as an industrial Hollywood project of narrative recycling. This narrative recycling comes up again when S. Evan Kreider makes a case for the importance of *Serenity* as a tool for the narrative completion of character and relationship arcs. He argues that *Serenity* plays a vital role in providing closure. H.S. Hobma looks at mortality in *Serenity*, and the Whedonverse more broadly, to question Western society's complex relationship with death and dying, framing the deaths of major, beloved characters in the film as significant markers of a society engaging directly with death and dying.

Aviva Dove-Viebahn compares River Tam to the ancient Greek figure Cassandra to explore the depths of the character's agency, set against and above her targeted (and historically gendered) victimization by the Alliance. In my own contribution to this collection, I explore *Serenity*'s generic identity, making the case that its engagement with Western themes expands on that of *Firefly* through its treatment of civilization. Ina Rae Hark veers away from standard generic readings of *Serenity* to consider it not only through a lens of sci-fi, Western, or horror, but rather through its many references to the history of crime films, offering new reading strategies for the film's many recognizable tropes.

Eric Benson identifies hints within *Serenity* as to the fate of "Earth-that-was," humanity's home planet, evacuated when it could no longer support life. Benson suggests that Whedon provides commentary on the state of climate change at the time of the film's release. Erin Giannini looks at the role of paratexts not only to market the film, but also as self-reflexive elements of the narrative and mise-en-scène, laying bare the complex relationships between *Serenity* and its own industrial context.

Andrew Howe uses the Alliance's crimes on Miranda to extrapolate *Serenity*'s broader engagement with power structures, both on the level of large-scale interplanetary governments and smaller communal dynamics aboard Serenity itself. Max Ferguson uses a public health lens to question *Serenity*'s depictions of mental health, most notably that of the Reavers and River Tam, humans made ill by a controlling government. Ferguson questions the dehumanization of these human subjects not only by their oppressors, but by the heroes who claim to fight for them. Joel Hawkes suggests that River, played by professional dancer Summer Glau, engages in a balletic dance in *Firefly*, and that her performance reaches it climax in *Serenity*.

Agnes B. Curry updates her essay, "'We don't say "Indian": On the Paradoxical Construction of the Reavers," originally published in *Slayage* 7.1 in 2008, in "'The Indians ride over the hill': Revisiting 'On the Paradoxical Construction of the Reavers.'" Here, Curry explores the racialized depictions of *Serenity*'s Reavers to suggest that Whedon undermines his own anti-colonial project by re-inscribing familiar stereotypes onto his sci-fi monsters. Renee St. Louis investigates the racial politics of *Serenity*, building on Curry's analysis while using the work of Toni Morrison to delve into the role of black identities in the film and particularly Mal's relationship to Shepherd Book and the Operative.

K. Brenna Wardell explores the collaboration between Whedon and his director of photography, Jack Green, and how the two established an aesthetic for *Serenity* that was distinct from that of *Firefly* while complementing and building on the feel of the overall series. Holly Randell-Moon and Arthur J. Randell zero in on *Serenity*'s use of sounds to signify narrative and tonal relations. Building on *Firefly*'s soundscapes and introducing entirely new ones, *Serenity*'s preoccupations can be read formally though its music, dialogue, and sound effects.

Works Cited

Abbott, Stacey. (2010). "'Can't Stop the Signal': The Resurrection/Regeneration of *Serenity*," in Rhonda. V. Wilcox and Tanya. R. Cochrane (eds.) *Investigating* Firefly *and* Serenity: *Science Fiction on the Frontier*. London: I.B. Tauris, 227–38.

Buchanan, Ginjer. (2004). "Who Killed *Firefly*?," in Jane Espenson (ed.) *Finding Serenity: Anti-Heroes, Lost Shepherds and Space Hookers in Joss Whedon's* Firefly. Dallas: BenBella Books, 47–53.

DeCandido, Keith R.A. (2004). "'The Train Job' Didn't Do the Job," in Jane Espenson (ed.) *Finding Serenity: Anti-Heroes, Lost Shepherds and Space Hookers in Joss Whedon's* Firefly. Dallas: BenBella Books, 55–62.

Espenson, Jane. (2004). "Introduction," in Jane Espenson (ed.) *Finding Serenity: Anti-Heroes, Lost Shepherds and Space Hookers in Joss Whedon's* Firefly. Dallas: BenBella Books, 1–3.

Goldman, Michael. (2005). "Tight Ship," in *Millimeter* 33.10: 10–20.

Hadlock, Tony, Jason Heppler, Jeremy Neish, Jared Nelson, and Brian Wiser (dir.). (2006). *Done the Impossible: The Fans' Tale of* Firefly *and* Serenity. Done the Impossible [DTI].

Pascale, Amy. (2014). *Joss Whedon: The Biography*. Chicago: Chicago Review Press.

Telotte, J.P. (2008). "*Serenity*, Cinematisation and the Perils of Adaptation," in *Science Fiction Film and Television* 1.1: 67–80.

Whedon, Joss. (2005). Serenity: *The Official Visual Companion*. London: Titan Books.

A Reaver
in the Writers' Room
The Cannibal Approach
to Box Office Fear

Lᴏɴᴅᴏɴ Bʀɪᴄᴋʟᴇʏ

"Indeed, if the other is us, then we are becoming increasingly savage in our civility, to the point where our civility is actually beginning to consume us."—Priscilla Walton [2004:34]

"I'm feeling something—I don't know what it is. Then I realized; It was fear."—Joss Whedon (2007), on listening to the final sound mixing of the Reavers in *Serenity*

The first time I saw Joss Whedon's film *Serenity* (2005) was in the theater, opening weekend, and I had not yet seen a single episode of *Firefly* (2002–03). I was attending the screening on the fervent recommendation of an acquaintance (also, at the time, a non–*Firefly* initiate) who had excitedly classified *Serenity* as a "hyper cool movie about zombies in space." This description of the hard-won film follow-up to FOX's canceled series is likely to make many diehard Whedonites cringe.[1] And yet, the statement is not necessarily wrong. *Serenity* is a lot more than a movie about space monsters, and one of its most impressive feats is the extent to which it can be very different things to very different people (examples of this can be found within this very book). But it is also, at least in part, a movie about zombie-like creatures in space. Rather than igniting any debate over the categorical genre(s) of the film, what is more compelling about this flippant but enthusiastic classification is that it illuminates a very basic truth about *Serenity* specifically, and adapted cinema more broadly—viewing the film as a pre-established viewer of the mythos, and viewing the film as a complete newcomer to the world *Serenity* inhabits, is a very different experience. On another level, the reduction of the film to its monsters suggests another much more surprising truth. For the uninitiated (those who did not arrive to *Serenity* loaded with a full-knowledge arsenal of backstory), the "space zombies," or rather the Reavers (ultraviolent cannibal killers haunting the dark outer ridges of deep space), in many ways provide the central point of story, conflict, and connection for those trying to navigate their first time through *Serenity*'s vast universe.

Placing that much narrative responsibility on the Reavers and/or deriving that much narrative purpose from their presence in the story is a tall order. Especially for such an evasive group of rampaging cannibals, who, although still a memorable monster in the television source material, only haunted the fringes of two episodes and were never actually seen during the series run. But a closer inspection of the Reavers' story (the tale presented within *Serenity*, and the journey of the Reavers' adaptation process from the small to big screen) reveals a creature that occupies a very curious place in "the 'verse" in terms of narrative function, both within the created world and within the creative industrial process of constructing the film. In the film, the Reavers occupy a central role, but in an oddly decentralized way. They are an element that, like many others, were imported into the film from the *Firefly* text. And yet out of all the adapted objects in this new space, they end up the most fundamentally transformed. As it turns out, these monsters can tell us a lot: (1) Unraveling why the Reavers can be such a big takeaway for new coming audiences provides a further understanding about the function and structure of the film itself. (2) Considering the Reavers of *Serenity* as they compare to the Reavers in the original *Firefly* source material illuminates parts of the adaptation process that went into creating a film narrative out of a televisual one. And finally, (3) Dissecting the kind of monsters that the Reavers are (and evolve into) on screen, helps us to more intricately comprehend how the reworking of the Reavers into the "big bad" of the big screen provides the film narrative with an essential element in expressing the full scope of horror and humanity in the 'verse.

The Adaptation of Worlds and Monsters

Before we delve further into the Reavers' tale, it is necessary to take a moment to first establish why *Serenity* presents such special narrative challenges for both its creators and the recipient audience, which comes down to a very different, more paratextual monster known as "adaptation." Adaptation of media forms is all about translating, reformatting, and remodeling one media form into the consumable shape of another media form. TV and film, although occasionally similar on the surface in terms of certain aesthetic crossovers, are not the same form, nor do they adhere to the same production process (see Hilliard 2011).

Firefly and *Serenity* creator Joss Whedon is well aware of the differences between the two platforms, and he suggests that the world of *Serenity* was always meant for TV. According to Whedon, the narrative concept "was designed to be a TV series, because I wanted to tell the boring stories about Han Solo smuggling when he wasn't involved with the Rebellion, I wanted to tell the stories about people who live in between, and the stories themselves that live in between greater stories.... It was a deliberately television idea" (Whedon 2005: 10). And for fourteen episodes (10 hours and 30 minutes of narrative screen time), telling the "in between stories" is exactly what *Firefly* did, complete with the slower pacing that allowed for the characters to come to know themselves and the series' audience to come to know the characters. Therefore, *Serenity*'s resurrection of the universe two years after *Firefly*'s abrupt cancellation proved a treacherous script-writing challenge. As Whedon observed on the process,

> A movie is a very different animal than TV ... they are as different as painting and pottery. It requires adjustment narratively, because you have to tell the bullet points of the story and you're not going to be able to go off on bizarre tangents. I found myself in a very unenviable position of having to re-introduce all of the characters, to be true to everything that had happened before without repeating it or contradicting it, and making it palatable to an audience who has never seen the show [2005: 18].

Or, put more succinctly, the narrative is constantly "balancing the fans who have seen the show with the people who haven't, and trying to pay respect to both" (Whedon 2005: 20).

The final script[2] succeeds at this balancing act, but in doing so ultimately becomes what is essentially two movies in one, with both answering to two very different audiences and studio demands. *Firefly*'s abrupt end left fans, cast, and crew yearning for closure, with *Serenity* stepping in to offer a bit of character-based narrative resolution. However, a theatrical release of a canceled TV series produced through Universal Studios requires the ability to watch the film as a standalone product. As a result, *Serenity* is, in one way, the continuation of a character-driven story of an already beloved ensemble crew undertaking another adventure in a long life of adventures. In this version, the specifics of the adventure are secondary, a vehicle to allow the crew a reason to continue to fly, fight, banter, and love across the screen. The second version is a hybrid genre film about politics and bioethics, in which the ensemble crew's interactions among themselves and their companions becomes the secondary plotline around which a galactic spectacle of action and horror unfolds.

The movie is also still an adaptation. Slight changes from the televisual text occur in order for the film to function on its own as well as it can.

Although the film never contradicts the series that came before it outright, details do on occasion mutate under the compressive weight of adaptation, inevitably altering some of the textual meaning of its content. Rather than simply decry these alterations as issues of continuity, there are, in these moments, valuable opportunities to observe the fingerprints of the adaptive process of recreating written worlds as they shift from one form to another— an opportunity, as we will come to learn, that is particularly strong with the adaptation of the Reavers.

Finally, interwoven with all the structural concerns of form and style, is the issue of identifying which stories floating around in the 'verse would make their way into *Serenity*. Whedon already knew, going in, who the protagonists would be, but deciding what conflict would anchor the story is a more acute challenge—one that began by scanning the skies to select a suitable box office monster.

Reaver Madness

On a quick survey of *Serenity*'s surface, monster hunting in the universe is an overwhelming prospect. After all, the opening sequences of *Serenity* are a parade of subtle horrors. The film flickers to life in a surreal garden, with children engaged in a debate about the local legends of border savages and cannibals. As the topic transitions into the benefits of government mind control, the scene is jarringly wrenched away from our gaze as the schoolteacher calmly crushes a steel needle into the forehead of a protesting child. Cut to the same young girl, River Tam (Summer Glau), older now and violently convulsing as she is strapped down and impaled by the same cranial invasion, surgically gloved men in government suits watching on. Cut again to a mysterious man introduced only as the Operative (Chiwetel Ejiofor). Hollow of human emotion and apathetic to suffering, he slices his way through bodies, coming to rest upon what turns out to be the holographic ghost of the tortured woman as he asks, "Where are you hiding, little girl?" Cut finally to a ship grinding, screeching, and rattling its way through the callous blackness of unforgiving space, the captain bursting into the engine room demanding to know if the convulsing mass of metal is going to fall out of the sky. There is, of course, a lot more exposition going on in these establishing scenes, but lurking beneath the specifics is a pulsating core of danger and primal fear. The created universe of *Serenity* is a holistically built and textured world of worlds, and all worlds are full of monsters.

It is curious then, that when asked in an interview about the Reavers' place in his created universe, Whedon singles these fringe-haunting border dwellers out as the "necessary" monsters of the tale (Arroyo 2005).[3] But what of the others? Why are the Reavers a necessary monstrosity in a realm of so many impending threats? The answer to this quandary once again has a lot to do with adaptation. As Whedon laments, reintroducing the nine protagonists that already had a history together was not the only hurdle. *Serenity's fabula*[4] is "also [already] dealing with an incredibly complex governmental and historical structure. There is the Alliance, the rule of the Alliance, the Parliament, the Rebels, the Browncoats, the Independents, a lot of central planets, [and] the outer planets," and for *Serenity* to use any of these factions as a point of conflict in a standalone film would mean a loss of moral nuances in favor of a flattened villain (Whedon 2005: 18). And above all else, Whedon did not want the film's adaptation to yield such a reduction, remarking that:

> The whole point of the show and the movie is to say that things are not simple ... to destroy the notion of absolute good and evil and black and white—what some people consider "sin," I consider human characteristics. The worst people in the world might have the best ideas and the best intentions might create the worst monsters [Whedon 2005: 18–20].

Serenity notably enforces that the majority of the perpetrators of these horrors are simply human. They are mortal, civilized men doing monstrous things for an array of personally justifiable reasons. And although the moral ambiguities interlaced throughout the film may be narratively refreshing, the effect can be lost on viewers previously unfamiliar with this world and its inhabitants, made available in just a two-hour run time. Whedon appears aware of this dilemma as well, suggesting that:

> [When] dealing with the gray area in a movie ... you still want people to get the feeling that they get from a movie that's morally black and white. You want to get that rising feeling of, "we want to fight back, we want to stand tall, we believe in these people." And to get that in a world that is so hard is very tricky [2005: 20].

The Reavers, on the other hand, ravenous, mutated, and blood-soaked, are not so tricky (or gray). Crashing into the screen as something that is "no longer man," or rather "forgot how to be," their snarling mutilated faces allow instead for a more classic sort of movie monster. The kind of familiar marker of "otherness" which, despite its uncanny affect, is narratively comforting in its stability.

For the first two acts of the film, the Reavers are the black spots on a gray canvas, their monstrous and mutilated bodies dropping into the film's narrative action almost immediately. In an early scene, the crew of Serenity is "up to some crime," and everything is going well enough until *they* show up. Evidently, the mere mention of the Reavers is enough to inspire fear. River is the first to utter their name. The young, psychically enhanced member of the crew catches a premonition of their impending arrival and collapses to the ground, barely managing to spit out the word "Reavers." This motion is mirrored with added energy and emphasis in the very next shot by Jayne (Adam Baldwin) rushing down into the vault. His is an ardent, echoing cry: "Reavers!"

Veterans of the *Firefly* mythos don't need to be told why the Reaver arrival is of dire significance. As Zoe (Gina Torres) succinctly informs us in *Firefly*'s pilot "Serenity" (20 December 2002), Reavers "will rape us to death, eat our flesh, and sew our skins into their clothing. And if we are very, very lucky, they will do it in that order." Newcomers may not have the full context, but it is not too difficult to figure out the Reavers' role on a basic, archetypal level. All of the faces onscreen know to fear them, to seal themselves in behind steel, or run. They understand that to shoot a man captured by the Reavers is an act of kindness—a sentiment established twice, first when Mal (Nathan Fillion) shoots a stranger that has fallen into the Reavers' swollen scraping hands, then again when Jayne demands of Mal that "you shoot me, if they take me."

As the scene plays out, the Reaver threat reaches a crescendo. The editing that follows is a calculated frenzy of rapid cuts in a montage of frantic violence. Reaver ships of twisted metal and bone drop off hoards of the humanoid creatures from the sky. Flashes of burnt and gashed skin appear through tilted camera angles as the monsters attack. The torso of a woman is stretched back into the open mouth of one of the Reavers, a man is ripped apart by another, while a further hoard grasps at a human corpse, only to let the body collapse to the ground when they realize it is no longer living. River, having regained her voice and composure, adds a helpful insight into the pathology of the Reavers' disappointment with the dead: "They want us alive when they eat us." Any still breathing pieces of flesh know the severity of the situation. They know what Reavers are, and, almost instinctively, the audience does too. This is a mindless sort of monster. One that cannot be reasoned with. One that will chase and shred and destroy. One that is ruled entirely by the three Cs—chaos, carnage, and cannibalism.

Narratively, this direct approach to conflict is a smart choice. With all the moving pieces of ethical ambiguity imported from the show and floating about in the 'verse, it is a helpful strategy to provide some sort of universal point of resistance, a classic symbol of definitive conflict that a new audience can latch onto. A newcomer to the 'verse may not (and likely will not) understand in just one prior establishing scene who all these people are, what they mean to each other, or if they as an audience should care about such characters, but everyone speaks the language and/or understands the semiotics of cannibals. As a result, this monster is an early access point for the uninitiated, creating a simpler current or simplified story thread of more clearly defined "predator and prey" into a *fabula* jam-packed with world building. It is a standard industry lifeline-technique when script writing to reduce the primary points of the narrative to a recognizable structure. Treating the early stages of the story as a monster-centric horror film functions as such a lifeline for Whedon. At this point in the narrative, a classic monster movie is what *Serenity* is. There is an ensemble cast, already familiar with one another, who, in the first moment of action, encounter a clearly signified monstrous threat that wants to chase them down and eat them indiscriminately.[5]

This does not imply, however, that new, uninitiated viewers are unable to handle narrative complexity or follow rapid exposition. The Reavers provide a more familiar access path into the 'verse, but those that take it still have their own cognitive work to do. As monstrosity scholar Jeffrey Cohen observes about the complex narrative function of monsters,

> The monster is born … at [a] metaphoric crossroads, as an embodiment of a certain cultural moment—of a time, a feeling, and a place. The monster's body quite literally incorporates fear, desire, anxiety, and fantasy (ataractic or incendiary), giving them life and uncanny independence. The monstrous body is pure culture. A construct and a projection, the monster exists only to be read: the monstrum is etymologically "that which reveals," "that which warns".… Like a letter on a page, the monster signifies something other than itself: it is always a displacement, always inhabits the gap between the time of upheaval that created it and the moment into which it is received, to be born again [2001: 12].

In short, the monster is a longstanding functional method of world-building through metaphor, and, upon its dissection, a monster can reveal a lot of things about the world it inhabits and the external/outer world that created it. If a film overflowing with information needs a conduit, a method of stuffing complex ideologies and metaphors into a visible filmable package, then building a monster is an excellent strategy. Once the monster is alive, it becomes the audiences' job to take it back apart. The dissection of a monster is always easier if one has seen it before and/or has something from its genus to compare its current manifestation to. The Reavers of *Serenity* are a particular and special kind of monster, with comparisons to be found within broader archetypal folklore (the boogeyman, the mindless cannibal, the zombie, etc.), while also deriving much of their cinematic identity from their former televised selves—the Reavers of *Firefly*.

Comparing what the Reaver will become in *Serenity*, to what the Reaver is in *Firefly* exposes a monster that occupies a very different space in the TV series than its silver screen companion. *Firefly* aired for 14 episodes, with the Reavers coming up (unseen) in only two: the show's original two-part pilot,[6] "Serenity," and the episode "Bushwhacked" (27 September 2002). The Reavers "appear" twice in the pilot. The first is a mention of the Reavers by name twenty-two minutes in during a conversation about a potential buyer of marked Alliance goods (one name is immediately crossed off the list on account of his "bein' dead"—the whole town burned down by Reavers). This foreign term is expounded upon 30 minutes later as the crew accidently finds itself in a Reaver ship's path. The crew reacts to their sudden proximity to the Reavers in varying shades of panic reined in by their methodically rehearsed responses to deep fear. For the few confused passengers on the ship that have only heard of these monstrous men as campfire stories, Zoe clarifies: They are real, and they will kill, rape, violate, destroy, and consume everything they touch. From a conceptual standpoint, Zoe's words (the first definitive description of Reavers) suggests that the actions of Reavers—what they do, and how they do it—are much more important to the early television narrative and its characters than what they are and where they come from. This is a stark contrast to *Serenity*, for which the Reavers' origin—the what and why—becomes the driving force of the narrative. But in the pilot, the Reavers do not perform any of their signature moves. The crew powers down, plays dead, and the threat floats on by.

There is, however, a hint of an origin tale insinuated during the Reavers' appearance in "Bushwhacked." Encountering the carcass of a ship, the crew boards to find an assemblage of mangled corpses along with a lone survivor who will later bisect his own tongue, carve up his face, and gut half the Alliance medical staff—the man's diagnosis: Reavers made him this way. Back aboard Serenity, Mal offers context to his crew in the form of a folktale. Reavers, he says, were once men who had "got out to the edge of the galaxy, to that place of nothin' and that's what they became." He echoes a similar existential sentiment again later in the same episode when speaking with an Alliance official, offering potential insight into how Reavers propagate their numbers. Men go mad when looking into the void says Mal, whether "the void" appears in the fringes of vast space, or in the chilling emptiness encountered when looking into the contagious face of one already tainted by the dark disease. The officer, however, having never seen a Reaver, doesn't believe in them nor in Mal's tales. As he tells Mal, he has seen too many men try to blame Reavers for their own crimes.

That is the full extent of the Reavers' presence in the television run. We encounter only fragments: legends and rumors, a Reaver ship seen from afar, mutilated bodies, and a survivor who copes with trauma by becoming a traumatizer. But evidence of the Reavers' existence is entirely circumstantial. The creatures themselves are never seen. They are the twenty-sixth century boogeyman, parables of destruction and devastation. And for all we know, maybe that is all these encounters amount to—men committing atrocities only to blame them on a philosophic darkness. The Reavers of *Firefly* leave us with a mysterious monster from the borderlands. The cold inaccessibility/invisibility of their forms creating shadow legends floating aimlessly in the dark reaches of imperial colonies. Alternatively, if we are inclined to believe in the Reavers, the genesis of their madness is mythically epic, but we are given no indication within the truncated TV 'verse to question it. *Firefly* as a televisual text has a bit more luxury in the form of time to explore space. The crew and its audience spend a lot of time "in the black" during the series, and it is not hard to believe that a man could go mad there.

Firefly's audience, transposed into the theatre for *Serenity,* carries these assumptions of origin with them, but the film is quick to dismiss such folklore. First, by quickly establishing that Reavers are indisputably real, and second, by providing a curious conversation of exposition between Jayne and Kaylee (Jewel Staite) once the crew is back aboard the ship:

> JAYNE: I don't get it. How's a guy get so wrong? Ain't logical. Cutting on his own
>   face, raping and murdering … these Reavers, the last ten years, they show up
>   like the boogeyman from stories. Eating people alive? Where does that get fun?
> KAYLEE: Shepherd Book said they was men who just reached the edge of space,
>   saw a vast-y nothingness and went bibbledy over it.
> JAYNE: Ah hell, I've been to the edge. Just looked like more space.

On an adaptive level, some very interesting things are happening here. Something—some *things*—have changed. Kaylee's personal translation of the madness of the void mythos is an explanation from the *Firefly* text, only these were Mal's words in "Bushwhacked," not Shepard Book's (Ron Glass). Furthermore, Mal's words were spoken in direct opposition to Book, who had indicated that Reavers are just men that have been outside of civilization too long and simply need the willingness to find their way back to heal. One could simply write this off as a continuity error, but that would be a rather wasted opportunity. There are few enough episodes of *Firefly*, a dedicated enough writing staff, and plenty of accessible comprehensive wiki sites to suggest that this is not an oversight in continuity. Something else is taking precedence over a strict adherence to the source material. It is a key moment in which we get to observe the fingerprints of adaptation smudged across the screen.

One of the primary, yet more general, things this alteration achieves is to slip in an early (re)establishment of the character of Shepard Book, his name drop an early plant for when he appears later in the film and an assurance for the established viewers that, despite Book's current absence from the ship, he is not forgotten. That this is accomplished through making Book the teller of the Reaver-tales, more specifically, in turn casts a fair bit of doubt over the authenticity of the Reavers' mysterious origins. An audience familiar with *Firefly* may take notice of the curious difference as a move that disrupts the perception of the canonical reality and/or the taken for granted truth of the 'verse carried over from the show, while those hearing this information for the first time are less likely to receive the echoed words of an unknown, off-screen character with the same level of definitive authority that Mal's central narrative position allots him in the series. Instead, Kaylee's words here in the film read a bit more like Reaver folklore, a reiteration of vernacular knowledge and a reinforcement of the role of monsters as a narrative tool used for social bonding among participants (i.e., those that share in the telling, beliefs, or traditions of the monster and its stories).

The scene is also riddled with mutations that offer carefully calculated narrative foresight. "I don't get it," says Jayne, asking the question for the audience, "how's a guy get so wrong?" Established viewers know that Jayne has heard the folktale version of their origins before. But even a newcomer might question why the man who seemed to have enough of a working knowledge of the creatures to recognize them by name and culinary preference would now ask such a question. As Jayne puts it, "it ain't logical." Unless, of course, he is providing the verbal cue to the audience that this is the question *they* should be asking. We have just met our monster and had the first narrow escape. And yet the first question we are presented with is not "how do we hide, run from, or kill the Reavers?" The question is "how did they come to be?" It is a question that is crafted into the film early, and it matters, derailing the expectations of a classic monster invasion plot structure into a subtler noir scape.[7] There is a mystery here, lurking beneath the sunlight.

This is further enforced by Kaylee's response, one that sounds even more like a slippery folktale version of the Reavers as she repeats the oral narrative that someone else told her. One perhaps Sheppard Book had himself heard from Mal. Or maybe, in the way oral folk stories go, the tale has been told by so many people in the 'verse that the tale-teller is not really the point. Although here, knowing both of these men, Mal's words, originally tinged with his more secular views on the very concept of nothingness, either become a strangely agnostic statement for Book (the preacher), or take on an even more spiritual meaning as a euphemism for men who had strayed into the wilds and "lost faith." Either way, "the reason" for the Reavers, so compelling and convincing within the *Firefly* text, rings entirely hollow in *Serenity*'s ship. Particularly cemented by Jayne's own quick dismissal, "Hell, I been to the edge. Just looked like more space."

For the most attentive viewers, there is a further piece of premonitory dialogue. The time stamp in Jayne's "last ten years" observation is quite suspicious, as the expansion into space has been a slow crawl that surely had exposed far-flying men to the insanity-inducing fringes way further back than just the past decade. There is an alternative version of this scene that teases the reason for this temporal curiosity. The moment still appears in the published official *Serenity* screenplay and is available as extra footage on *Serenity*'s DVD release. In it Kaylee attempts to change the topic to River and Simon, at which point Jayne gets in one last Reaver remark by pointing out that River "is no saner than one of them Reavers" (Whedon 2005: 78). Kaylee dismisses this statement, but for very careful viewers, the comparison creates a dark alliance between River and the Reavers, cryptically foreshadowing the Reavers' true origins. River is insane. Or rather she was driven insane by bio-scientific experiments sanctioned by the Alliance. She is also further addled by the government secrets gleaned from key members of parliament (i.e., the truth of the Reavers' origins). The dialogue hints at their intertwined stories. This is further visually captured and continuously relayed as the film presses on through the frequent use of montage (visually reflecting River's fractured mind) that splice together images of River as a child at school, the Alliance, a forbidden planet littered with the dead, and the Reavers' ravenous, biting faces, all set to a mixed loop track of the Reavers' grinding guttural sounds.

We soon find out that the embedded coding in the script is indeed a hint at the horrors to come. As the crew aboard Serenity will discover, there is a hidden planet in the 'verse named Miranda, which the Alliance ter-raformed and colonized 12 years prior to the film's events. At the time of its conception, Miranda, tucked away in the outer edges of the galaxy, recruited aspiring workers and their families with the promising horizons of a new frontier. Once dozens of cities were established and flourishing, the unified government system set about trying to improve things, striving to build a better civilization through a better version of its citizens —a bright civil new world which was never heard from again. Investigating this enigma is a per-ilous challenge as the area surrounding the planet has since been overtaken by Reavers. Up to the task, Serenity forges ahead.

Taking on the guise of a Reaver ship in order to sneak through the dark fleet of monsters that surround the planet, the crew pierces through Miranda's atmosphere to land in a glistening, anesthetized (and over-exposed) metrop-olis. It is a city plagued by the dead, a classic setting for a zombie infestation, only none of the passive and rotting corpses gently lain throughout the city seem to have it in them. The only remnant of life on the planet is a holo-graphic recording that enlightens the crew and the viewers about the atrocities that happened here. The Alliance, thinking they could make people "better" and doing so "for their own good," had been adding chemicals in the air processors "to calm the population, [and] weed out aggression." "It worked," but too well. The people just stopped caring, stopped eating, and finally just stopped living. But a small percentage of the population exposed to these experiments reacted with an opposite effect: they became hyper aggressive until aggression was all that was left, fueling an insatiable hunger for destruc-tive consumption. Unable to find sustenance among the dead, these now mindless, ravenous men took to the skies, their unconscious rebellion of vio-lent cannibalism a stark contrast to the placidly starving dead left behind on Miranda. Wash (Alan Tudyk) first realizes and vocalizes for the audience what this means: "the Reavers, they created them." With the Reavers' secret origins revealed, the film undertakes its final act as the ensemble crew risks their lives to unveil the truth to the 'verse.

As the crew races to broadcast the Reaver secret to the universe, the audience has time to ruminate on what this re-contextualized monster really means. This is also the point when considering Reavers as an example of "space zombies" begins to help us unpack the culturally informed nature of their monstrosity. Although the Reavers might evade the more recent image of the zombie as a revenant dripping with rapid decay, the zombie as a cultural monster has a much broader history where the Reaver finds its place quite comfortably. As Peter Dendle suggests, consistently throughout historical usage, "the essence of the 'zombie' [(as both a literary and legendary figure)] at the most abstract level is supplanted, stolen, or effaced consciousness"— an essence which has in turn been utilized throughout the twentieth and twenty-first centuries for a variety of metaphorical purposes (2007: 47).

Dendle further observes that the incarnations of the zombie in the early 20th century "flourished ... [within] a century whose broad intellectual trends were preoccupied with alienation. [And where] Existentialism vividly brought out problems of solitude, of the possibility of true connections between individuals, and the very nature of the self" (2007: 47–8). As the living dead ambled through the twenty-first century alongside a growth in capitalism, corporate governance, and civil morality, the zombie became the centralized hoard, moving its metaphorical potential from that which is "other" to that which is "us" (See Dendle 2007; Walton 2004). This new modernized zombie was particularly signified by its frantic cannibalism through an increased rabid and singularly focused appetite for human flesh. As Pricilla Walton argues, such figurative representations of contemporary cannibal anxieties "embodies one of the fundamental axes" of contemporary culture, as "the fear of consumption and the apprehensive willingness to consume animate the movements and maneuverings of everyday life in a surprisingly pervasive and invasive manner" (2004:7). Augmenting this surface tension of consumption, expansion, and the body as raw material, the cannibal-frenzy zombie "embodies a wanton, unfettered pursuit of immediate physical cravings, a fear of raw power ... It is the sign of an over-leisurely society lacking in broader spiritual or communal purposes, left to the impulses of its unchecked power and its desires for consumption" (Dendle 2007: 54).

Serenity's universe (an expanding, spreading mass of civilization into the never-ending black) is one of these societies, over-leisurely in its opulence, unchecked in its unification efforts to govern all of space, and steadily consuming everything within its reach. Whereas the Reavers of *Firefly* manifest as the apex of the "alienation zombie" of the twentieth century (as lone men confronted with the existential crisis of stark solitude at the edges of black, blank space), *Serenity*'s climax pulls the Reavers back into the full clutches of society as the twenty-first century's "over-civilized hoard" of mindless, cannibalizing consumption. These wild men who in *Firefly* strayed too far away from civilization and into their own solitary madness had, in reality, not run far enough. The film as adaptation maintains the mythos of its television source material while reworking the Reavers into a more contemporary cinematic creature, a combination that repositions the Reaver as both predatory, ravenous, cannibal killer *and* the institutionally harvested, preyed-upon human waste of others. As a result, the film's monster becomes a stitched-together metaphor of fractured zombie and cannibal(izing) tropes, at once the self "othered" through alienation in "savage lands" and the central collective horde reduced to the chewed-up, spit-out refuse of civilization.

This adapted hybridized monster acts as the core point of conflict for the Serenity crew. And yet the core of the monster codex is that the monster, and more specifically the zombie, is rarely (if ever) the true source of the threat. When physically present, zombies are the more immediate danger, as they will tear humans (literally) and humanity (figuratively) apart. But it is almost always the case that something "made" the zombie into what it is. Be it a bokor, sorcerer, soul crushing slave labor on a plantation, de-humanizing peddling in the depression-era, mind-numbing dreg work in an office building, a biochemical spill, weaponized contagion, alien pathogen, (or an Alliance experiment), etc., the true threat lurks behind the zombie as an insidious catalyst of degenerative agency. However, the crux of film as a visual medium means that a film narrative must visualize the conflict in some way, even if what the audience sees is merely the symptoms of an infection. The cinematic monster fulfills this demand as an embodied tool to deliver the message of danger to the screen in a more visually accessible medium. In this way, a culture's monsters are often, as their namesake insinuates, revelatory signs and warnings of less visible, but ever-present, horrors hidden within its world.

The expansive scope of *Serenity*'s vast 'verse and all its disquiet shadows are hard to glean in a condensed film frame, but burning brightly in the center of the screen, the Reaver is one such synecdoche, or monstrous byproduct and mutated mirror-image, of its textual world. And *Serenity*'s cinematic harvesting of the televisual text (a process containing its own sort of auto-cannibalization) combined with feeding off of recognizable signifiers from the greater cultural cache of archetypal zombie and cannibal monstrosity, provides the audience with all the tools it needs in order to view, consume, digest, and understand the Reaver as code. Through first isolating the Reaver as *Serenity*'s monster and then decoding the Reavers' embodied admonishments, the audience comes to learn that the Reavers themselves are simply a brash visual symptom of a much more dangerous domestic disease.

As the film's Reaver-climax reveals, the true rapidly pulsating wounds festering at the narrative's core are an ambiguous mix of hubris, optimism, and a blind belief in progress. Each of these social illnesses born and germinating from well-intending governments and scientists who continuously fail to fully consider the consequences of institutional power and the ethics of experimentation. Only unlike the signified monstrosity of the Reavers' snarling ravenous visages, the convoluted ethics of scientific advancement and the quite horrors of governed well-meaning civility is a difficult villain to construct, fight, and conquer in a two-hour run time. This is particularly further challenging when placed alongside Whedon's insistence that all men on all sides of the 'verse remain morally grey and yet his simultaneous resignation that a film "needs a villain." The Reavers step in as a filmic compromise to the dilemma. Filtering the film's conflict through the coded monstrosity of the Reavers allows the narrative a recognizable, familiar system through which to introduce larger ideologies and dormant issues, while also offering tangible figures with which the principle crew can engage in at least some semblance of a visual struggle or physical fight.

In this spirit, by the final scene, the crew wins its small victory by slaying the collection of Reavers that had pursued them through deep outer-reaching space and into the final act on the home front. A hard-won battle which yields to the crew's larger success in uploading and projecting the message—the truth of the Reavers' civil utopian origins —across the Allied planets. This moment of triumph, as the now-retired Operative informs Mal, has roused the unified planets, inspiring political uproar in the form of protests and riots. But Mal is not mollified, countering, "'Verse wakes up a spell. Won't be long 'fore she rolls right over and falls back asleep." Mal's choice in words is unsettling, evoking those who lay down to sleep forever on a forgotten planet. The callous cynicism of the idea is rather chilling, hinting that the world(s) may already be on an inexorable slouching path towards a new Miranda, mentally complacent and morally lethargic. Meanwhile—since merely discovering the disease does not immediately cure it—the Reavers are still out there, hungry and violent, living ghosts of "progress" circling around the borders.

A Not-So-Brave, Not-So-New World

Whedon has remarked that he thinks of *Serenity*'s final product as "Mal's story told through River's eyes" (2007), and yet, for an audience unfamiliar with *Firefly*'s pre-established story lines and character development (especially Mal's), the film functions more as the Reavers' story told through River's eyes. The Reavers are present in the film's first action sequence, and they return for the final fight. When they are not in the center of the action, they still haunt the film from the fringes. They are whispered about by school children, projected in quick bursts across the screen as fragments of chaos in River's fractured mind, invoked by every narrative utterance of "Miranda," headlining the news in the bar, and representing the one thing that will rattle, if only for the briefest moment, the Alliance's "meddling" efforts at civil control.

The "othered" Reavers of *Firefly*—parables of hubris, existential crisis, and the potential limits of human capacity to process empty "space"—are a wonderful monster in their own right. But as the former markers of solitary madness on the small screen cinematically reenter as an enriched hybrid of horrors condensed into an entangled mass of pulp, bone, and biochemical conspiracy, the adapted Reaver within *Serenity* transmutes into a monstrous cultural reflection masked to hide a more mundane, yet no less potent, fear tailor-made for a box office release.

In the end, the true horrors in both *Serenity*'s and the audience's worlds do not stay constrained to legend, folktales and monsters. The more dangerously concealed threats simmering beneath the monster's mask are a convoluted bureaucracy, short term memory of the public when it comes to atrocity, apathy to mindless expansion, unethical submissions to scientific progress, irresponsible applications of biotechnology, a blind faith in systems, and the dismissal of the consequences of "civilization."

And for viewers who have never themselves encountered the empty void of deep space, who instead watch *Serenity*'s tale unfold on a big, brightly lit screen of a multiplex theater while eating company popcorn and breathing processed air from commercial ducts among a collective of strangers in their ticketed seats in neatly ordered rows, the Reavers as "civil accident" become a more impactful and insidious threat. The Reaver is an old monster in new skin, and this shiny new world projected onto the screen may not be so new after all.

Serenity's universe is one that the film audience knows well, one as hauntingly familiar as the film's monstrous and cold, lit stars. And as the film follows and consumes the Reavers' theatrical tale to the bitter end, the audience is left to digest the exposed central nerves of the universe while the scrolling black screen of the credits roll. The crew aboard Serenity lives on to fly another day, but an anxious aftertaste remains, which carries with it an effectively disturbing take on horror and humanity in "the 'verse." The monster is the messenger and—through its adaptation—the Reaver's message is resoundingly clear: The "other," as it turns out, has always been "us." Be it the twenty-sixth century, or right here in the twenty-first, we do not need to venture out into "the black" to experience the existential crisis of horror and madness. True horror is central, it is civilized, and it is what we call home.

Notes

1. The "zombie" classification might not be so outrageous after all. Joss Whedon has used the classification himself, remarking on the film's DVD director's commentary that the final showdown with the Reavers is "essentially a zombie fight."

2. The adaptation process of this balancing act was so difficult that Whedon turned in an initial 190-page draft pitch entitled "The Kitchen Sink," taking another eight months to edit it down to the final screenplay (Whedon 2007).

3. Whedon adds that "the movie deals with the Reavers in a way that *Firefly* would have as time went on.... Every story needs a monster. In the stories of the old west it was the Apaches." Whedon would also claim to have removed the racial aspect of the Apache metaphor through the Reavers: "I used that example by saying that anyone who goes out into space and goes mad can become a monster" (Arroyo 2005).

4. "*Fabula*" is a term borrowed by film studies from the Russian formalist school of narratology. In essence, the *fabula* is the raw material of the story and/or all the things an audience knows about the chronology of the story and its world (through direct viewing or inference). This contrasts to the *syuzhet*, which is the organization and representation of events through selected film choices (narration, metaphor, camera angles, editing order, montage of longer temporal events, etc.).

5. Whedon himself has mentioned that, with the Reavers, he "was trying to evoke horror, and the horror movie" (2005: 25).

6. The Fox Network notoriously originally aired the series' episodes out of sequence, making "Serenity" one of the last episodes to air. This was later corrected on the *Firefly* DVD release and all streaming platforms.

7. For a more in-depth exploration of variant forms of monster movies, including the "monster invasion" plot structure, see Andrew Tudor: 1991.

Works Cited

Arroyo, Sam. (2005). "Joss Whedon—Panel at Wondercon: Full Report." Online. Available HTTP: http://www.whedon.info/Joss-Whedon-Panel-At-Wondercon.html (30 May 2017).

Cohen, Jeffery Jerome. (2001). "Monster Culture (Seven Theses)," in Brandy Blake and L. Andrew Cooper (eds.) *Monsters*. Southlake: Fountainhead Press, 11–33.

Dendle, Peter. (2007). "The Zombie as Barometer for Cultural Anxiety," in Niall Scott (ed.) *Monsters and the Monstrous: Myths and Metaphors of Enduring Evil*. New York: Rodopi, 45–60.

Hilliard, Robert. (2011). *Writing for Television, Radio, and New Media (Broadcast and Production)*. Boston: Cengage Learning.

Hutchings, Peter. (2004). *The Horror Film*. Harlow: Pearson Longman.

Kerner, Aaron Michael. (2015). *Torture Porn in the Wake of 9/11: Horror, Exploitation, and the Cinema of Sensation*. London: Rutgers University Press.

Sconce, Jeffrey. (2013). "Dead Metaphors/Undead Allegories," in Leon Hunt, Sharon Lockyer, and Milly Williamson (eds.) *Screening the Undead; Vampires and Zombies in Film and Television*. London: I.B. Tauris, 95–111.

Shapshay, Sandra. (2009). *Bioethics at the Movies*. Baltimore: Johns Hopkins University Press.

Skal, David. (2001). *The Monster Show; A Cultural History of Horror*. New York: W.W. Norton & Company.

Tudor, Andrew. (1991). *Monsters and Mad Scientists: A Cultural History of the Horror Movie*. Hoboken: Wiley-Blackwell.

Walton, Priscilla. (2004). *Our Cannibals, Ourselves*. Champaign: University of Illinois Press.

Whedon, Joss. (2012). Firefly: *A Celebration (Anniversary Edition)*. New York: Titan Books.

Whedon, Joss. (2007). *Serenity*: Director Commentary, Universal Studios Home Entertainment. DVD.

Whedon, Joss. (2005). Serenity: *The Official Visual Companion*. London: Titan Books.

Completion of Character
and Relationship in *Serenity*

S. EVAN KREIDER

The most obvious reason to make *Serenity* (Joss Whedon, 2005) was the need for a sense of completion, since the single season of *Firefly* (2002–3) left too much unanswered. Much of the discussion of this has treated *Serenity* as a means to tie up important threads in the plot (What will happen to River [Summer Glau]?) and fill in the gaps in the setting of the 'verse (Where did the Reavers come from?). However, less has been said about how *Serenity* acts as a vehicle for completion of character and relationship. Prime examples of character completion include Jayne (Adam Baldwin), who becomes a hero rather than a mere hired gun; Mal (Nathan Fillion), who finally comes to term with the kind of person he is, deciding that he does indeed believe in something after all, after years of disillusionment; and River, who finally becomes an autonomous person rather than a broken child or a dangerous weapon. Examples of relationship completion include Mal and Inara (Morena Baccarin), who initiate a romantic relationship; Zoe (Gina Torres) and Wash (Alan Tudyk), whose marriage culminates in a tragic and yet inevitable manner; Kaylee (Jewel Staite) and Simon (Sean Maher), who finally consummate their eventual romantic relationship; and River, who enters into an adult sibling relationship with Simon, and also develops a relationship with the rest of the cast as a full member of the crew. These examples demonstrate how *Serenity* served as much more than a double-length plot finale, but also as a way to show us who these characters are and what they really mean to each other.

Jayne undergoes a remarkable personal transformation through the events of *Firefly* and *Serenity*, especially in contrast to what we learn of him prior to his time on the crew. In his early life, he seemed concerned for no one but himself, and perhaps also his immediate family (especially his mother, who knits him rather cunning hats), and is portrayed as largely self-interested, sometimes to the point of amoral. As we learn in the flashback episode "Out of Gas" (25 October 2002), Jayne betrayed his former crew to join *Serenity* for the promise of a better cut, and more importantly, a nicer room. In "Jaynestown" (18 October 2002), we get more evidence of Jayne's duplicitous nature as we learn that he had no problem leaving a partner behind to face imprisonment and torture as long as he himself was able to escape (with their shared stolen cash). This is certainly not a portrait of a virtuous person.

However, there is some movement, though incomplete, toward a more virtuous character for Jayne during the run of *Firefly*. One particularly notable example takes place during the aforementioned "Jaynestown" episode. Misunderstanding Jayne's accidental dropping of the stolen money as a kind of Robin Hood activism, the workers have created a mythology around Jayne's heroism, and treat his arrival as a sort of Second Coming. Eventually, events come to a head when his old partner, released by the Magistrate to wreak mutual vengeance, attempts to kill Jayne, but is prevented from doing so by a young worker who bravely sacrifices his own life to stop the bullet. Later reflecting on that act, Jayne asks Mal why the young man would do such a thing, and "why that eats at me so." Mal explains that the people needed a hero, whether he really was one or not. This triggers some of the earliest of Jayne's development into a more heroic figure, one that makes especially good sense within the context of an Aristotelian account of virtue. For Aristotle, the good life involves, in large part, the development of a virtuous character, one for which good deeds are performed from virtuous motives rather than ulterior ones. As Grinnell notes of this scene, Jayne is finally "beginning to care about his behavior and what it reveals about him as a person to himself and to others. The kind of character excellence emphasized by Aristotle … is starting to take root" (2011: 98). The last line of the episode is Jayne's "Don't make no sense," but we can already tell that the selfless act, which he did not deserve, has made him think seriously about the virtues of heroism.

Another example of the beginnings of this sort of reflection on Jayne's part takes place in "Ariel" (15 November 2002). Jayne plans to betray Simon and River, turning them over to the Alliance for reward money, rationalizing that they are not really part of the crew anyway. After being betrayed himself by the Alliance, he helps them escape. Once again, he is the recipient of undeserved praise for heroism: Simon exclaims: "He was amazing…. We wouldn't be standing here if it weren't for him. Thank you." Mal, however, is not fooled, and later threatens quite literally to throw Jayne from *Serenity* mid-flight. At first, Jayne seems not to understand why Mal is so angry, but Mal explains: "You turn on any of my crew, you turn on me. But since that's a concept you can't seem to wrap your head around, then you got no place here." Mal seems only to relent once Jayne expresses sincere regret and shame for his behavior, asking of Mal "Don't tell 'em what I did." What this scene also shows us is the social dimension of character development.

According to Aristotle, humans are naturally social creatures, and so our social groups play an important role, for good or ill, in our development into virtuous people. Thus, the truly happy life is available "not to a person on his own, living a solitary life, but to a person living alongside his parents, children, wife, and friends and fellow-citizens generally, since a human being is by nature a social being" (Aristotle, 2000: 11). Jayne's most important social group, though it takes him a while to see it, is Serenity's crew. As noted by Kowlaski about this scene: "Because the interests of the crew have grown together so tightly, harming one means harming everyone.... Mal relents only after Jayne exhibits genuine remorse" (2011: 82). Once again, being mistaken for a hero makes Jayne realize his lack of heroism, and in this instance, experience legitimate shame for his unvirtuous behavior, especially relative to its social dimension.

However, it is only during *Serenity* that we see this transformation truly take effect. Near the beginning of the film, Jayne seems almost to have reverted to his former self. He still seems to have a fairly limited sense of personal loyalty or altruism, continuing to tell Mal that Simon and River "ain't your crew," and he is happier than anyone at the idea of them leaving the ship. He also continues to be at odds with Mal over the way he runs the ship: when Mal asks, rhetorically "You wanna run this ship?" he answers enthusiastically "Yes!" At this point, early in the film, he still seems like little more than a common criminal. He expresses some minimal sense of what it is to be on a crew, but he does not extend that concept very broadly, and he still conceives of it primarily in terms self-interest.

Jayne finally starts to become the hero that others keep mistaking him for as the film's central narrative begins to unravel. For the first time, he begins to take seriously that there are greater things to fight for than personal profit, and he is genuinely moved by Mal's call to "misbehave," his own response to which is a quote from Shepherd Book (Ron Glass): "If you can't do something smart, do something right." This is a particularly interesting quote, because it contains more than a little irony. On the surface, it seems to imply that doing what is right is the opposite of doing what is smart. That is, of course, exactly how the old Jayne used to think of things, since to him "smart" meant nothing more than "self-interested," whereas the new and improved Jayne has finally come to realize that there is more to life than the pursuit of self-interest. However, even this Jayne still hopes that doing what is right need not always conflict with self-interest: when Zoe asks, in the final battle against the Reavers, "Do you really think any of us are gonna get through this?" Jayne responds hopefully "I might!" Jayne is certainly more heroic than before, but there remains a healthy dose of self-preservation there.

River is another character who undergoes completion of character during *Serenity*, but in her case, it is less about virtue, and more about human subjectivity or personhood itself. Because of her enormous personal gifts and potential, she has been subjected to cruel experiments by the Alliance that have turned her into a lethal weapon, while leaving her psychologically unwell. Simon, during a solo undercover operation to break River out from an Alliance research facility in *Serenity*'s opening scene, asks the head researcher to explain River's state. He responds: "Well, obviously, she's unstable. The neural stripping does tend to fragment their own reality matrix.... Given the right trigger, this girl is a living weapon." The entire run of *Firefly*, and the majority of *Serenity*, provides numerous examples of both River's dangerous abilities and her psychotic tendencies.

A helpful framework for making sense of this is Immanuel Kant's notion of personhood. According to the Second Formulation of Kant's Categorical Imperative, it is our moral duty to "act in such a way that you treat humanity, whether in your own person or in the person of another, always at the same time as an end, and never simply as a mere means" (1983: 36). Because human beings are rational, autonomous beings, they may not be used as objects with mere instrumental value, but must be treated as beings with intrinsic value— in possession of a certain dignity, and valuable as ends in themselves. The contemporary philosopher Thomas Mappes, operating from a Kantian framework, elucidates this in terms of "voluntary, informed consent" (2006: 171).

Because River is not fully rational and autonomous during the run of *Firefly* and for most of *Serenity*, she is generally treated more like an object than a person. Certainly the Alliance sees her as nothing more than a weapon, and even Mal has a tendency to view her as an object and to use her as a means to an end on occasion. We see this in his very first interaction with her, when he discovers that Simon has smuggled her on board. Mal jumps to the conclusion that she may be objectified as a victim of human trafficking. He certainly does not approve, but that is nevertheless his initial reference point when looking at her. As pointed out by Alyson Buckman, "Mal immediately asserts her status as an object; he assumes she has been purchased as a sex slave for Simon or another buyer" (2008: 42). Mal may not harm or take advantage of her to quite the same degree as the Alliance, but he does still treat her as a useful object at times, as we see early in *Serenity* when he brings her along to serve as a mind reader during a heist.

This all comes to a head in *Serenity*. Determined to track down the mysterious "Miranda," Mal confronts River: "The government's man, he says you're a danger to us. Not worth helping. Is he right? Are you anything but a weapon? I've staked my crew's life on the theory you're a person, actual and whole, and if I'm wrong, you'd best shoot me now." Mal may not always have treated River as a whole person, but he has at least come to that realization at this point, and is willing to do what he can to help her become "actual and whole." Once the crew journeys to the planet Miranda and discovers the Alliance's experiments in social control (which accidentally spawned the Reavers), something clicks for River. The secrets she uncovered as a result of her programming and that triggered her psychological fragmentation no longer have such an effect on her, and she finally achieves a full measure of rationality and autonomy, arguably restoring personhood itself.

As such, she is no longer an object, or even a helpless child, but another adult alongside the others. This allows her to step up and take care of others instead of always being taken care of herself, especially by Simon: during the last big battle against the Reavers, River saves them all, saying to Simon in particular: "You've always taken care of me. My turn." This also allows her to serve as a full member of the crew, taking over as pilot after the death of Wash (Alan Tudyk), and surprising Mal with her flying expertise: "So, you gonna ride shotgun with me, help me fly? Think you can work out…" but he interrupts himself when she expertly takes off. "Okay, clearly some aptitude." She is now a member of the crew, and a person among other persons.

The most obvious instance of a character undergoing a kind of completion from *Firefly* to *Serenity* is of course Mal, the main character of the series, and captain of the ship. In his case, the completion involves an interesting intersection of virtue and personhood, a completion of personal authenticity, in which Mal finally comes to believe in something in which he can place personal value, and by which he can make important choices. As we know from the events of and backstory presented in *Firefly*, Mal was a believer of sorts at one point. As we learn during a flashback scene in the original pilot episode for *Firefly*, "Serenity" (20 December 2002), Mal fought for the Independents; as such, we can infer that he had political beliefs motivating enough for him to fight and possibly die. We also see in the flashback that he was at least nominally religious, as he is depicted as wearing a Christian cross, and even kissing it at one point, presumably for God's protection and guidance.

In the later events of *Firefly* and throughout most of the film *Serenity*, Mal has lost his beliefs, or at least his desire to act authentically in accordance with them, to some degree or another. With regard to religion, Mal has clearly lost faith and has no desire to regain it. He makes it clear to Shepherd Book right away that, while he is welcome on the ship as a paying traveler, he should in no way try to minister to Mal. Mal even describes religion as "a long wait for a train that don't come." With regard to his political beliefs, things are a bit murkier. He claims on occasion not to believe in such things, and to act only to make a living and protect his crew. However, there are still instances of him acting and talking in such a way as to suggest that they are still there, if buried under a layer of denial most of the time. In "Bushwhacked" (27 September 2002), the crew is detained by the Alliance, who are looking for River and Simon. During his interrogation, Mal denies caring about his old affiliation with the Independents: "It's not 'Sergeant'. Not no more. War's over."; however, he also says of the Independence army: "May have been the losing side. Still not convinced it was the wrong one."

Mal's behavior to this point serves as an example of what Jean-Paul Sartre termed "bad faith," a denial of one's own freedom, choice, and values: "we say indifferently of a person that he shows signs of bad faith or that he lies to himself ... bad faith is a lie to oneself" (1984: 87). In Mal's case, bad faith takes place in two ways. With regard to religion, Sartre would have no problem with Mal's rejection of belief in God; Sartre himself was an atheistic existentialist. However, Mal operates as though the non-existence of God necessarily entails the non-existence of any real value or belief, and that sort of defeatist nihilism is something that Sartre rejected. With regard to politics, Sartre would characterize Mal's lack of honesty with others and even himself about his values as bad faith. Clearly, he still believes in the basic political ideals behind the Independence movement such as freedom and political autonomy, but he often pretends not to, taking on the bad faith role of the mere "scoundrel" character. What Sartre would recommend for Mal instead is to live in "good faith," in which he chooses something to believe in and lives according to those beliefs, and is honest with himself and others about it. This shift towards good faith takes place in two key scenes in *Serenity*.

First is Mal's last conversation with Shepherd Book, just before Book dies. In an earlier conversation, Book had counseled Mal: "Only one thing is gonna walk you through this, Mal. Belief." When Mal protests that he has no interest in religion, Book continues: "When I talk about belief, why do you always assume I'm talking about God?" What Book is telling Mal is that he needs to believe in something, whatever that is, but that mere action untethered to strong belief will not see him through. As Kowalski notes: "Book is pleading with Mal to discover some sort of anchor or cornerstone that reenergizes his moral core" (2015: 26).

The other scene is Mal's final confrontation with the Operative (Chiwetel Ejiofor) in one of the film's last scenes. The conversation between the two of them is quite telling:

> MAL: I know the secret. The truth that burned up River Tam's brain. Rest of the 'verse is going to know it, too. 'Cause they need to.
> THE OPERATIVE: Do you really believe that?
> MAL: I do.
> THE OPERATIVE: You willing to die for that belief?
> MAL: I am.

Here we see Mal taking Book's counsel and choosing to believe in a fully authentic way. It is only at this moment that Mal truly becomes the complete hero that the series always hinted he could be. In this way, he stands in stark contrast to the Operative, the villain to Mal's hero. Though the Operative is also a man of belief, he allows those beliefs to substitute for his own free will. As Foy and Kowalski note: "Unlike Mal, who owns his beliefs … the Operative is owned by his belief in the Alliance, a belief that completely displaces his identity" (2011: 157). Mal, however, creates his own identity by choosing for himself what to believe, heroism in contrast to the Operative's villainy, good faith in contrast to bad.

Inara (Morena Baccarin) goes through a process of character development similar to Mal's, also in terms of authenticity and good faith. Inara struggles with decisions about her personhood, values, and priorities; her time spent on Serenity are a reflection of that. She too has some issues with fully honest behavior towards herself and others, which makes it difficult for her to operate in good faith relationships with others or herself. For one most obvious example, she is not completely honest with herself or the rest of the crew about her romantic feelings towards Mal. It is also occasionally suggested that she is not fully honest with her clients about their relationships, as we see when one client suggests that her clocks may run fast in order to shorten their time together, and when she herself suggests to a female client that she cannot be fully herself in the company of men. We also learn from outside the confines of the show itself that Inara's full story arc would have involved a cancer diagnoses, serving as a major reason for her leaving her home and travelling aboard Serenity—a fact she never shares with the rest of the crew, but which was revealed by series writer and producer Tim Minear in the 10-year *Firefly* anniversary TV special *Browncoats Unite*. As I have noted elsewhere: "If anyone is entitled to know about our serious health issues, it would be close friends, family, and lovers. Such people make a serious investment in their relationships with us, and take on a considerable amount of emotional risk in doing so. In that regard, one might argue that they are entitled to know what they are getting into, and to withhold such information is disrespectful" (Kreider 2015: 17). Between Inara's problems with Mal and her personal struggles, she eventually abandons Serenity too, leaving the ship sometime between the events of the television series and the movie.

During *Serenity*, however, Inara takes the essential first steps toward completing her character in good faith, and also completing good-faith relationships. For one, Inara and Mal actually have one of their first honest exchanges about their feelings for each other when Mal admits to her "But you fog things up. You always have. You spin me about." Though she doesn't verbalize it at that moment, it is obvious from her reaction that she takes seriously his expression of his feelings, and makes no bad faith attempt to deny their romantic tensions. This seems to prompt some self-reflection on her part, culminating in their last exchange in the movie when Mal asks her if she is "ready to get off this heap, back to civilized life," to which she replies "I, uh … I don't know." They give each other a knowing, intimate look, and Mal responds, smiling: "Good answer." There is a lot that is unspoken, but still very clear to the audience: Inara may finally be ready both to admit her true feelings for Mal and to pursue a relationship with him, and to admit to herself that Serenity is her home and that she herself is part of the crew, not just a passenger. There's certainly no suggestion that it will be an easy "happily ever after," but for the first time, she is ready to engage in good faith. This complements the theme of completion of character with the completion of relationship. In Mal and Inara's case, we merely see the very first steps towards romance, but completion occurs in the sense that no explicit romantic relationship existed before, while one now begins before us.

On the other end of the relationship spectrum, we find Zoe and Wash. From the beginning, we are tempted to think that their relationship is already a complete one, dramatically speaking. Of course, we do see some of the backstory of their pre-marital interactions during Wash's recruitment in the *Firefly* episode "Out of Gas" (25 October 2002), but they are already married by the "present-day" events of *Firefly*. There is also a minor bit of marital discord that needs resolving when it is revealed that Wash harbors some jealously about Mal and Zoe's relationship, but this is quickly resolved among the three of them. For all appearances, it is a complete and harmonious relationship, one meant only to serve as contrast to the more difficult relationships in the show, and one that can even serve as a bit of comic relief. During "Bushwhacked," we get a laugh out of the contrast between the way that Zoe reacts to questions by Harken about her marriage ("Don't see that it's any of your business, is all. We're very private people.") and Wash's responses ("The legs. Oh yeah, definitely have to say it was her legs. You can put that down. Her legs, and where her legs meet her back. Actually, that whole area. That, and above it.").

So, what could completion mean for a seemingly perfect relationship in a Whedon universe? Any die-hard fan of Joss needs only a moment to see the obvious answer: someone has to die. In a way that brings to mind the inevitable fall of a naive character in a Greek tragedy, Wash does not always take seriously the dangers of a relationship with a spouse who is a soldier. The unexpected twist is that it is not Zoe who dies, but rather Wash who, even in his final moments, enjoys the perceived safety of the ship. Wash saves the crew from both the Alliance and the Reavers through savant-like feats of piloting, only to die from a Reaver spear that pierces Serenity after the more or less successful landing. "I am a leaf on the wind. Watch how I soar," he proclaims, barely finishing the phrase before his sudden demise. In retrospect, the moment should not have been so surprising, as there was simply no other dramatic conclusion for such a relationship.

There is also a sort of middle ground between Mal and Inara's newly budding relationship and Zoe and Wash's violently truncated one, found in the relationship between Kaylee and Simon. Throughout *Firefly*, Kaylee spends a great deal of time and emotional energy pining after Simon. Simon himself is aware of Kaylee's feelings, and even occasionally suggests that he reciprocates, but at no point does he open himself up or allow for a romantic relationship to develop. This keeps Kaylee in a continual state of confusion about whether Simon does have feelings for her, or if he simply thinks he is too good for her. In the episode "Safe" (8 November 2002), Simon picks up an item at a store that Kaylee was admiring, and says, "They're asking money for this crap?" Kaylee, upset but hiding it, pretends to sympathize by saying "Hard to believe, ain't it?" In one of the few exchanges in which he even seems to admit to liking Kaylee, he ends up ruining it, and reinforcing Kaylee's fears that he considers himself too good for her, when he jokingly characterizes her as the only woman in his universe who is not either married, a relative, or a companion, inadvertently implying that he could do better in normal circumstances.

Serenity once again provides the opportunity for completion by allowing Simon and Kaylee finally to consummate their relationship. During the final battle scene, Simon says to Kaylee (who has just admitted her fear that they will all die):

> SIMON: I never planned anything. I just wanted to keep River safe. Spent so much time on Serenity ignoring anything that I wanted for myself. My one regret in all of this is never being with you.
> KAYLEE: With me? You mean to say, as.... Sex?
> SIMON: I mean to say.
> KAYLEE: To hell with this, I'm gonna live!

And after the danger is over and the crew is back on board, we see that Simon and Kaylee have indeed lived and can finally have said sex.

Serenity also provides the opportunity for Simon and River to complete their relationship as siblings. A major premise of the show and the movie is that River is little more than a psychologically broken child, a little sister for whom Simon must care. To his credit, Simon does just that, and very much from a sense of love rather than just duty. As the Operative points out, after watching the video footage of Simon breaking River out of the Alliance facility where she was held: "The boy spent his entire fortune developing the contacts to infiltrate this place, gave up a brilliant future in medicine as well." When the Head Researcher exclaims "It's madness," the Operative responds: "Madness? Have you looked at this scan carefully, Doctor? At his face? It's love, in point of fact. Something a good deal more dangerous."

Once again, the final battle scene in *Serenity* provides the occasion for the relationship to move away from the one-sided care-giving relationship between Simon and River to a more complete relationship of adult siblings who can care for each other as needed. When Simon is severely wounded, it finally snaps River out of her semi-catatonic state and motivates her to save the crew, especially Simon. "You take care of me, Simon. You've always taken care of me. My turn," she says, before throwing herself into harm's way. Earlier, this example served to illustrate River's personhood, but it also serves as an example of a complete relationship, especially in the context of the ethics of care, as described by the philosopher Nel Noddings: "When I am in this sort of relationship with another, when the other's reality becomes a real possibility for me, I care. Whether the caring is sustained, whether it lasts long enough to be conveyed to the other, whether it becomes visible in the world, depends on my sustaining the relationship or, at least, acting out of concern for my own ethicality as though it were sustained" (2013:14). What was an incomplete relationship before finds completion in *Serenity* only when River is able to do her part in caring for Simon, acting from a sense of the reality of his needs and concerns.

River also serves as the lynchpin in the final and arguably most important sense of completion for the series, and that is the completion of the crew. Certainly, most if not all of the above examples contribute to that already: Mal has to become a complete person in order to be the best captain he can be, Jayne must become a hero in order to serve as a genuine member of the crew, and so on. However, River is the character that ties all of this together. Throughout *Firefly*, she is barely more than cargo, a point made in a rather explicit way by having her loaded onto the ship in a literal cargo container. It is only after she becomes a complete person that she is able to become a complete member of the crew herself, not only caring for Simon, but also contributing in the important role of pilot now that Wash is gone. Her move into that role also gives Mal the opportunity to summarize this completion, in a manner that once again echoes Noddings' care ethics:

> MAL: It ain't all buttons and charts, little albatross. You know what the first rule of flying is? Well, I suppose you do, since you already know what I'm about to say.
> RIVER: I do. But I like to hear you say it.
> MAL: Love. You can learn all the math in the 'verse but you take a boat in the air that you don't love, she'll shake you off just as sure as the turn of the worlds. Love keeps her in the air when she ought to fall down, tells you she's hurting before she keels. Makes her a home.

This last speech explicitly provides the major theme of the *Firefly* universe, whether romantic love, love between siblings, or love between a crew and her ship. *Firefly* is a story of love, and a story that only finds completion in *Serenity*.

WORKS CITED

Aristotle. (2000). *Nicomachean Ethics*. Trans. Roger Crisp. Cambridge: Cambridge University Press.

Buckman, Alyson R. (2008). "'Much Madness is Divinest Sense': *Firefly's* 'Big Damn Heroes' and Little Witches," in Rhonda V. Wilcox and Tanya R. Cochrane (eds.) *Investigating Firefly and* Serenity: *Science Fiction on the Frontier*. London: I.B. Tauris, 41–52.

Foy, Joseph J., and Dean A. Kowalski. (2011). "Seeking Authenticity in the Whedonverse," in Dean A. Kowalski and S. Evan Kreider (eds.) *The Philosophy of Joss Whedon*. Lexington: University Press of Kentucky, 151–167.

Grinnell, Jason D. (2011). "Aristotle, Kant, Spike, and Jayne: Ethics and Character in the Whedonverse," in Dean A. Kowalski and S. Evan Kreider (eds.) *The Philosophy of Joss Whedon*. Lexington: University Press of Kentucky, 88–102.

Kant, Immanual. (1983). *Ethical Philosophy*. Trans. James Ellington. Indianapolis: Hackett Publishing.

Kowalski, Dean A. (2015). "Letting That Belief Be Real Enough": Shepherd Book as the Embodiment of Religious Non-Realism in the Whedonverse," in *Slayage: The Journal of Whedon Studies* 13.2.

_____. (2001). "Plato, Aristotle, and Joss on Being Horrible," in Dean A. Kowalski and S. Evan Kreider (eds.) *The Philosophy of Joss Whedon*. Lexington: University Press of Kentucky, 71–87.

Kreider, S. Evan. (2015). "To Live and Die in the 'Verse: A Re-Evaluation of Inara," in *Slayage: The Journal of Whedon Studies* 13.2.

Mappes, Thomas. (2006). "Sexual Morality and the Concept of Using Another Person," in Thomas A. Mappes and Jane S. Zembaty (eds.) *Social Ethics: Morality and Social Policy* 7th ed. New York: McGraw-Hill, 170–83.

Noddings, Nel. (2013). *Caring: A Feminine Approach to Ethics and Moral Education*. Berkeley: University of California Press.

Sartre, Jean Paul. (1984). *Being and Nothingness*. Trans. Hazel E. Barnes. New York: Washington Square Press.

Death in the 'Verse

H.S. HOBMA

In contemporary Western culture, most individuals remain distant from death in their day-to-day lives (see Durkin 2003 and Howarth 2007). Western culture is often still referred to as a death-denying society, and death is often considered a taboo topic, uncomfortable, unseemly, or morbid. And yet, paradoxically, death is ever-present in our media and popular culture (Gibson 2007). Some of the most popular and successful TV shows and movies feature death front and center—see, for example, *The Walking Dead* (2010–), *Game of Thrones* (2011–), *Vikings* (2013–), *Dead Like Me* (2003–2004), *Twin Peaks* (1990–1991, 2017), and a slew of others. Death is also heavily featured in video games, where players take the act of killing into their own hands, as well as in music, plays, and all other forms of entertainment. Through these mediums, death is often subtle, but nevertheless pervasive. Death can be sensational and pornographic, but also personal and quiet. When celebrities die, fans mourn, often publicly and collectively. Celebrity graves, haunted buildings, crypts and mausoleums are popular tourist destinations (Blom 2000). It is almost ridiculous to observe the fascination with death, dying, and tragedy among Western peoples while still labeling the West as death-denying.

Pop culture is not only a reflection of the society that creates it, but is also a medium of exploration for subjects that both fascinate and terrify us. Perhaps this is the reason celebrity lives become so interesting to regular people: the rest of us get to see how the rich and famous live, while eventually seeing their humanity revealed when they die. But the same can be said for death and dying in general. Because we have so little real, direct connection to one of the few experiences that are shared by literally every person on the planet, the subject of death and dying becomes entrenched in our popular culture, perhaps as a way to witness it, explore it, or to form some kind of connection with it before our own time is up. In her YouTube series *Ask a*

Mortician, Caitlin Doughty, a professional mortician, answers viewers' questions about death and the macabre. In one such video, "Body Worlds (& Other Forever Corpses)" (2015), she attempts to answer the question as to why Gunther Von Hagens's *Body Worlds*, along with other similar traveling shows involving plastinated bodies, remain so popular despite "op-eds and religious leaders in every country asking 'what does going to see a disgusting, flayed-open corpse say about us as a society?'" She answers, "What it says about as us a society is that we made a bunch of dead bodies the most popular touring attraction in the world. It says we're really interested in death and want to see corpses." Doughty's observation in this particular case emphasizes the complex relationship we have with death in Western society. On the one hand, we feel repulsion. On the other, we are fascinated and seek death out.

Viewers can often invest a lot of time, energy, and emotion in a TV show. After spending a number of hours watching a character grow, change, make choices, and live, viewers can, and do, become quite attached to the fictional characters depicted onscreen. When these characters die, there often follows a period of collective mourning. In many ways, the feelings present at these moments are real, tangible emotions that should not be dismissed (Gibson 2007: 418).

Fans of Joss Whedon are all too familiar with the pain of losing a cherished character, and know all too well that Whedon certainly does not shy away from killing our favorite protagonists. These deaths are often sudden, unexpected, shocking, and important. See, for example, "The Body" (27 February 2001), an episode of *Buffy the Vampire Slayer* (1997–2003) centered on the moments and days following the death of the protagonist's mother. After the cancellation of *Firefly* (2002–03), the short-lived space Western that garnered an unprecedented cult following, fans of the series were rewarded for their hard work and patience with the film *Serenity* (2005)—and with the sudden deaths of two major, beloved characters. However, through examination of the world of *Serenity*, its genre, environment, and the specific character deaths, it becomes clear that *Serenity*, as much as it is about River's (Summer Glau) deteriorating mind and the search for the truth, is also about connection, loss, war, and family. In this essay, I use *Serenity* as a case study on the representation of death in pop culture, and how the film is at odds with a conception of Western culture as death denying.

Death in Western Society

The belief that Western society is death denying came about in large part due to the denial of death thesis, a well-known thanatological theory on the Western attitudes towards death, primarily popularized by Gorer (1955 and 1965) and Ariès (1981). The theories of both are problematic and have been heavily criticized (for varying reasons), but they are credited with starting a valuable coversation (Walter 1991). The continued argument, then, is whether or not Western cultures and socitieties are actually death denying. The current common consesus is that we are *not* death denying, despite the repeated proclamation that we are, even by contemporary writers (Durkin 2003; Gibson 2007; Warraich 2015; The Commuter 2015, among others) and among those in the deathcare industry (see Doughty 2011 and Anon. 2015). In their own research, Zimmerman and Rodin (2004) found that the sociological argument against the denial of death thesis is largely ignored in clinical literature. This literature ultimately still supports the argument that Western culture is death-denying (Zimmerman and Rodin 2004, 121). Why this may be is better discussed in other articles, like Zimmerman and Rodin's work in the field of medicine, and Walter's and Howarth's in sociology, but it is important to lay the foundation of Western attitudes towards death in this essay so we can properly examine how death is portrayed in a movie like *Serenity*.

In this section, I focus on Allen Kellehear's 1984 essay "Are We a Death-Denying Society: A Sociological Review," largely because he closely examines the death-denying thesis and systematically explains how it is flawed and inaccurate. His paper (as well as Walter's paper [1991]) is also often cited by contemporary authors as evidence that we are not death denying, and may never have been (see, for example, Walter 1991 and Zimmerman and Rodin 2004).

Kellehear attempts to reconcile the two primary arguments on the perception of death in contemporary Western society; the first being that Western society is death denying, the second that Western society is death accepting, or at least simultaneously denying and accepting of death, as suggested by Dumont and Foss (1972). Kellehear argues that the widely agreed-upon theory that western society is a death-denying one is false, and that the evidence given to support this theory is mostly anecdotal and therefore inherently flawed. In *In Our Hour of Death*, Ariès (1981) argues that, commonly and historically, individuals were constantly aware of their own mortality and impending death, and when the time came, were ultimately accepting of it. However, this has since changed due to the rise of secularism and the lack of religious rites and traditions in death rituals (Ariès 1974; Gorer 1965; Feifel 1959), which has left individuals lost and without support in times of loss. Subscribers to this theory argue that the increased reliance on the medical industry to prolong life, coupled with the practice of withholding terminal prognoses—something that has only just begun to change (see Kellehear 1985: 718; Zimmerman and Rodin 2004: 121; and Warraich 2015)—and the perception that an "untimely death" (any death that occurs for any other reason than old age) is a failure of medical science. Furthermore, the view that hospitals are sterile and clean and where patients go to "cheat death," has created a contradictory image of death being dirty, contaminating, and embarrassing (Kellehear 1985: 716 and Doughty 2011), and should therefore be hidden away. Additionally, the proliferation of the funeral industry has removed the care of the body from the family and home (the private sphere), and placed it in the hands of hired professionals in the public sphere, essentially turning death into a commodity (Doughty 2011 and Warraich 2015).

Another common argument for the denial of death in Western societies draws on the universal fear of death suggested by Freud (1915), which, however, is not true: the fear of death is certainly not held by every person, or even every culture. A third argument, the twentieth-century crises of individualism (Kellehear 1984: 717 and Ariès 1974) states that the loss of autonomy over one's own death and reduced reliance on death rituals have robbed the individual of a self-subscribed "good death," which results in what Ariès calls a "crisis of individualism" (Ariès 1974). In his essay, Kellehear goes on to explain how none of these theories actually support the argument for death-denial in Western societies through a sociological lens, stating that these theories gloss over or oversimplify the individuals and the societies that are supposed to house these feelings.

In addition to the aforementioned theories and studies, Kellehear breaks down the anecdotal evidence often given to support the denial of death thesis, and explains why the evidence either fails to support death denial, or may even point to a death-accepting culture (1984: 718–720).

He begins by tackling the funeral industry and different products created by that industry often portrayed as an attempt to hide death. For instance, the use of caskets, which look like boxes, instead of coffins specifically made to look like they hold bodies, are often used as evidence that we are entering/have entered into a death-denial state. Kellehear argues that although a coffin "may look like furniture rather than a disposal box this is merely another example of aesthetic styles transcending the practical" (1984: 718). Another funerary practice is embalming, which is intended to preserve a body and make it look like the person is merely sleeping. However, Kellehear argues that embalming is more a product of capitalism and is likely "structurally a carry over, a logical continuation, of the cosmetic industry for the living" (1984: 718). Furthermore, embalming was created as a practical method of preserving bodies for transportation during the civil war, and has merely become expectation (Fitzharris 2015).

Kellehear goes on to point out that many point to the existence of religious beliefs and practices as proof of denial of death by arguing that the belief in God and immortality dissuades the finality of death. However, Kellehear argues that religion instead offers a social network that lends support to the bereaved, making it easier for communities to cope and move on from the death of a loved one rather than inviting death denial (1984: 719).

As mentioned earlier, it is commonly believed that the reluctance to talk about death is often seen as proof of death denial. This is perhaps a seemingly obvious piece of evidence, and is arguably the most widely accepted proof of death denial, or death as a "taboo" topic (see Ariès 1974; Durkin 2003; Feifel 1959; and Doughty 2011). However, Kellehear argues that death and grief are taboo because, like sex, they are seen as socially unacceptable topics of conversation, and that the individual chooses not to talk about death and grief for fear of offending those around him (1984, 719). Death may indeed be sad or painful, but this is not evidence of its denial.

Kellehear concludes by stating that the evidence of Western death denial is not convincing enough, and that it ultimately ignores the various institutional and individual organizations around death and dying. He argues that the individual will always experience death privately, and that some will deny death, but also "become angry, laugh or feel sorrow in relation to death" (1984: 720). He also states that societies specifically "do not deny death, but instead organise for it and around it," by subscribing rituals for the dead and defining what is considered a good death (720). He concludes by stating that the societal response to death is

> always complex and historically unique. In the Middle Ages the essential sociological meaning of death was religious. Today this meaning is medical. There are signs already that tomorrow this meaning may be a legal one [720].

This, perhaps, is the most important statement: that the response to death, individually and socially, changes and is dependent on a given society.

In my own research, I have found that most recent literature on Western attitudes towards death rely heavily on the argument for the medicalization of death and the institutionalization of the death industry (see Durkin 2003; Howarth 2007; Oritz 2016; and Doughty 2011). In particular, the Death Positivity movement (Doughty 2011) argues that the movement of the dying and the dead from private to public (i.e., from the home to the hospital) has removed the personal from death, and therefore has created a disassociation with death in Western societies. The Positivity movement is attempting to (re-)normalize death, which, as Oritz states, should not be perceived as an obsession with the morbid, but rather an appreciation of life (2016). By more openly talking about death and dying, by acknowledging it in the everyday, by *seeing* death in its many forms, the Death Positivity movement proclaims that it can remove the stigma from the dead and dying, and improve the healing of those who have experienced loss, something that media and pop culture can help with.

Death in Pop Culture and the Media

Keith Durkin reviews the many ways death and dying are portrayed in popular culture, exploring music, coverage of celebrity deaths, television, movies, print media, etc. Indeed, death and dying are ubiquitous throughout all aspects of human history. What changes are the attitudes towards death, how death is handled from generation to generation (2003). Just as we can look to the Victorians and their *memento mori* to see that death was so much a part of daily life that it became fashionable to mourn (Kucich, 1980), we can look to our own portrayal of death to see how we relate to it. Because lacking time and distance may make it more difficult to analyse our own culture, we are faced with many conflicting theories on contemporary Western attitudes towards death and dying. It will do us good to remember that these attidutes are always changing, and they are never simple. Durkin does offer, briefly, two differing theories that may explain the seemingly paradoxical coupling of Western fascination and denial (2003, 47).

First, Durkin argues that the most obvious (or superficial) interpretation of the paradox is that the U.S. is not as death denying as many writers contend. Second, Durkin argues that the most compelling theory is that the saturation of death themes in American media, as entertainment and as humor, is a way to cope with the trauma and anxiety of death by way of neutralizing it. This over simplifies the argument, as we have seen earlier, since it relies too heavily on the flawed theory of the universal fear of death. It is far more likely that we never became death denying, but that our perception and relationship to death has changed from that of our ancestors.

Contradicting Durkin, in her essay "Death and mourning in a technologically mediated culture" (2007), Margaret Gibson argues that Western societies are not death denying, but that because of modern technology, death is placed at the forefront of our media. This creates an interesting experience for the average person in that he or she may witness thousands of "fake" (fictional) or "distant" (as reported on the news) deaths a year without ever directly experiencing death in his or her own life (2007: 415–16). She examines the different ways contemporary individuals consume images of death and the dead, what these relationships may mean, and why they exist. She argues that "fake deaths" are created within the frame of a narrative and influence viewers into perceiving the death for a specific purpose. For example, deaths on crime shows like *CSI* (2000–15), a show about scientists gathering data and evidence to solve a murder, are often cold and clinical (417). Contradictorily, the "real" but "distant deaths" of public figures, such as Princess Diana, have a profound effect on millions of people who have no personal connection to them, and often result in mass mourning (421). These are two very different responses to death within one culture, because the experiences and representations of these deaths are different: one is manufactured for a specific reason while the other is organic. However, both of these situations remind us of the same thing: that death can happen to anyone.

In these two simple examples, we can see the complicated and conflicted relationship we really have with death in Western society. This paradoxical relationship is born out of our immediate, if mediated, access to global death and disaster contrasted with distance and unfamiliarity of death and bereavement in many of our lives. Through the portrayal of death in fiction, those in the West have the opportunity to build a relationship with death. Indeed, the disassociation with death invites curiosity and fascination with death, resulting in a desire to see and experience it, even remotely, through aspects of media and pop culture. This is especially interesting when looking death in the Whedonverse.

Death and Whedon

Fans of Whedon are undoubtedly familiar with his habit of killing fan-favorite characters. From Wesley Wyndam-Pryce (Alexis Denisof) in *Angel* (1999–2004), to Penny (Felicia Day) in *Dr. Horrible's Sing-Along Blog* (2008), to Agent Coulson (Clark Gregg) in *The Avengers* (2010), to nearly every major character in *Buffy the Vampire Slayer* (1997–2003), including Buffy (Sarah Michelle Gellar) herself, and, most relevant here, Shepherd Book (Ron Glass) and Hoban Washburn (Alan Tudyk) in *Serenity*. Whedon has a terrible habit of killing the innocent, the heroic, and the beloved. Death is featured so prominently and traumatically in Whedon's creations that he has been dubbed TV's Grim Reaper (Barton 2011), and has inspired article (Monsour 2009) after article (Payne 2012) and list (Holm 2012) after list (Narasaki n.d.) about the worst, the most heartbreaking, and the most shocking deaths in all his projects. Many attempt to parse Whedon's motives behind these deaths, and the director constantly fields questions about them during interviews.

For the purpose of this essay, I will focus on the two major character deaths in *Serenity*: Wash and Shepherd Book. Neither actor could commit to a *Serenity* sequel (Paur 2015), so Whedon would have had to explain their absences if a sequel was ever made. He chose to kill them off instead. Fans were heartbroken, of course, especially, and interestingly, in the case of Wash. Fans have been asking why Whedon made this choice ever since the character deaths were released, because certainly there are other, less final ways to explain a character's absence. During a 2006 interview on Fanboy Radio, a listener asked Whedon a question that reveals the profound effect that Wash's death had on at least two fans (the listener and his wife), an effect echoed by countless others: "When we saw *Serenity*, the moment that took our breath away and stunned us, and stunned us for hours afterwards, was Wash's death. What creative process brought that character death about?" In response (after jokingly stating how much he hates Alan Tudyk) Whedon offered the following reply:

> The fact of the matter is that it's a great point of contention with many people. Very simply, without it the movie would have been two hours of blather. I made a whole big thing about heroes getting people killed, and the dangerousness of Mal actually becoming somebody who believes in something and how much they were laying [sic] on the line ... I realized, you do this one thing that nobody sees coming, the rest of the movie has enormous resonance ... you take away somebody you love, and then every card is on the table. It's not pretty, but it's the way to make something creative. I hate movies that lie. I hate movies like *Jurassic Park* where just the bad people die, because I don't believe in a just and all-knowing dinosaur. I believe it should be more random than that. The only way to really sell the sacrifices they're making is to make one.

It is clear that Whedon finds death to be a necessary evil in his storytelling. What makes him stand out is that he attempts to make these necessary deaths respectful, meaningful, relevant, and resounding. Whedon is so successful at keeping his audience's attention even in the wake of major character deaths because he never trivializes these deaths, treating these characters instead with respect. By doing so, the audience becomes more connected to the remaining characters, and therefore become more involved, attached, and immersed in the outcome.

You can take this explanation and apply it to any of the major character deaths throughout Whedon's various projects, because it is a compelling and convincing reason. But it goes deeper than making the fight appear real: yes, it makes the audience feel that the fight, the war, is as dangerous has been claimed, but it also gives us something more to relate to. Perhaps the simplest explanation for why Whedon always includes death in his creations is that we, as human beings, need death. We need to see it, to experience it, even if vicariously through fictional characters. This brings us to *Serenity* itself, and my argument that, despite its many other themes, *Serenity* is a movie about death. Indeed, Ina Rae Hark, in her essay "Decent Burial or Miraculous Resurrection," presents the movie as a dead television show brought back to life.

Genre

Genre plays an important role in how audiences react and interact with a film. Audiences have been conditioned and trained to expect certain conventions from a film depending on its genre. An action movie will have less space to develop a romantic plot than a drama would, for example, and a romantic comedy will likely not feature a space fight. However, some films successfully cross genre boundaries, or are able to blend them, and so feature multiple characteristics not dependent on genre, or else dependent on competing genres. Whedon is adept at blurring genre boundaries, at working within the rules of genre and successfully breaking them to make a point, as is evident in *Serenity*. Whedon himself classifies *Serenity* as a "space Western" (Maio, 2014), blending American Western elements and science fiction. Many argue that science fiction is a genre built on exploration, of exploring "the final frontier" (as *Star Trek* fans will recognize), and as such already shares a great deal with Westerns (Maio 2010: 202); Whedon more purposefully combines both genres in *Firefly* and *Serenity*. His is a world that features horses and spaceships, six shooters and laser pistols, a futuristic wild west with advanced technologies and struggling frontier colonies.

By highlighting both genres, both of which display dangerous new worlds, the death motif becomes even more prominent, as both traditions deal with conflicts of person vs. person, or person vs. nature, or person vs. machine. Not only is the Serenity crew fighting the Alliance, but they are also in constant conflict with their environment, as their ship is an oasis surrounded by inhospitable space. The audience then, even if not totally aware of it, is made to feel the fragility of life on board the ship. *Serenity* is a movie built on likelihood of death, and our awareness of it. From the world building, to the lore, to the character development, every part of the movie is designed to remind the audience what it means to survive in the 'verse.

At its heart *Serenity* features a world that is in constant conflict with itself: along with science fiction and Western elements, the history of the 'verse is deeply influenced by the Unification War between the Union of Allied Planets (the inner planets) and the Independent Planets (the outer planets), echoing, quite consciously, the American Civil War. The loss of that war by the Independents defines almost everything that our heroes do. Even more so than the others, the loss of that war has infected Malcolm "Mal" Reynolds' (Nathan Fillion) very character. Even his ship is named after war's final battleground, where the Independents lost at the Battle of Serenity Valley. Fans of the series *Firefly* (2002–03) are all too familiar with the crew of Serenity's propensity for being on "the losing side," beginning when the Independents lose the war. Whedon has combined science fiction, Western, and war film conventions, subverting the expected tropes of heroism to tell a story about history's losers.

The Environment

The Alliance is the Big Brother (or Big Bad) of the 'verse. The Alliance has infinite resources and power, is everywhere, and sees everything. The

Alliance is constantly tracking the crew of *Serenity*, not only because they are "outlaws" in their own right, but also primarily because they are harboring high-value fugitives: River and Simon Tam (Summer Glau and Sean Maher, respectively). The Alliance is thus presented as an almost impossible enemy to fight, and one that is a constantly present threat. Indeed, it seems that everything bad in the 'verse boils down to Alliance control.

Another looming threat comes from the Reavers. They are the bogeyman of the 'verse, the constant threat that comes without warning, to rape and kill without discrimination. They are everything that is inhuman. They are a myth to those on the inner planets, but a very real, very deadly threat the further out one travels. In *Serenity*, Reavers become the literal obstacle between the crew and the Alliance secret they are investigating. But they are also the answer to the mystery: the Reavers have a deadly connection to the Alliance who, in their attempt to control the population using a chemical added to the air (the Pax), effectively killed a thriving planet, and turned the few survivors into Reavers.

The planet Miranda effectively becomes a giant grave, where the bodies of those killed by the Pax remain. Miranda is ironically named after the character in the Shakespearean play *The Tempest*, who speaks the famous lines: "How many goodly creatures are there here! / How beauteous mankind is! / O brave new world, / That has such people in't!" (Act 5 Scene 1 lines 190–193). Only, the brave new world in *Serenity* becomes a representation of the danger of attempting to control people, to "make them better," as Mal says.

The very environment of *Serenity* sets viewers up to expect danger and death (or at least to comprehend the threat). Even if death is never openly talked about—despite being joked about, balancing the movie's more serious components with moments of levity—death is constantly present in the 'verse, a quiet shadow that follows every character.

"Good Death"

Before moving forward, I want to further explore the principle of the Good Death, mentioned above. Unfortunately, this essay does not lend itself to a thorough discussion of the Good Death, but it is important to discuss briefly nonetheless, since it provides valuable context for the deaths in *Serenity*. The Good Death is a complicated term, because it is entirely dependent on culture and society. For example, there are certainly cultural taboos surrounding suicide in contemporary Western societies. However, this is not the case in modern Japan, which has a high rate of suicide, often framed as *seppuku* (Pierre n.d.). *Seppuku* is the ritualized, honorable suicide by disembowelment, performed primarily by the warrior class Samurai in Feudal Japan

(Pierre n.p.). For these ancient warriors, a Good Death was one that demonstrated resolve, courage, discipline, and that one was fully in control of oneself, a perception that has lasted through generations. In contrast, in contemporary Western society, a Good Death typically happens naturally, preferably due to old age, and is painless, preferably taking place during sleep (Emanuel and Emanuel 1998 and Howarth 2007).

However, what is deemed an appropriate Good Death on television or in film is something completely different; a Good Death may depend on genre, setting, and characterization, and if a character's death is not deemed "acceptable," audiences respond negatively. We often become quite attached to our favorite onscreen characters, and when they die, we generally demand that their deaths be thoughtful, important, and dignified, and we want their deaths to drive the story forward, and to connect us to those who are left. *Serenity* features two such deaths. Although they differ quite drastically from each other, they each play significant roles in the story of *Serenity*, and they both motivate the future actions of the remaining characters. But before I get into the literal representations of death (those of Wash and Book), I will explore the metaphorical representation of death in the Operative and River Tam.

Symbolic Death

One of *Serenity*'s opening scenes reveals the Operative's investigation into the escape of River Tam, with help of her brother Simon, from an Alliance facility. Audiences learn quite a bit about who the Operative is in this short scene. We learn that he is an agent of the Alliance, and that he has the highest security clearance, despite technically not "existing" in government records. We can also glean that he is smart, intuitive, calculating, careful, and terrifyingly dangerous. And we also learn that he is honorable, or at least that he lives according to a code of ethics that he deems honorable. A major part of his code of honor, we soon learn, is a propensity to kill: he values death as penance. We know this in part because of his bizarre bastardization of *seppuku*: "You know, in certain, older, civilized cultures, when men failed as entirely as you have, they would throw themselves on their swords." But the Operative forces Dr. Mathias (Michael Hitchcock) to "throw himself on his sword" by incapacitating him and placing the sword in front of him. When the scientist falls, the Operative says, while looking the dying man straight in the eyes: "This is *a good death*. There's no shame in this, in a man's death, a man who has done fine works. We're making a better world; all of them better worlds" [emphasis added]. From this moment on, the Operative becomes exceedingly dangerous, tracking the crew of Serenity across the solar system, killing anyone and everyone that gets in his way. He effectively becomes the embodiment of relentless death. He is also, not so coincidentally, the personification of the Alliance.

And then we have River Tam, who is the near exact opposite of the Operative, but shares similarities with him nonetheless. First, she is a 17-year-old teenager who has been "created" by the Alliance, operated on, experimented on, and modified into a literal weapon. However, in contrast to the Operative, she has little control over her thoughts or actions. She has been conditioned to turn into a weapon at a seemingly random trigger, and then effectively "shut down" by way of a safe word. When triggered, she acts entirely through programming, and fights and kills indiscriminately. It is not until after the crew unveils the secret on Miranda that River experiences a kind of purging of her psychological demons. Suddenly she has control over her weaponized body, which she uses to save the crew during the final battle with the Reavers, just when it seems like all hope is lost and death is inescapable. She both saves her crew from death and inflicts death upon those who would kill them.

Literal Death

Both Wash and Shepherd Book's deaths act as narrative devices to drive the movie forward, despite the deaths being contractually necessary (neither Alan Tudyk nor Ron Glass could promise availability if there were ever to be a sequel). Each death is important in its own right, and without them the movie would lose much of its emotional impact and narrative meaning.

Book was no longer a passenger or crewmember in *Serenity*, but rather ran a settlement on the planet Haven. The crew of Serenity hide out at Haven while on the run from the Alliance, but it is heavily implied that they have hidden there before, since the crew is on friendly terms with the colonists: as soon as they land, a child runs up to Kaylee (Jewel Staite), who warmly embraces him immediately, while we see Jayne (Adam Baldwin) warmly shake hands with a male settler. Shepherd Book, despite being a major character throughout the *Firefly* series, is only in two short scenes, but he serves his usual purpose. In his first scene, Book and Mal talk about ways to deal with the Alliance. The audience is reminded here that Book served as Mal's conscience and spiritual guide in the series, despite Mal's firm lack of faith. The audience is also reminded that Book has a mysterious and unknown past, clearly entwined with the Alliance somehow, as revealed in the series and in his extensive knowledge of Alliance protocols.[1]

In the second scene, the crew returns to Haven only to discover that the Operative has already been there, and has killed everyone and destroyed everything. Mal finds Shepherd Book alive, but dying. One significant difference between Wash and Shepherd Book's deaths is that Book gets to say his final words (and even crack a few jokes in his final moments). Book's death also certainly has meaning, because he takes down the Alliance ship tasked with Haven's destruction, avenging his and his fellow colonists' deaths.

We know, or at least suspect, that Book has some warrior in him, possibly even a military past, and so it is fitting that he dies a warrior's death. And ultimately, Book's death is the catalyst for Mal's commitment to taking on the Alliance once and for all. Prior to this scene, the crew's strategy is largely centered on running away; Mal says as much to Book. But with the destruction of Haven, Mal comes to realize that if he does not do anything, more people are going to die. The irony is that members of Mal's crew die when he does nothing, and they die when he resists, as we see in the case of Wash.

In the earlier Whedon quotation, he states that Wash's death was a point of contention for fans. For some reason, fans were more upset about Wash's death than even Book's. In her essay, "Decent Burial or Miraculous Resurrection," Hark highlights the fans' visceral reactions to Wash's death:

> Some fans became so upset by his random death just after he had miraculously landed the severely damaged ship that they said they would boycott the movie. One review thread that berated Whedon for this choice had the title "Joss, I'm Calling You Out" ('Archive). Other fans began letter-writing campaign urging Universal to recut the film so that Wash lived [132–133].

Hark suggests that this is because Wash is a central character to the Serenity crew, even more so than Shepherd Book, but that he also represents the "everyman" (132). Even 12 years later, viewers and fans of *Serenity* are still talking about Wash's death. Kyle Hill, fan and scientist, uses physics in an attempt to prove that the projectile that kills Wash could not in fact have pierced the window of Serenity, concluding, "the movie is wrong" (2013). Hill's math unfortunately fails to deny the pilot's death. Eric Ravenscraft of *Kinja* explains that Wash's death is necessary. He argues that everyone on board Serenity has lost something or someone at some point in their lives, except for the audience. He states that, in order for audiences to feel what the crew of Serenity feels, we have to lose someone too (2014). I cannot help but agree, at least to a point. Loss changes us. It reminds us that life has to be lived, fought for, and felt. It reminds us that we are human. Wash's death is shocking, and violent, and sudden, and it raises the stakes just as it seemed impossible for the stakes to get any higher. And his death is certainly not senseless. The crew is at war, and in war, death is expected. Wash's death may not have been a Good Death (one with autonomy, preparedness, or final lines), but he does die a hero, having just safely landed the beat-up Serenity; he makes sure his crew is alive and able to continue to fight.

Possibly what makes Wash's death difficult to see is Zoe's reaction to it.

Zoe has always been the warrior woman: Mal's Corporal, fellow Browncoat, and one of 150 survivors of the Battle of Serenity Valley. She is unflappable, stoic, brave, and loyal. When Wash dies onscreen, Zoe is allowed just a beat in which to be vulnerable, and her initial disbelief is completely heart wrenching. It is in small moments like this that the characters onscreen become real, and become an outlet that the audience can relate to. Zoe's grief is our grief. It is required, or else death means nothing. Her subsequent disregard for her own safety, as well as her disbelief that any of them might come out of the fight alive,[2] is realistic in the immediate aftermath of her husband's death. When the one person in the world Zoe loves most dies suddenly and tragically, why would her own survival matter? In contradiction to Zoe's reaction, Mal stays on course. He has a job to do, and Wash's death is just one more reason why he must prevail.

Conclusion

Even more important for the audience than the onscreen deaths is seeing the remaining crewmembers continue to live their lives. Our society so often does not know how to deal with the aftermath of a death. How long are we allowed to grieve for? How loudly, how openly, how publicly can we grieve before it becomes unbearable for those around us? When are we supposed to be able to move on? Additionally, how do we talk to someone who has experienced a recent loss? What are we supposed to say, or are allowed to say? There is so much mystery surrounding expected behavior when it comes to death, grief, and loss that it often results in anxiety and stress in an already stressful time. So it becomes even more important for audiences to see the fictional characters memorialize their loved ones, grieve, and continue on with their lives. We see the crew rebuilding the ship, which was nearly destroyed in the final battle, and whose "own repair and rebirth concludes the film" (Hark 2012: 132). This rebuilding after extreme loss shows us that it is okay to keep on living after death touches our lives.

It is easy to believe in Western society as death denying, considering how death is often an uncomfortable topic. We have seen, however, that much of the literature disagrees with such a reading of the West. Rather, there is a distinct disassociation with death for those who live in Western countries. Dying most often takes place in hospitals and hospices, surrounded by professional healthcare workers and machinery. Care for the dead takes place in morgues and funeral homes by professional deathcare workers. Bodies are cleaned, prepared, and dressed up by strangers who make them presentable and palatable, but have no connection to the person who used to inhabit them. The institutionalization and medicalization of death and dying has created a distance between death and the average person. But despite all of this, death? pervades our media and entertainment. It is because of this disassociation that there is a fascination with death and that our entertainment and pop culture are steeped in it.

In Whedon's *Serenity*, fans get to see death done right. Not only does it depict two central characters' deaths onscreen, but the entire movie embodies the theme of death. We see the heroic death in Book, which becomes motivation for Mal's actions against the Alliance, as well as the unexpected and tragic death of Wash, which becomes Mal's motivation to complete the mission at all costs. But, most importantly, viewers get to see the remaining crew survive, and continue to live, and their connection to death and grief becomes just a bit deeper because of it.

Through depictions of death, either symbolically or literally, in popular culture, Western society is essentially attempting to respond to its own distance from death and dying in everyday life. Losing death in the home means that we search for it elsewhere, almost creating an obsessive fascination with death and dying. By placing death and dying directly in front of us, on screen, through music, plays, etc., we are working to acknowledge and naturalize death. *Serenity* is one of many such examples.

Notes

1. His past is revealed later in the Dark Horse comic *The Shepherd's Tale*.

2. Humorously, and in contradiction to Zoe's reaction, Kaylee becomes more determined to fight in the end when Simon confesses his regret at not pursuing a relationship with her when he had the chance.

Works Cited

Anon. (2015). *CINDEA*: Homepage. On-line. Available HTTP: http://www.cindea.ca/ (1 June 2017).

Ariès, Philippe. (1981). *The Hour of Our Death*. 2nd ed., Trans. The Franco-American Foundation. London: Allen Lane.

_____. (1974). *Western Attitudes Toward Death from the Middle Ages to the Present*. Baltimore: Johns Hopkins University Press.

Barton, Kristin M. (2012). "TV's Grim Reaper: Why Joss Whedon Continually Kills the Characters We Love," in *PopMatters*. On-line. Available HTTP: http://www.popmatters.com/feature/139167-tvs-grim-reaper-why-joss-whedon-continually-kills-the-characters-we-/ (10 June 2017).

Blom, Thomas. (2000). "Morbid Tourism—A Postmodern Market Niche with an Example from Althorp," in *Norwegian Journal of Geography* 54.1: 29–36.

Bowman, Donna, and Noel Murray. (2012). "*Firefly: Serenity*," in *The A.V. Club*. On-line. Available HTTP: http://www.avclub.com/tvclub/firefly-serenity-86206 (23 January 2017).

Doughty, Caitlin. (2015). "Body Worlds (& Other Forever Corpses)," in *Ask a Mortician*. On-line. Available HTTP: https://www.youtube.com/watch?v=ID7M4k_k3-Q (16 September 2017).

_____. (2011). "Home Death Care," in *The Order of the Good Death*. On-line. Available HTTP: http://www.orderofthegooddeath.com/death-planning-test (7 February 2017).

Dumont, Richard, and Dennis Foss. (1972). *The American View of Death: Acceptance or Denial?* Cambridge, MA: Schenkman.

Durkin, Keith F. (2003). "Death, Dying, and the Dead in Popular Culture," in CD Bryant (ed.) *The Handbook of Death & Dying,*. Thousand Oaks: SAGE Publications Inc., 43–9.

Emanuel, Ezekiel and Linda Emanuel. (1998). "The Promise of a Good Death," in *The Lancet* 351: 21–9.

Feifel, Herman. (1959). *The Meaning of Death.* New York: McGraw-Hill.

Freud, Sigmund. (1974). "Thoughts for the Times on War and Death," in James Strachey (ed.) *The Standard Edition of the Complete Psychological Works of Sigmund Freud.* London: Hogarth Press, 275–300.

Gibson, Margaret. (2007). "Death and Mourning in Technologically Mediated Culture," in *Health Sociology Review* 16.5: 415–24.

Gorer, Geoffrey. (1965). *Death, Grief, and Mourning in Contemporary Britain.* London: Cresset.

_____. (1955). "The Pornography of Death," in *Encounter* 5.4: 49–52.

Hark, Ina Rae. (2010). "Decent Burial or Miraculous Resurrection: *Serenity*, Mourning, and Sequels to Dead Television Shows," in Carolyn Jess-Cooke and Constantine Verevis (eds.) *Second Takes: Critical Approaches to the Film Sequel.* Albany: University of New York Press, 121–37.

Hill, Kyle. (2013). "Saving Lives in *Serenity*: Can a Fanboy and Physics Change a Movie?" in *Scientific American.* On-line. Available HTTP: https://blogs.scientificamerican.com/guest-blog/saving-lives-in-serenity-can-a-fanboy-and-physics-change-a-movie/ (20 April 2017).

Holm, Barbara. (2012). "The 7 Most Tragic Deaths Caused by Joss Whedon," in *Dorkly.* On-line. Available HTTP: http://www.dorkly.com/post/45215/the-dorklyst-the-7-most-tragic-deaths-caused-by-joss-whedon (10 June 2017).

Howarth, Glennys. (2007). *Death and Dying: A Sociological Introduction.* Cambridge: Polity Press.

Kellehear, Allan. (1984). "Are We a 'Death-Denying' Society: A Sociological Review," in *Social Science & Medicine* 18.9: 713–23.

Kübler-Ross, Elisabeth. (1969). *On Death and Dying.* New York: Macmillan.

Kucich, John. (1980). "Death Worship Among the Victorians: The Old Curiosity Shop," in *PMLA* 95.1: 58–72.

Maio, Barbara. (2010). "Between Past and Future: Hybrid Design Style in *Firefly* and *Serenity*," in Rhonda V. Wilcox and Tanya Cochran (eds.) *Investigating* Firefly and Serenity: *Science Fiction on the Frontier.* London: I.B.Tauris, 201–211.

Monsour, Celeste. (2009). "Joss Whedon's 16 Most Painful Character Deaths," in *Fandomania.* On-line. Available HTTP: http://fandomania.com/joss-whedons-16-most-painful-character-deaths/ (10 June 2017).

Narasaki, Rosie. (n.d.). "Ranking Joss Whedon's Most Heartbreaking Character Deaths," in Hollywood.com. On-line. Available HTTP: http://www.hollywood.com/tv/ranking-joss-whedons-most-heartbreaking-character-deaths-57379669/ (10 June 2017).

Oritz, Jen. (2016). "The Women Who Love Death," in *Marie Claire.* On-line. Available HTTP: http://www.marieclaire.com/culture/a22236/women-in-death-positivity-movement/ (1 May 2017).

Pateman, Matthew. (2010). "Deathly Serious: Mortality, Morality, and the Mise-en-Scene in *Firefly* and *Serenity*," in Rhonda V. Wilcox and Tanya Cochran (eds.) *Investigating* Firefly and Serenity: *Science Fiction on the Frontier.* London: I.B.Tauris, 212–23.

Paur, Joey. (2015). "13 Fun Facts About Joss Whedon's *Serenity*," in *Geek Tyrant.* On-line. Available HTTP: https://geektyrant.com/news/13-fun-facts-about-joss-whedons-serenity (15 April 2017).

Payne, Rob. (2012) "Joss the Beloved Character Slayer: Deconstructing One of the Director's Most Common Tropes," in *Pajiba.* On-line. Available HTTP: http://www.pajiba.com/think_pieces/joss-the-beloved-character-slayer-deconstructing-one-of-the-directors-most-common-tropes.php (10 June 2017).

Pierre, Joseph M. (2015). "Culturally Sanctioned Suicide: Euthanasia, Seppuku, and Terrorist Martyrdom," in *World Journal of Psychiatry* 22.5: 4–14.

Ravenscraft, Eric. (2014). "In Defense of Wash's Death," in *Kinja.* On-line. Available HTTP: http://ericravenscraft.kinja.com/in-defense-of-washs-death-1510067085 (14 April 2017).

Seale, Clive. (1998). *Constructing Death: The Sociology of Dying and Bereavement.* Cambridge, UK: Cambridge University Press.
TheCommuter. (2015). "Our Death-Defying, Death-Denying Society," in *allnurses.* On-line. Available HTTP: http://allnurses.com/nursing-activism-healthcare/our-death-defying-773839.html (1 June 2017).
Walter, Tony. (1991). "Modern Death: Taboo or not Taboo?" in *Sociology* 25.2: 293–310.
Warraich, Haider Javed. (2015). "The Rituals of Modern Death," in *Opinionator* (*The New YorkTimes*). On-line. Available HTTP: https://opinionator.blogs.nytimes.com/2015/09/16/the-rituals-of-modern-death/ (4 February 2017).
Zimmerman, Camilla, and Gary Rodin. (2004). "The Denial of Death Thesis: Sociological Critique and Implications for Palliative Care," in *Palliative Medicine* 18.2: 121–8.

Cassandra Revisited

River Tam, Hysteria and the Politics of Ecstatic Revenge

AVIVA DOVE-VIEBAHN

And whether you believe all this or not,
it does not matter. What is coming, comes.
And soon, you will yourself stand here and say,
in pity, that all my words were all too true.—Cassandra,
Agamemnon [2003: 87]

I get confused. I remember everything. I remember too
much, and some of it's made up, and some of it can't be
quantified, and ... there's secrets.—River Tam, "Safe" [8
November 2002]

Introduction

A meditation on her upbringing, schooling, torture, and rescue from
the Alliance, the film *Serenity* (Joss Whedon, 2005) foregrounds River Tam
(Summer Glau) as its wispy, erratic hero around whom the other characters'
lives—and deaths—coalesce. If not an ode to River, *Serenity* is, at the very
least, arranged to play in her key. The central narrative arcs in both *Firefly*
(2002–03) and *Serenity* work to repudiate River, from confused and damaged
child to impressive "psychic warrior" (Beeler 2008: 45). By the end of the
prematurely canceled television series, River endears herself to the crew after
ingeniously outsmarting a bounty hunter set on her recapture in "Objects in
Space" (13 December 2002). By the end of the film, River takes things a step
further and prevails twofold against the traumatic legacy of her captors. In
a startling display of martial skill, River defeats a vicious, frenzied horde of
Reavers, killing machines born of Alliance incompetence and maleficence.

In doing so, she buys enough time for her captain, Mal Reynolds (Nathan Fillion) to overcome the Parliamentary Operative (Chiwetel Ejiofor) and broadcast the Alliance's misdeeds on the planet Miranda into the 'verse.

River's physical victory over the Reavers and her psychic victory over the Operative, whose hunt for her ends after she reveals the secrets he was meant to conceal, provide a few chinks in the Alliance's monolithic armor. But, the long-term impact of River's double victory is unclear. The Alliance is vast and Serenity small. The 'verse is still full of Reavers. Serenity will still encounter all the everyday threats facing a smuggling vessel and her crew. Ostensibly free from her captors, River proves herself a potent weapon and crucial asset to her family and friends, but will it be enough to afford her an unfettered life?

Then again, rather than concern itself with River's future, *Serenity* obsesses over her past. Like many heroes before her, River's greatest curse is also a source of tremendous strength. While River was "weaponized" by the Alliance, she was chosen as a subject for such experimentation precisely because of genetic and intellectual aptitudes she possessed as a child (Marano 2007: 40). An unequivocal genius, both River's protectors and her pursuers consider her special, although the connotation of that specialness is inconsistent, from Simon's (Sean Maher) insistence that she is "gifted" in "Serenity" (20 December 2002) to Mal's concern that she's still "crazy" despite her brother's careful treatments in *Serenity*. River herself is also a host of contradictions. She looks slight and frail, but is unbelievably strong and fast; she is psychic, but not always comprehensible; and she is plagued by a slippery form of agency so often the provenance of madwomen in literature, film, and television—at her most powerful only when she is not herself.

During moments of coherence and socially acceptable interactions with the crew, River presents as a vulnerable, if precocious, child. During fevered fits of rage or ostensibly psychotic lapses, River holds the fate of the crew in her hands both literally and figuratively. It is her mercurial agency and the perception of her clairvoyance as madness that has led to a few comparisons between River and the ancient Trojan priestess Cassandra. Alyson R. Buckman, for example, writes that "While the possibility exists for a simple, traditional, sexist representation of River as a disabled madwoman, instead she is represented as a Cassandra figure with knowledge that is unacknowledged: the audience and then the crew gradually come to realize that River is not insane but gifted" (2008: 45). Karen Beeler identifies River as one of several "postfeminist Cassandras" on contemporary television, an anti-heroine whose categorization as "dangerous and abnormal" should not "devalue" the character, but instead makes her a "unique illustration of postfeminist 'girl power'" (2008: 39).

While others have likened these two psychic misfits, the Cassandra-

River connection deserves further investigation. By considering River in relation to Cassandra, whose life and death is also so intimately bound to her captors' misdeeds, we can see how both women's so-called hysteria manifests instead as a form of incisive intelligence. In the case of Cassandra, featured frequently in ancient Greek mythology and drama, the prophet finds herself cursed by the god Apollo with the power to see the future but to never have her predictions believed. As such, she functions as a troubling symbol of the consequences of psychic violation and its unintended, sometimes brutal effects. Dismissed as a crazed madwoman by Trojans and Greeks alike, Cassandra warns against the pitfalls of betraying one's kin and choosing profit over honor, all while her warnings go largely ignored. Thus, when Troy is sacked and she becomes a captive, Cassandra's agency as a slave is far greater than her counterparts; she is given leeway to speak and act against the grain, performing a narrative of ecstatic revenge on her Greek captors without the punishment such rhetoric would usually inspire. When Cassandra eventually meets her foretold death, she does so with a brazen kind of bravery, knowing her murder will be avenged and that this vengeance will mean utter ruin for the family of her enslavers.

River's defeat of the Reavers also functions as a cathartic moment of retribution and redemption through which she both destroys the crew's immediate enemy and guarantees her own legitimacy as a psychic, as a fighter, and as an irreplaceable asset to Serenity's crew. While River survives and Cassandra does not, these characters embody the ways in which patriarchal interference can both irreparably damage the innocent and create horrifying monsters. Acting as articulations of the effect of an invasive and oppressive force, River and Cassandra employ strategies of vengeance in which they risk or sacrifice their own lives in ways that seem "crazy," but actually make perfect sense in the context of their prophetic knowledge. This essay explores these acts of madness and vengeance through a close analysis of Cassandra's characterization in two ancient Greek dramas and a consideration of River's trajectory in *Serenity* as a fantasy of feminist revenge against a masculinist terror. Misunderstood and misjudged, River and Cassandra are simultaneously encumbered and freed by their stark difference from those around them, their "madness" a blessing and a curse.

A Prophet's Revenge

Greek playwrights Aeschylus and Euripides leave us with two different, but no less captivating, representations of the priestess Cassandra at moments when she turns her own doomed fate and tragic powers of clairvoyance into unexpected courage and strength. In her youth, Cassandra receives her prophetic powers from the god Apollo, only to rebuff his sexual advances despite his assumption of a *quid pro quo* arrangement. Enraged that Cassandra reneged on their agreement, Apollo inflicts on her a particularly cruel curse: to see the future, but never be believed (Aeschylus 2003: 85–6). In both *Trojan Women* and *Agamemnon,* the Chorus, her captors, and even her own mother only understand Cassandra when she is speaking of the past. Otherwise, all they hear and see is madness and folly—a hysteric flitting before them in the throes of psychosis—even while her words ring true to the audience, whose knowledge of the Trojan War and its aftershocks throughout the Greek mythos verify Cassandra's claims.

Euripides' *Trojan Women* (415 BCE), written later than Aeschylus' play but recounting an earlier episode in Cassandra's life, highlights the despair and fear felt by the losers of the Trojan War. With the city's warriors slain, all who remain in Troy are the women and girls, led by their dethroned queen, Hecuba, who wait miserably to hear from the Greek messenger to which of the conquering Greeks they will each be distributed as spoils of war. Now slaves whose best case scenario is to find themselves allocated to a "good" master who will not beat or rape them, the remaining women react with shock when Hecuba's daughter, Cassandra, whirls her way onto the stage in the throes of joy over her impending "marriage" to Mycenaean king Agamemnon. In her seeming madness, Cassandra equates her slavery to a wedding, not because she feels anything but loathing for her Greek captor, but because she knows what their journey back to his homeland portends: "Agamemnon, marrying me, will make / A marriage more disastrous than Helen's. / Our wedding night will be a night of death / And devastation for his house; I'll kill him, I'll / Avenge my father and my brothers' blood" (Euripides 2009: 43). Cassandra compares herself to Helen, whose elopement with Cassandra's brother, Paris, sparked the Greek siege on Troy and the city's ensuing destruction. Cassandra's vengeance will be nothing less than the knowledge that Agamemnon's family is destined for utter ruin, even if she dies in the process.

That said, Cassandra's reference to "killing" is not literal, but by proxy: Agamemnon's wife Clytemnestra and her lover Aegithus plan to murder him upon his return. Cassandra's vengeance takes hold in the role she knows she has to play in this impending drama, as she asserts that "when you take me from this land / You'll take with you a Fury, one of three" (47). Upon their arrival, Cassandra knows her presence will only infuriate Clytemnestra further and solidify the queen's resolve, hence the prophet can cast herself in the role of avenger rather than victim. Even though her foreknowledge also provides her with a brutal depiction of her own death and her body that they will "slash and dump in some ravine" where she will "lie, naked, for wild beasts to feed on (46), Cassandra remains confident that vengeance will be hers. This is especially remarkable in a play in which all the other women must submit to their captors and bow before their will. For example, Cassandra's sister-in-law, Andromache, forced to marry the son of the man who killed her husband, can do nothing but watch in horror as the Greeks rip her young child from her breast and hurl him from the city walls. Cassandra, thought delirious, is given free rein to speak to the point that the Greek messenger, Talthybius, confesses, "If Apollo hadn't made you crazy, / We'd punish you for hurling at our leaders / Such evil omens as they leave your country" (45). While she has no possibility for physical resistance, Cassandra's free speech is a form of agency quite remarkable for a woman in this time period, no less a prisoner of war.

Even during her entrance in Aeschylus' *Agamemnon* (458 BCE), Cassandra stands defiant in the returned king's war chariot, refusing to respond to Clytemnestra's demands that she enter the house—a house in which the Trojan woman knows the queen is preparing to slaughter both the king and his new slave. Only once Clytemnestra leaves does Cassandra begin to speak to the Chorus, telling them about both the royal family's bloody past and its fatal future. "Yes, soused on human blood / to utter recklessness, a home-brewed, / rioting band of Eryines [Furies] is dwelling there, / not easily driven out," Cassandra says of the past, and the Chorus understands her perfectly, marveling that she knows the dark story of Agamemnon's father, Atreus, who killed, cooked, and served his brother's children to him in order to punish the brother for seducing Atreus' wife (Aeschylus 2003: 85). But, moments later, the Chorus cannot comprehend her when she foretells her own murder and that of Agamemnon, avowing that his children Orestes and Electra will in turn kill their mother and her lover in a final act of revenge that will bring the family's bloody narrative to a close. Through her death, Cassandra has the satisfaction of fulfilling her fate as retributive force against a powerful family of Greeks and defying the god who ruined her life.

Like in *Trojan Women*, it is not Cassandra's role to enact revenge herself; she is a catalyst for action who calls for vengeance in her final words on stage, before she walks knowingly to her own slaughter: "I pray to the sun's last shining / that my avengers will exact a bloody / payment from my foes, for my murder too, / for murdering a slave, a harmless prey" (89). When the Chorus commends her for her bravery, she explains that there is no use in fighting when she cannot change the outcome of events. And yet, Cassandra again performs a shocking act of rebellion, renouncing her bond to Apollo, whose ceremonial staff, priestly robes, and garlands she rips from her body and tears apart just prior to her death (88). Here, she both blames Apollo for her death ("And the prophet has destroyed his prophetess, / escorting me off to meet my fate right here, / right now.") and recognizes that through her death a part of him will be lost as well ("At least I can destroy you / before my own destruction!") (88).

Apollo may have given Cassandra her powers of foresight, but he doomed her almost in the same breath. While the Greek gods enact far harsher punishments for disobedience throughout the ancient mythos, Cassandra's plight seems particularly bleak, most notably because of its extended duration and wide impact. Apollo's curse results in death not only for his priestess, but also for a majority of the population of Troy and a well-respected Greek king. By refusing to follow through on their agreement of sex in exchange for her clairvoyance, Cassandra sets into motion a disproportionately cataclysmic chain of events while still paradoxically benefiting—if one can call it that—from the power given to her by Apollo. Much like River, Cassandra's struggle emerges from this split between her impressive powers and their undesirable side effects. Both women appear to others as crazy, hysterical, or otherwise mentally ill, but are only perceived in these ways because of powerful forces that attempted and failed to fully bring these women under their control. For example, in a compelling move that will prove useful in my following analysis of *Serenity*, a number of scholars attribute Cassandra's appearance of hysteria to her friction with patriarchal culture writ large.

As Krista Ratcliffe asserts, "Cassandra comes down to us through a tradition of patriarchal myths as a wise women to whom no one pays the slightest heed" (1995: 63). Laurie Schapira provides some historical specificity, as well, identifying Cassandra's "hysteria," in particular her acceptance and then subsequent refusal of Apollo's sexual advances, to the uncertainty of the priestess' social position during a time when Troy's matriarchal culture and systems of worship were being subsumed—and, ultimately, destroyed—by Greece's patriarchal values (1988: 19). Schapira later elaborates, "Cassandra personifies the archetypal conflict between matriarchal and patriarchal values, both vying for supremacy and with no eros to connect them. Hysteria has long been a manifestation of this psychic split" (37). Cassandra does not fit into the new culture she confronts, chafing at knowledge she should not have and cannot share. River oscillates between frightened girl and assertive assassin, while struggling to negotiate a mind that the Alliance has tampered with in profound ways. It is no wonder that both women find solace in the destruction of those who seek to control them.

The Alliance and Its Discontents

As a show, *Firefly* illustrates the many ways Serenity's crew position themselves in opposition to the Alliance, which strives for order, obedience, and extreme pragmatism in all things. A smuggling vessel, Serenity is built for speed and stealth, a contrast to the imposing hulk of many Alliance ships they encounter. Mal and Zoe (Gina Torres) fought outright against the Alliance in the past, and while other crewmembers may be mercenaries (Jayne, played by Adam Baldwin) or taking advantage of the crew's nomadic lifestyle for professional purposes (Inara, played by Morena Baccarin), everyone on Serenity seems, at the very least, content to buck Alliance protocols with impunity. Mal especially resists the repressive and homogenizing will of the Alliance, aligning himself with the figure of the outlaw rather than the hero, as frequently observed by fans and scholars alike (see Buckman 2008 and Hill 2009). Along these lines, the *Firefly*-verse simultaneously embraces and challenges generic conventions of Westerns and science fiction in an effort to dismantle viewers' expectations of norms of behavior and narrative structure. River functions, then, as a prime example of the characters' constant pushback against any attempts to define or constrict them. As Matthew Hill elaborates:

> Ephemeral and in perpetual motion, she embodies her namesake, at the cost of any sense of coherent, stable subjectivity. In this sense, Whedon models with River the dangerous side of "mobility" as a response to trauma: taken to its logical extreme, psychological mobility borders on the dissolution of the conscious mind, a total instability in personality [2009: 499].

While River's mental instability can be linked back to the trauma she faced at the hands of the Alliance, it is instructive to return for a moment to Cassandra. Her ostensible madness may prevent Cassandra from saving her family, but it does allow her to disrupt social mores and, eventually, "kill the very ones [she] hate[s] the most" (Euripides 2009: 45).

River also unravels the fabric of social expectations, and her oddness manifests itself in a number of ways throughout the series, to the extent that she is often underestimated, ignored, belittled, feared, laughed at, pitied, and condescended to—even by her own brother. In "Safe" (8 November 2002), River's powers of perception cause the religious townsfolk to accuse her of witchcraft, and they naturally attempt to burn her at the stake. Even as Simon jumps up to protect her, and even though he tentatively believes in her mind-reading abilities, he continues to doubt her, not understanding that when she tells him that they will be saved by "daddy," she is predicting the inevitable rescue by Mal and his crew, not suffering a psychotic break. Not fully trusted by anyone, including her own brother, River breaking free of Alliance imprisonment and experimentation seems simple compared to the far greater challenge that awaits her on the outside. Now, she must make sense of a vast network of secrets and lies that only she knows; she must make others see and understand what she sees; and then she must help the others understand that her way of seeing the world is not crazy, but just unlike anything they have seen before. As such, Buckman argues that River "enacts resistance to the Western system of language and logic" (2008: 45). She pushes back against our understanding of what a girl should be and how she should speak, and her words, though comprehensible as such, often come across as indecipherable to the crew.

The portent of Cassandra's words is also mostly indecipherable to friend and foe alike, but in both *Trojan Women* and *Agamemnon*, her first utterances are not words at all; she shrieks and keens, and her nonverbal outcries of woe and warning are then followed by sinister, initially vague predictions of harm: "The terrible labor of / true prophecy whirls me around, and I / am shaken to the core with darkening preludes!" (Aeschylus 2003: 86). River, too, begins her time on Serenity with a scream in "Serenity." She screams frequently, she wails, she falls to the ground, she holds her ears, she shakes, she whimpers, and she mutters. River's voice often disrupts the space of the ship and damages the "calm" of the crew (as Jayne declares, when River becomes overwhelmed on Miranda). In *Serenity*'s opening scene, young River tells a teacher that the reason people rebel is because the Alliance is meddlesome and "people don't like to be meddled with." The teacher's response is to stab a fountain pen through her pupil's forehead just as the scene cuts to teenage River screaming in a darkened laboratory, a needle through her cranium and equipment and scientists monitoring her every thought. Whether the schoolhouse vision is a dream, a memory, or a premonition, River's powers of insight resonate in this moment, pulling us into the film's world through physical signs of her trauma (the outcry) and her profound awareness of the Alliance's pernicious interference with people's lives.

The imagined/remembered classroom makes another appearance later in the film while River is locked in what passes for Serenity's brig after being triggered by a subliminal message and indiscriminately attacking a bar full of people. Again, she dreams of the bucolic, yet sterile, outdoor classroom, this time free of other children and all the more haunting for it. The lighting of the scene is overly bright, whites bleeding and hazy at the edges, but River is in sharp focus, wearing the grey leggings and hospital gown she had on when Simon rescued her from the laboratory at the beginning of the film. Blood trickles down her forehead from the aforementioned needle, linking these two schoolhouse visions together. Barefoot as usual, her steps are deliberate and sure, but her face betrays suspicion as she gazes down at a running electronic tablet on one of the desks. Chinese characters scroll by as the camera zooms in and the focus shifts to a planet and moon reflecting on the black screen. Zooming in further, the camera enters the screen and flips; suddenly the planet appears in the foreground, River on a white screen suspended above it, looking down. When the shot cuts back to a profile of River's face in the washed-out classroom, we only hold on her for a moment before a rapid succession of static images of dead bodies and the sound of swarming flies take her place. Then we are back to River's profile, but only for a moment:

suddenly, a Reaver grabs her face, forcing her gaze onto its rotting flesh and open, toothy mouth. Rather than another scream, the vision ends with River back in the brig, calm and suddenly in full control of her faculties. Moments later, she fights her way past first Jayne and then Simon to make it to the bridge and redirect the ship to Miranda.

In this scene, several things come to the fore, including how River's visions alternatively haunt and empower her and how her psychosis and her psychic-ness are so closely aligned. *Serenity* blurs the line between River's ability as a "reader," as Mal calls her, and her seeming hysteria so completely that it is never clear whether the Alliance's attempts to create a psychic assassin caused River's mental instability or if her apparent madness is merely a form of growing pains as she learns to harness her psychic (and other) abilities in order to make them functional in relation to the more conservative minds of "normal" others. The scene also highlights River's connection to two other unintended consequences of Alliance experimentation gone wrong: the millions dead on Miranda and the brutal Reavers. Beeler elaborates on this connection by drawing on the homonymic qualities of the words "River," "Reaver," and "reader":

> The link between being a "reader" or a woman of vision, and a "Reaver," a mad creature, is not unusual in the context of how women with visionary and psychic abilities have been constructed in literature and culture. Cassandra was presented as a mad seer because people did not believe her prophecies and because the impact of the visions was so strong that it affected her psyche and her body [2008: 43].

Like River, Miranda and the Reavers are secrets the Alliance wants to keep. In order to protect itself, the Alliance hid Miranda by vanishing the entire planet from maps and history books, an easy thing to do because the dead are silent and tell no tales (except to River). The Reavers and River, too erratic to be silenced, are instead disavowed and made unbelievable. Even a well-educated man like Simon initially thinks Reavers are just "campfire tales" ("Serenity"), and whole settlements frequently fall victim to their raids, suggesting either a lack of awareness of the danger they pose or skepticism regarding the existence of Reavers on the part of some settlers.

The Alliance's approach to dealing with River is far more insidious. At the beginning of *Serenity*, just before being subjected to a forced ritual suicide by the Operative, one of River's doctors attempts to minimize the depth of her ability: "Whatever secrets she might have accidentally gleaned," he says, "it's possible she doesn't even know she knows them, that they're buried beneath layers of psychosis." Later, River tells Simon, "They show me off like a dog. Old men covered in blood, never touched them, but they're drowning in it. I don't know what I'm saying. I never know what I'm saying." Perhaps recalling an incident where the Alliance made her perform some of her more fatal "tricks," River also reveals an essential detail. Whether the Alliance deliberately caused River's mental instability or not, her hysterical presentation clearly works to their advantage, obfuscating River's own understanding of her visions and undercutting her believability just as Apollo did so successfully with the doomed Cassandra.

Thinking of River as similarly doomed, however, is counterproductive. Buckman assures us, "River cannot be encapsulated by traditional employments of women as lunatics or witches. She is far too complicated, and her excesses enable the transgression of these limits" (2008: 47). While Buckman hones in on the "force of community" that allows River to "de-center" masculine discourse in order to revise it (48), her use of French philosopher Helene Cixous to link River to the "bodies of hysterical women" who wield feminine discourse like a weapon provides a more apt parallel to the agency both River and Cassandra reflect when they embrace and are ultimately able to leverage the burden of nonconformity and apparent madness inflicted on them by the meddlesome powers that be. Cixous articulates the way women's writing can be used to undercut and dismantle oppressive patriarchal linguistic systems. Putting aside her essentialist assumptions regarding the man/woman binary and woman's inherent differences, it is worth remembering Cixous' philosophy operates both actually (via her subject: women's writing) and metaphorically, in terms of how reinforced and embraced difference can shatter paradigms and force authoritarian regimes to loosen their stranglehold on "correct" behavior and restrictive social norms.

Cixous sees the potential of feminine discourse as both destructive and rehabilitating. She writes,

> If woman has always functioned "within" the discourse of man, a signifier that has always referred back to the opposite signifier which annihilates its specific energy and diminishes or stifles its very different sounds, it is time for her to dislocate this "within," to explore it, turn it around, and seize it; to make it hers, containing it, taking it in her own mouth, biting that tongue with her very own teeth to invent for herself a language to get inside of [1976: 887].

By creating her own language, woman can begin operating from within a space that is truly her own rather than a set of norms created by (masculine) others. There is quite a bit to say about the role gender plays in *Firefly* and *Serenity* (see Taylor 2004 and Marano 2007). However, even though River's gender may be crucial to her disempowerment and eventual reclamation of agency, the linguistic and structural points drawn out by Cixous and illustrated by River and Cassandra extend far beyond the gendered experiences of an individual character. Just as the overly rational, borderline fascist Alliance operates as a foil for the ragtag, contradictory community of Serenity's crew, we can see in the Reavers and the Operative opposing ends on a spectrum of patriarchal/masculinist terror that only River's starkly divergent way of seeing the world—her madness—can defeat.

Miranda overwhelms River with its cacophony of silent dead, all of whom gave up living when Alliance scientists pumped the air full of a chemical meant to calm the populace. In this scene, River spins, and the camera spins with her as she pulls at her face and clothes, again enacting her break with normality bodily and verbally:

> [Merciful God, please take me away!] Make them stop. They're everywhere. Every city, every house, every room—they're all inside me. I hear them all. They're saying nothing. Get up. Please get up. [I will close my ears and my heart and I will be a stone.] Please God, make me a stone [bracketed portions translated from the Chinese in Sullivan 2014].

In this moment, the lack of voices in her head is River's undoing. She begs to become a stone, begs to be made inert and unfeeling, a curious choice given her horror at those on Miranda who met more or less this exact fate. Attempting to create a peaceful and pliant citizenry, the Alliance instead orchestrated a mass suicide by people who lost all will to be human, to be anything but stones.

The Operative aligns himself with this haunting vision of the future and Mal taunts him with his own proclamation that he is fighting for a "world without sin." When Mal defeats the Operative at the end of the film and broadcasts the Miranda transmission throughout the 'verse, the captain assures him, "I ain't gonna kill you. Hell, I'm gonna grant your greatest wish. I'm going to show you a world without sin." Just as willing to kill children as he is willing to sacrifice himself for his mission in his single-minded pursuit of silencing River, the Operative exemplifies the purest and worst manifestation of Western rationalism over and above concerns regarding ethics, liberty, or humanity. On the other hand, the Reavers, also products of the Alliance's chemicalized air, evince the worst of stereotypically masculine violence and aggression as they rape, murder, and cannibalize with impunity. When River confronts these forces, however, she is not just a girl, nor is she a madwoman-*qua*-monster. She represents the intrinsic advantage given to those who see the world through fresh and divergent eyes.

River's willingness to engage with her own emotions, especially fear, only strengthens her resolve, as it does with Cassandra. River comes by her fear honestly enough: she knows what people are thinking and knows, to a certain extent, what obstacles lie in the path of the crew's survival and success. Tellingly, River tries to warn Simon that her presence on the ship is not safe for their friends just before her assassin persona takes control in the bar, but Simon, still thinking of his sister as "just a girl" misunderstands her pronouncement and shows concern only for River's safety until it is almost too late. By the time River tearfully warns Simon that "things are going to get much, much worse," there is little any of them can do to stop the cascade of events that have been set in motion. In *Trojan Women*, Cassandra tells the

Chorus how she predicted the fall of her home city of Troy, all for naught: "But what good came of it? There was / no cure to save the city from what / it had to suffer. Now I, too, am / on fire/ I, too, will crash to the ground" (Aeschylus 2003: 84). Like her, River initially succumbs to hopelessness in the face of catastrophic horror. It is this ability to feel, understand, and embrace fear and regret that undergird the resolve of both priestess and psychic.

River may recognize terror in others and feel it deeply, but she does not concern herself with the possibility of failure nor is she burdened by others' idea of ideal behavior as she defies them at every turn. Through Cixous, we can again see the power evinced by River's refusal to bow down before normative expectations around emotion and action: "We're stormy, and that which is ours breaks loose from us without our fearing any debilitation … we never hold back our thoughts, our signs, our writing; and we're not afraid of lacking" (Cixous 1976: 878). While Cixous cites non-normative discourse as essential to dismantling structural oppression, Michael Marano's analysis of Whedon's "weaponized women" relies on the notion of hope to reinforce how the *Firefly*-verse sets River apart from other characters and subsequently allows her to succeed: River diverts the

> punishing, meddling, Patriarchal authority that, Zeus-like, seeks to control us through force and fear [and] represent[s] the hope of overcoming or subverting that authority. These women use that hope and actualize that hope by actualizing themselves, by taking control of their destinies in another directed way that is a boon to those of their immediate home and family spaces, and also to all of society [2007: 46].

River both refuses to bear the burden of conformity and eventually sees hope in the face of seemingly insurmountable adversity. However, what's truly unique about River is her brazen acceptance of her role in what will come to pass, which allows her to transform what passes for madness into a dance of ecstatic revenge.

Conclusion: The Dancer and the Dance

By way of conclusion, let us consider two moments when River performs acts of apparently irrational, but ultimately brilliant bravery in order to protect those she loves. I want to particularly interrogate these moments as ecstatic ones, utilizing the original ancient Greek definition of the word— *ekstatis,* standing outside oneself. Contemporary philosopher Jules Evans elaborates that Platonic philosophy asserts two articulations of ecstasy: "the way of the philosopher or mystic, who over years and years of contemplation frees their soul from ignorance and finally attains an ecstatic knowledge of the Divine," and "the way of the artist or seer, who suddenly gets seized by

God and goes into an ecstatic trance, a sort of divine madness" (2013). The lack of ignorance, ecstasy in knowledge, and "divine madness" of sudden insight are all crucial to an understanding of River's ability to enact vengeance where others cannot. In fact, the respectively triumphant and explosive climaxes of *Firefly*'s final episode and *Serenity* illustrate the ways River stands outside of herself as not just a sage or a seer, but as both.

At the end of "Objects in Space," River outsmarts bounty hunter Jubal Early (Richard Brooks) by pretending to become Serenity. The episode takes great pains to acknowledge how River feels ostracized by the crew, making her merging with the ship seem, for a moment, a desirable and understandable turn of events, especially in light of her admission to Early that she "[Doesn't] belong. Dangerous like you. Can't be controlled. Can't be trusted." In this storyline, River aligns herself with Serenity in such a way that, despite illustrating how she does not fit in and that the space of the ship is too confined to contain her, emphasizes how integral River and her psychosis/psychic abilities are to the crew's survival. In other words, River is just incongruous enough in her surroundings that her plan to pretend she's "melted" into the ship seems plausible. After Early has been overpowered and jettisoned into space, River enjoys a brief respite from the crew's concerns over her sanity, their gratitude outweighing their worries. Here, River masquerades as not herself, pretending instead to be Serenity and playing a clever, if absurdly dangerous, game of chess with the bounty hunter. The mental game River plays with Early and its effects, however, do not hold a candle to River's climactic battle with the Reavers at the end of *Serenity*.

The scene itself is short, particularly considering its agonizing prelude. Pursued by Alliance cruisers and Reavers, Serenity crash lands, and a Reaver harpoon impales and kills pilot Wash (Alan Tudyk). This shocking death of one of the film's main characters clouds the finale with a sense of true precarity. No life is sacred and any of them—all of them—could die. Her husband dead, first mate Zoe becomes a stoic soldier bent solely on killing as many Reavers as possible. When Jayne admonishes her to concentrate on strategy rather than recklessly throwing herself into battle, Zoe's bleak response emphasizes the dire situation in which they find themselves:

> JAYNE: You can't be thinkin' on revenge if we're gonna get through this.
> ZOE: Do you really think any of us are going to get through this?

As the Reavers begin fighting through the barricades, everything, as River predicted, gets much, much worse. By the time she steps in, the fate of the crew does appear quite hopeless: Zoe has been partially incapacitated with a deep gash along her spine, engineer Kaylee (Jewel Staite) is beginning to suffer paralysis from a poisoned dart, and they have all been forced to retreat into a narrow corridor with no useable exit. Moreover, the blast doors separating them from the Reavers refuse to close completely, while Simon has left his medical bag on the other side of the door.

While early in the battle, River suffered a meltdown, overwhelmed by the Reavers' rageful and ravenous minds, by this time she is fretfully engaged in watching the action, twitching as her eyes flit from person to person, assessing damage, her hair hanging limp and sweaty in front of her eyes. When Simon is shot through the gap in the doors and subsequently apologizes to his sister for not keeping her safe as he bleeds out on the floor, River kneels beside him, calmer than before but with her voice high and girlish: "You take care of me Simon. You've always taken care of me." As she stands, we see the shift in her from impotent to determined; even the lighting around River changes as if she is suffused with a warm glow from within. "My turn," River intones before running headlong toward the narrow opening left in the blast doors, diving through it, and rolling straight into the lion's den. She takes down two Reavers immediately and seals the door from the outside, tossing her brother's medical bag into the corridor just before the opening closes and she is physically dragged into the fray by the Reaver horde.

At this point, the film interrupts River's action to focus on Mal overcoming the Operative for many suspenseful minutes. It is not until Mal has prevailed, trapping the Operative and broadcasting the Miranda transmission, that we learn of River's fate. Whether dead or alive, her sacrifice will have not been in vain. As the camera cuts back to River, her fist connects with a Reaver's face in slow motion and then the scene shifts into a rapid-paced melee with River in the center, wielding a sword and an axe, picking off Reavers with the skill and finesse of a practiced warrior and balletic grace befitting both River's love of dance (mentioned explicitly in "Serenity," "Safe," and *Serenity*) and actor Summer Glau's background as a dancer (Anon. 2005). During the fight, the camera and lighting sway and swerve to encapsulate the frenetic energy of the Reavers alongside River's own preternatural calm and effortless martial skill. When the blast doors finally open, River stands poised in victory in her flimsy grey dress, blood dripping from her weapons, the bodies of Reavers littered around her in one of the most iconic images of the film.

River's act of reckoning is an ecstatic dance through which she achieves revenge for herself, for Zoe, for Miranda's dead, and for her friends and brother who have been hounded by the Alliance and its misdeeds. Cixous' articulation of how women's writing—a feminine discourse of madness, release, relinquishment, and difference—empowers and liberates proves instructive here:

> As a militant, she is an integral part of all liberations. She must be farsighted, not limited to a blow-by-blow interaction. She foresees that her liberation will do more than modify power relations or toss the ball over to the other camp; she will bring

about a mutation in human relations, in thought, in all praxis: hers is not simply a class struggle, which she carries forward into a much vaster movement [1976: 882].

Understanding River's revenge as ecstatic does not necessitate that she must take pleasure in that violence; rather, River operates outside herself, on a higher plane than her comrades knowing that all of their actions have consequences far outreaching the confines of their last stand. When taken captive, Cassandra sings an ecstatic lyric monody to celebrate her pyrrhic future victory over the Greeks who stole her homeland; she suffers literally from a divine madness of Apollonian origins (Euripides 2009: 41–2). In her final moments, though, the priestess renounces the god and walks calmly to her own death because she is outside of herself and can see the expansive ripples of change beyond her own death (Aeschylus 2003: 90).

River, who despairingly prays to God to "make me a stone" on the planet Miranda, has no real gods to defy, only expectation. Up until this point, everyone has been taking care of her, with Simon so fixated on keeping his sister safe that he has not allowed either of them to really live. Beyond the Reavers, though, River sees life—not just for herself, but for them all. It is her ability to see outside herself, via the permeable boundaries of other peoples' thoughts, as well as her clear-sighted confidence in herself and the future that allow River to emerge victorious. Understood and embraced by the crew and, hence, freed from her apparent madness through their acceptance and celebration of her difference, River does not have to die like Cassandra to enact vengeance. Previously haunted by secrets and pursued by her captors, River's most potent revenge rests in her freedom from others' demands. In the film's final scene, River co-pilots Serenity alongside Mal, once again holding the lives of the crew in her hands. This time, though, the burden of trust is one freely given with River willingly taking the reins.

WORKS CITED

Aeschylus. (2003). *Agamemnon*, in *The Oresteia*. Trans. Alan Shapiro and Peter Burian. Oxford, UK: Oxford University Press.

Anon. (2005). "Dance of the Telepathic Space Assassin," in *The Telegraph*. On-line. Available HTTP: http://www.telegraph.co.uk/culture/3646900/Dance-of-the-telepathic-space-assassin.html (22 June 2017).

Beeler, Karin E. (2008). *Seers, Witches and Psychics on Screen: An Analysis of Women Visionary Characters in Recent Television and Film*. Jefferson, NC: McFarland.

Buckman, Alyson R. (2008). "'Much Madness Is Divinest Sense': *Firefly*'s 'Big Damn Heroes' and Little Witches," in Rhonda Wilcox and Tanya R. Cochran (eds.) *Investigating* Firefly *and* Serenity: *Science Fiction on the Frontier*. London: I.B. Tauris, 41–9.

Cixous, Helene. (1976). "The Laugh of the Medusa," in *Signs* 1.4: 875–93.

Euripides. (2009). *Trojan Women*. Trans. Alan Shapiro. Oxford, UK: Oxford University Press.

Evans, Jules. (2013). "Modern Ecstasy, or the Art of Losing Control," in *Philosophy for Life, and Other Dangerous Situations*. On-line. Available HTTP: http://www.philosophyfor life.org/modern-ecstasy-or-the-art-of-losing-control/ (3 July 2017).

Hill, Matthew B. (2009). "'I Am a Leaf on the Wind': Cultural Trauma and Mobility in Joss Whedon's *Firefly*," in *Extrapolation* 50.3: 484–511.

Marano, Michael. (2007). "River Tam and the Weaponized Women of the Whedonverse," in Jane Espenson and Leah Wison (eds.) *Serenity Found: More Unauthorized Essays on Joss Whedon's* Firefly *Universe*. Dallas: Benbella Books, 37–48.

Ratcliffe, Krista. (1995). "Listening to Cassandra: A Materialist-Feminist Expose of the Necessary Relations between Rhetoric and Hermeneutics," in *Studies in the Literary Imagination* 28.2: 63–77.

Schapira, Laurie Layton. (1988). *The Cassandra Complex: Living with Disbelief: a Modern Perspective on Hysteria*. Toronto, CA: Inner City Books.

Sullivan, Kevin. (2014). "*Serenity* (movie)," in *Firefly-Serenity Chinese Pinyinary*. On-line. Available HTTP: http://fireflychinese.kevinsullivansite.net/title/serenitymovie.html (1 June 2017).

Taylor, Robert B. (2004). "The Captain May Wear the Tight Pants, but It's the Gals Who Make Serenity Soar," in Jane Espenson (ed.) *Finding Serenity: Anti-Heroes, Lost Shepherds, and Space Hookers in Joss Whedon's* Firefly. Dallas: Benbella Books, 131–8.

"Better worlds"
Western Heroes
and the Civilized 'Verse

FREDERICK BLICHERT

The legacy of *Firefly* (2003–03) is impossible to divorce from its engagement with genre. The series rather forcefully and anachronistically blends science fiction and the American Western. And it was very much marketed in a way that highlighted that seemingly unlikely pairing. FOX capitalized on the bizarre nature of this genre blending with ad campaigns that stressed just how "out there" the show was (Pascale 2014: 215). In reality, there is little about the science fiction Western that could be labeled "out there," though *Firefly* does take the aesthetic disjunction between genres farther than most texts. Just as the original *Star Trek* (1966–9) was sold to NBC as "*Wagon Train* to the stars," Joss Whedon's follow-up to his popular *Buffy the Vampire Slayer* (1997–2003) was clearly aiming for a similar generic marriage, if more obviously so (Buchanan 2004: 47). Nevertheless, it fits into a long tradition of Western gunslingers and cattle ranchers finding their analogues in outer space. *Star Trek*'s "final frontier" is a rather on-the-nose acknowledgement of this, but that frontier pops up elsewhere remarkably often.

It must have been at least a bit of a shock for audiences when *Serenity* (Joss Whedon, 2005), the feature film sequel to the canceled *Firefly*, toned the Western elements of the series way down, opting for a more recognizably futuristic sci-fi narrative. The characters remained, as did a number of clear markers of cowboys-in-space Western-ness, but the unrelenting nods to the Western genre in *Firefly* were certainly tamed in favor of a film more wholly aligned with high-tech, futuristic science fiction. This is not to say that *Serenity* sheds its allegiance to the Western. In fact, its investment in the themes and iconography of American frontier myths is one of the film's most prominent and rewarding features, even if they are less aesthetically overt than in

Firefly. If anything, *Serenity* may be engaging with the Western genre far more meaningfully than the series ever did.

Cowboys in Space

Of course Westerns and science fiction can be blended together in very different ways, and certain categorical difference are important. John Wills breaks down how *Firefly* taps into the various iterations of science fiction Westerns. In fact, he proposes that the science fiction Western is itself distinct from the "space Western." This distinction is largely predicated on the existence of two frontiers: the literal Western frontier of nineteenth century America and the futuristic "final frontier" of undiscovered space. For Wills, *Firefly* plays with both, as in its first aired episode "The Train Job" (20 September 2002), which uses Western iconography to suggest a literal Old West setting before eventually revealing the show's science fictional outer space setting: "The opening scene of *Firefly* thus begins with one frontier and ends with another" (2015: 2). Here, our expectations are destabilized, and possibly doubly so. The characters seem to be in the old west, but even before they are revealed to exist in the future, in an entirely different solar system than that of the old west's Earth, there remains a momentary possibility that they could be situated in an alternate historical America with futuristic technology.

Overarchingly, *Firefly* is an example of what Wills calls the space Western, a subgenre of both science fiction and the Western "where themes and features of the American West are applied to a space setting" (2). The space Western is a rather common blending of genres, and includes quite popular examples like *Flash Gordon* (Frederick Stephani, 1936), *Star Trek*, *Star Wars* (George Lucas, 1977), *Outland* (Peter Hyams, 1981), and *Avatar* (James Cameron, 2009), not to mention countless examples in print media. *Firefly* certainly conforms to this tradition, but it manages to tap into the more standard science fiction/Western hybrids set firmly in the old west itself. *Firefly* certainly is not situated there or then, but it recreates that old west within its outer space setting in an *almost* literal way. That is to say that the 'verse, taken at face value, is not an altogether convincing future setting. The world of *Firefly* contains the iconography of the Western frontier far more intensely than do other space Westerns. In fact, Wills suggests that *Firefly* engages quite directly with the Western frontier, that it "fast-forwards" the frontier.

Of course, the "authentic" frontier itself has also often provided a backdrop for science fiction, so *Firefly* should be differentiated at least somewhat. The link between science fiction and the old west may not be at first intuitive, but it is nonetheless fitting. Westerns are historically heavily invested in technological innovation, building narratives around the coming of the railroad and advancements in telecommunications. Such technologies often serve a purpose similar to that of the "novum": science fiction's new thing or innovation that distinguishes the story world from our own. The first ever science fiction dime novel is in fact a Western and provides a perfect stand-in for the steam engine in the form of a steam-powered iron robot (Bleiler, 1990: 220). *The Steam Man of the Prairies* is very much a science fiction Western in its historical setting and themes. An early and typical example of the "Edisonade," its hero is remarkable for his inventiveness and technological innovation, in this case creating a steam-powered iron man. The tradition of "weird west" and steam punk novels and comics make similar use of the American frontier to tell stories of strange encounters and miraculous inventions.

Another way to consider these differences would be to look at Rick Altman's distinction between the semantic and syntactic approaches to genre. Roughly, the science fiction Western makes use of the semantic features of the Western, while space Westerns use the syntax of the genre. For Altman, Semantic qualities of the Western are rather specific. They are the "building blocks" of the genre, like the American West setting, the mid- to late-nineteenth-century setting, the stock characters, the dust, etc. (2004: 684). The semantic elements, on the other hand, "isolate a genre's meaning-bearing structures" (685). So here we get the Western's emphasis on thresholds— between nature and civilization, past and future, criminality and order, etc. As a rule, a "true" Western, if such a thing can ever be identified, would have both the semantic and syntactic elements of the genre. This is reductive, as no text can check off every item on the list, and different, competing lists of such characteristics abound. Nevertheless, the basic breakdown and subdivision into semantic and syntactic is useful. For example, while Westerns about a manhunt like *The Return of Frank James* (Fritz Lang, 1940) and *The Searchers* (John Ford, 1956) share a great deal, narratively and structurally, with *The Proposition* (John Hillcoat, 2005), the latter is set in Australia and thus lacks a central semantic feature of the genre. They can all be discussed as Westerns, but it is nearly impossible to consider *The Proposition*'s Western features without addressing its subversion of such a basic building block of the genre.

In a sense, *Firefly* functions on all of these levels. By "fast-forwarding" the frontier, we are left with narratives that, while not literally set in the American west, are nonetheless too rooted in their referent to function purely as metaphors. Unlike the loose thematic links between *High Noon* and its resetting in space in *Outland*, *Firefly* is too blunt in its aesthetics to only be thought about purely as a space Western. In other words, the series is semantically tied to the Western. In contrast, *Serenity* very much is a space Western, divesting itself of the almost absurdly literal Western-ness of *Firefly*. Even its color-palette veers towards the cold blues of sci-fi instead of the warm, earthy

Western hues of *Firefly*. While some semantic elements carry over from *Firefly*, what rises to the surface far more are the syntactical elements of western cinema. J.P. Telotte emphasizes this distinction and even states that, "While the film adaptation necessarily retains many of its dual generic markings, as well as the archaic speech patterns of its central characters, it is also a work that is far more intent on establishing a primary generic lineage in sf" (2008: 71). He points to *Serenity*'s overt and self-reflexive engagement with media production as well as references to science fiction texts like *Forbidden Planet* (Fred M. Wilcox, 1956) and *Star Wars* as evidence of this generic departure.

Telotte is right. To the extent that any text set in the future and outside the U.S. can be semantically Western, *Firefly* is certainly such a text. It provides the iconic accouterments of the genre, like six-shooters, dusters, desert settings, saloons, and chases on horseback. It even explicitly recreates political dynamics in which central "cities" hold power and capital, while "frontier towns" fend for themselves, while under the authority of big city politicians. Of course these last details are more syntactic. These are not cities, but rather central planets that function, in their entirety, as urban centers. And the frontier "towns" are actually planets on the outer rim of colonized space.

Semantically, *Serenity* does tone down the Western feel of *Firefly* and goes for the high-tech sheen and self-reflexivity that Telotte describes. But I would argue that more than any episode of *Firefly*, *Serenity* offers up a fundamentally Western syntax through its engagement with the themes of civilization and savagery, a syntactic staple of the Western genre, as Altman suggests. While that one feature of *Serenity* is enough to fundamentally tie it to the Western, it is also worth pausing to reflect on the overall Westernness of the film and to consider how it elaborates on generic markers absent from or only hinted at in *Firefly*.

Foremost among these is the treatment of the Reavers, who are never seen in *Firefly* and thus had to be visually coded from scratch in *Serenity*. That coding is quite overtly racialized, as Agnes B. Curry convincingly argues elsewhere in this collection. Presented as clear stand-ins for the Native American Other, the Reavers provide a strong metaphorical link between *Serenity* and the "cowboys and Indians" variety of Western film. Such a referent is unambiguously tied to questions of civilization, but while I argue for more metaphorical illustrations of the civilization/savagery dichotomy, it is important to note that the Reavers are indeed coded as "Indian" in a number of ways. They are visually racialized and discussed in terms of "packs" and raiding parties, their presence is signaled by non-diegetic drumbeats, and their reputation for sexual violence and cannibalism is a sad reminder of the racist tropes of Western cinema. The final showdown between Serenity and the Alliance also features the unexpected arrival of Reaver ships, visually reminiscent of the Western trope of an army of Natives appearing on the horizon to overwhelm the white heroes (exemplified in John Ford's *Stagecoach* [1939], *Fort Apache* [1948], and *The Searchers* (1956] among others). None of these links are coincidental.

Our heroes also tap into the tradition of "going Native" when they "desecrate" their ship in order to fly through Reaver space undetected. Serenity's captain Mal (Nathan Fillion) orders that the crew adorn the ship with corpses and red paint, presumably to look like a bloody reminder of past violent exploits. In this moment, the scene also harkens back to *High Plains Drifter* (Clint Eastwood, 1973), in which the Stranger (Clint Eastwood), tasked with protecting the town of Lago, tells the townsfolk to paint every building red.[1] Zoe's (Gina Torres) use of the word "desecrate" in *Serenity* also finds a analogue in *High Plains Drifter*'s priest, who is scandalized and asks, "You can't possibly mean the church too?" "I mean especially the church," the Stranger replies. His plan is to turn the town into a living hell. It is both a threat to the approaching outlaws, and a reminder to the townsfolk of their own complicity in their violence. *Serenity* sheds the sense of guilt attached to such an act, though the notion of sullying one's own home and presentation has at least a somewhat similar goal. Certainly one could also argue that the crew of Serenity is complicit in ignoring the plight of the Reavers. They are unambiguously humans, and rather than reacting to their suffering (are they not clearly sick?), the 'verse, including Serenity's crew, has turned its back on them. Regardless of how far this analogy goes, the act of painting one's home red certainly has a precedent in Western cinema, even when the trope of "going Native" is removed from the equation.

Outside of these elaborations on the Western-ness of *Firefly*, the film also does carry over a great many elements of the show that are quite unambiguously tied to Western cinema. Whedon calls *Firefly* "a Stagecoach kind of drama with a lot of people trying to figure out their lives in a bleak and pioneer environment" (2006: 6). The central characters of the series (who carry over into the film) are indeed largely modeled on the Fordian archetypes, like the funny driver, the "prostitute with a heart of gold," the man of faith, and the charming outlaw, represented in *Firefly* and *Serenity* by Wash (Alan Tudyk), Inara (Morena Baccarin), Shepherd Book (Ron Glass), and Mal respectively. Other Western archetypes come into play too: the genteel city doctor, the damsel in distress, the warrior woman, and the southern belle, most notably. None of these are necessarily so strictly tied to the Western, but they are consciously borrowed and used in such a way as to provide a continuous thread between not only the series and film, but between the fictional universe of *Serenity* and the history of Western cinema. While the film's engagement with the concept of civilization is arguably its strongest connection to the Western, *Serenity* as a whole is undoubtedly steeped in Western motifs, both semantic and syntactic.

Better Worlds

The concept of civilization is important in Western cinema. Civilization is customarily pitted against savagery, which can take the form of racist tropes of Native American violence, or simply the lawless frontier, where criminals run free on the doorstep into the unknown wild where humans have no authority. Jeanne Heffernan suggests that this is indeed one of the main tropes not only of the Western, but of American culture itself:

> We are pioneers taming the savage West, so the myth goes, a civilized people imposing order on a recalcitrant landscape populated by unruly Indians. The Western is famous, or infamous, for confirming this myth of American identity [1999: 147].

Indeed, it is. Western heroes often fight off the Native American Other to protect "civilized" communities. And even when the threat comes from within the settler community, it is frequently presented as a threat against further civilization.

Some obvious examples of the nature/savagery binary come up in the films of John Ford, particularly *The Searchers* and *The Man Who Shot Liberty Valance* (1962). John Wayne plays the liminal figure in both, whose role is to usher in civilization through the kind of violence associated with savagery. This is a compelling contradiction of the American Western myth—that civilization is achievable only through that which it seeks to negate. In the now-iconic final scene of *The Searchers*, Wayne's Ethan Edwards literally stands at the threshold of civilization, as he looks through the open door of a typically domestic space: his brother's home. Edwards is ostensibly welcome to follow the family in, having just saved his niece from the Comanche tribe that kidnapped her. He has, through violence and a distinctly uncivilized ability to navigate the wilderness, spent years searching, attempting to restore order and allow the "rightful" progression of American society. This final scene demonstrates his own self-awareness. Edwards may well be capable of championing civilization, but he has no place there. He knows his place, and rather appropriately wanders off into the desert. This is a frankly melancholy play on the image of the cowboy riding off into the sunset, though the underlying idea is the same. Having served his purpose (usually saving a town from outlaws or "Indians"), the cowboy cannot remain *within* the civilized space he has carved out.

Wayne's Tom Doniphon in *The Man Who Shot Liberty Valance* serves a similar function, though Ford seems even more dedicated to playing with the myth of the civilizing hero here. While Doniphon kills the tyrannical Liberty Valance (Lee Marvin), protecting the town of Shinbone and opening the door to further civilization (culminating in the arrival of the railroad), he refuses to accept credit for the act, recognizing its symbolic importance.

Instead, he gives the title of "man who shot Liberty Valance" to Ransom Stoddard (James Stewart), the genteel city lawyer who does have what it takes to "civilize" Shinbone, but has no ability to stand up to Valance without getting himself killed. Ford plays with the formula by giving us Wayne's classic hero, who fades back into obscurity once the job is done, while acknowledging that the myth of the Western hero will be necessary to Stoddard's success. He will become a governor, then senator, and always a symbol of civilization in part because of the legend of savagery projected onto him. One Shinbone reporter comes to realize that such a myth is necessary, when he refuses to report the truth. In the west, "when the legend becomes fact, print the legend," he says. The fact of the division between civilization and savagery is simply distasteful, when one fundamentally always relies on the other.

These films are not alone, of course. *Shane* (George Stevens, 1953), *The Magnificent Seven* (John Sturges, 1960), *A Fistful of Dollars* (Sergio Leone, 1964), and *The Wild Bunch* (Sam Peckinpah, 1969) all provide variations on the theme, as do countless other films. This is a well-worn trope, no doubt. And it extends to science fiction variations as well. Han Solo (Harrison Ford) is constantly on the edge of ditching the rebellion in *Star Wars* and its sequels. In *The Force Awakens* (J.J. Abrams, 2015), we discover that he has finally turned his back on the Republic, now that it is more or less stable (or civilized). Somewhere between a cowboy, a pirate, and a mercenary, Solo always refuses to stick around to enjoy the stability he helps to usher in. He helps fight for a civilized future while never quite fitting into it.

Serenity takes these themes to the extreme. While Whedon plays down some of the semantic elements of the Western, he takes full advantage of this syntactic feature to plumb its applicability to the high-tech future of his space Western. He does this in rather overt ways at times, though throughout the film, civilization through savagery is always hovering somewhere beneath the surface.

First, the narrative of Miranda is one of a failed civilization project. The act of terraforming an uninhabitable planet is, in and of itself, a part of the colonial project of civilization, but Miranda exemplifies more than that. Miranda represents a failed attempt to civilize not only a planet but also its people. In attempting to tame its populace, to forcibly, if secretly, quell any dissent and encourage productivity, the Alliance kills most of Miranda's population, turning the rest into monsters through the use of an airborne drug, the Pax, administered without the population's consent. While Native Americans are typically those either killed or "civilized" in Westerns, *Serenity* rather conspicuously projects this familiar narrative onto the settlers themselves, removing, for better or worse, much of the racial and historical baggage of the Western, while maintaining the treacherous essence of the civilizers, here the Alliance, controlling its subjects from a distance. Had the Pax worked on

Miranda, its people would have literally been drugged into submission, enslaved for the benefit of the central government.

The violence of civilization is turned inward here, which, in some ways, intensifies the paternalistic function of the civilizing government, seemingly acting with good intentions. There is certainly something unsavory about removing the racial implications of population control that are so clearly a part of *Serenity*'s referent, but at the same time, using the inhabitants of Miranda in such a way allows them to *become* monsters at the hands of the Alliance. It is only once the settlers of Miranda have been infected by their government that they are transformed into a racially coded villain (Reavers). The function of this reframing highlights the relative innocence of the people upon whom the Reavers are based. Westerns are rather complicit in turning Native Americans into monsters. By ascribing "savage" traits onto their Other, these settler texts "create" the very monsters that they need in order to justify the project of civilization:

> The incidents of Indians capturing whites during the nineteenth century were rather minuscule in relation to the systematic program of genocide by the U.S. government against that Native population, beginning before the formal inception of the nation, continuing in earnest with the 1830 Indian Removal Bill of Andrew Jackson, yet tales of Indian crimes against whites saturate Westerns" [Sharrett, 2006: 6].

Serenity plays with this historical reality by suggesting that while Reavers do capture innocents, their violence is eventually explained by the violence enacted upon them. If we allow the metaphor to remain contained in such a way, it provides a productive, if not unproblematic, intervention into Western history.

This inversion of good guys and bad guys runs deep, as indeed conceptions of civilization are turned on their head throughout the film. This subversion of the trope is perhaps best personified by the Operative (Chiwetel Ejiofor), who articulates the paradox of the Western hero quite directly after killing innocents in the name of catching Mal and the crew of Serenity. The following exchange, in which the Operative explains himself to Mal, is quite telling:

> MAL: I don't murder children.
> THE OPERATIVE: I do, if I have to.
> MAL: Why? Do you even know why they sent you?
> THE OPERATIVE: It's not my place to ask. I believe in something greater than myself. A better world. A world without sin.
> MAL: So me and mine gotta lay down and die so you can live in your better world?
> THE OPERATIVE: I'm not going to live there. There's no place for me there any more than there is for you. Malcolm, I'm a monster. What I do is evil—I have no illusions about it—but it must be done.

The Operative here is Ethan Edwards looking into his brother's home. The civilization he seeks to usher in (a "better world") is not for him because he represents the costs of creating it rather than the civility of living it. He says as much. He is a "monster," but his monstrosity—murdering children, for example—is something that he "has to" do. What he believes in is explicitly greater than him and it exists beyond his own personal, monstrous limitations.

At the end of the film, the Operative literally stands at an open door, looking in. Or, more precisely, he looks into the open cargo bay door of Serenity, watching Mal load supplies into the ship, having been defeated in his attempt to champion the Alliance. Now a loner, directionless in the universe, it would make some kind of sense for the Operative to join Mal's crew, but that is not in the cards for him. "Like to kill you myself, I see you again," Mal says to him. Serenity represents a different kind of civilization that the Operative cannot be a part of either. It is a sanctuary from the top-down systems of power that would accept the costs of "civilizing" planets and people—costs that include murder, biological pacification, and keeping state secrets.

Mal has his own Western-hero moment, standing in a doorway, shot from a dark space outside the door. Here the *Searchers* finale is quoted far more directly, with the framing and lighting evoking Ford's iconic scene far more than the scene with the Operative ever does. There is a major difference between Mal and Ethan Edwards though. While Edwards is shot from within the domestic space and looks into it, Mal has his back to us, and he stands firmly *within* Serenity's communal domestic space: the dining room. This scene tells us a great deal about the identity of Serenity and its crew. The shot through the doorway introduces a scene in which Mal definitively declares war on the Alliance. He goes through why the crew needs to act to inform the 'verse about the creation of the Reavers and ends with the war cry "I aim to misbehave."

The crew is with him; even Jayne (Adam Baldwin), who frequently stands apart, unwilling to do the right thing if it means risking his own neck. Here Jayne invokes the recently deceased Shepherd Book as a sign that he is in fact invested in joining Mal and the rest of the crew: "Shepherd Book used to tell me, if you can't do something smart, do something right." Mal and his crew are indeed outsiders, but unlike the cowboy outsiders, their politics and way of life are not necessary evils used to usher in civilization, but rather an alternative in and of themselves to the Alliance's notion of civilization. Mal literally turns his back to the world outside his ship to plan his next steps. His makeshift family is who he turns to to challenge the "better worlds" offered by the Alliance.

Conclusion

Joss Whedon would have been hard-pressed to remove the signature Western elements of *Firefly* when he adapted the series to the big screen. His choice to play down the more overt Western tropes of the series may have been quite wise, though, at least from a marketing standpoint. Ginjer Buchanan argues that one of the reasons for the series' demise was its reliance on a genre that had lost its viability decades earlier (Buchanan, 2004: 53). Nevertheless, he had a pre-existing fanbase to please and a need for at least some consistency between the television and film outings.

Perhaps more to the point, *Serenity* was a product of fandom. Without the promise of a fierce following, it is unlikely that a canceled series would be revived on any platform, and *Firefly* certainly owes at least some of its cult status to its playful engagement with genre. While some of the more obvious nods to the Western (horseback riding, dusty backwoods planets, etc.) are absent from the film, other intergeneric content appears. For one, the Reavers are presented as variations on the zombie, giving *Serenity* very clear horror overtones. Tangentially related to the Western, the Operative is aligned with eastern dress and wields a sword clearly inspired by katanas and the samurai traditions of feudal Japan. Samurai films and Westerns famously borrowed quite liberally from one another, with certain classic Westerns like *A Fistful of Dollars* and *The Magnificent Seven* being directly adapted from the films of Akira Kurosawa. This generic cross-referencing makes its way into *Serenity*, with both traditions remaining more or less intact but transposed into space and blended with the science fiction tradition.

All of this engagement with genre is in service to a narrative that is overwhelmingly invested in social change, mirroring questions of civilization and frontier "savagery" that belong to the Western. The underlying themes of power depicted in the film have some of the strongest claims to the Western label of any Whedonverse text. This includes *Firefly*, ostensibly Whedon's most overt Western work, but perhaps a more surface-level example of the genre than the more thematically and syntactically resonant *Serenity*.

NOTES

1. Thank you to Hayley Paskevich for pointing out this parallel during a lecture on *Serenity* and the Western at the University of Calgary.

WORKS CITED

Abbott, Stacey. (2010). "'Can't Stop the Signal': The Resurrection/Regeneration of *Serenity*," in Rhonda. V. Wilcox and Tanya. R. Cochrane (eds.) *Investigating* Firefly and Serenity: *Science Fiction on the Frontier*. London: I.B. Tauris, 227–38.

Altman, Rick. (2004). "A Semantic/Syntactic Approach to Genre," in Leo Braudy and Marshall Cohen (eds.) *Film Theory and Criticism* (6th ed.). Oxford: Oxford University Press, 680–90.

Bleiler, Everett Franklin. (1990). *Science-Fiction, the Early Years: A Full Description of More Than 3,000 Science-Fiction Stories from Earliest Times to the Appearance of the Genre Magazines in 1930*. Kent, OH: Kent State University Press.

Buchanan, Ginjer. (2004). "Who Killed *Firefly*?," in Jane Espenson (ed.) *Finding Serenity: Anti-Heroes, Lost Shepherds and Space Hookers in Joss Whedon's* Firefly. Dallas: BenBella Books, 47–53.

Hark, Ina Rae. (2010). "Decent Burial or Miraculous Resurrection: *Serenity*, Mourning, and Sequels to Dead Television Shows," in Carolyn Jess-Cooke and Constantine Verevis (eds). *Second Takes: Critical Approaches to the Film Sequel*. Albany: State University of New York, 121–37.

Jeanne, Heffernan. (1999). "Poised Between Savagery and Civilization": Forging Political Communities in Ford's Westerns," in *Perspectives on Political Science* 28:3: 147–51.

Pascale, Amy. (2014). *Joss Whedon: The Biography*. Chicago: Chicago Review Press.

Rabb, J. Douglas, and J. Michael Richardson. (2010). "Reavers and Redskins: Creating the Frontier Savage," in Rhonda V. Wilcox and Tanya R. Cochran (eds.). *Investigating* Firefly *and* Serenity: *Science Fiction on the Frontier*. London: I.B. Tauris, 127–38.

Sharrett, Christopher. (2006). "Through a Door, Darkly: A Reappraisal of John Ford's *The Searchers*," in *Cineaste* 31.4: 4–8.

Telotte, J.P. (2008). "*Serenity*, Cinematisation and the Perils of Adaptation," in *Science Fiction Film and Television* 1.1: 67–80.

Whedon, Joss. (2006). Firefly: *The Official Companion: Volume One*. London: Titan Books.

Wills, John. (2015). "*Firefly* and the Space Western: Frontier Fiction on Fast Forward," in Michael Goodrum and Philip Smith (eds.) Firefly *Revisited: Essays on Joss Whedon's Classic Series*. Lanham, MD: Rowan & Littlefield, 1–17.

The Miranda Job
Serenity *as Crime Film*

INA RAE HARK

Genre hybridity is a defining feature of *Firefly* (2002–03), a space opera that is also a Western, signaled by the iconic shot in the opening credits in which the ship Serenity flies low over a herd of galloping horses. Perceptions of the genre of its cinematic sequel *Serenity* (Joss Whedon, 2005) are less monolithic. Sharon Sutherland and Sarah Swan agree with several other scholars in seeing the film as set in a world of "horror, science fiction, and Western" (2008: 89); they also cite Whedon's pronouncement of his 'verse's design as "Western noir ... a kind of Hong Kong sensibility" (Whedon 2005: 25). An aggregate of reviews at Rotten Tomatoes to be sure contains descriptions of the film as "a well-balanced blend of whooping Wild West action and space opera" (Robinson 2005), a "near-future Western" (Rocchi 2005), and a "quirky blend of frontier rough-and-tumble and sci-fi space opera" (Greydanus 2005). Many other critics overlook the Western elements and slot the film, with its group of rebels going up against an oppressive government, within the familiar generic territory traversed by *Star Wars* (George Lucas, 1977), comparing Malcolm Reynolds (Nathan Fillion) to Han Solo (Harrison Ford) rather than Jesse James and praising its success against the disappointments of the *Star Wars* prequels.

Rotten Tomatoes itself labels the film "action & adventure, science fiction & fantasy" ("Serenity" 2005). A variety of other hybridites surface in the reviews: "an ultra-sophisticated chase movie" (Thomson 2005); "sci-fi buccaneer swashbuckler" (Lane 2005); "cobbles together elements of Westerns, space epics, new-age mysticism and even zombie-horror films" (Vice 2005); "equal parts deadly action, deadpan comedy and knotty mystery" ("Review: Serenity" 2005). All these generic possibilities do not, however, include one genre that I would assert *Serenity* unequivocally partakes of: the crime film, especially its subgenres of the heist/caper movie and the paranoid political thriller. This essay will delineate the film's crime genre bona fides, speculate upon why most critics and scholars have overlooked them, relate how they intersect with the predominant space opera/Western mash-up, and use theories about crime films to analyze the film's textual meanings.

A Crime Film Hiding in Plain Sight

That *Serenity* rarely receives consideration as a crime film is especially surprising because Malcolm Reynolds and his crew are criminals, a fact reviewers and scholars readily acknowledge. Nick Funnell describes their occupation as a "semi-legal transporting trade" (2005). References to them as outlaws, renegades, smugglers, and pirates recur throughout the critical literature. When the Operative (Chiwetel Ejiofor) looks into Mal's background, he finds a record of his being "bound by law" five times. In "The Train Job" (20 September 2002), the hastily-commissioned second pilot for *Firefly*, and the series' first broadcast episode, the crew undertakes a train robbery, a crime also committed in the seminal early Western *The Great Train Robbery* (Edwin S. Porter, 1903). Kieran Tranter devotes an essay to the entire *Firefly/Serenity* megatext's "outlaw intra-text" (2012: 279) and sums up the crew's "lawful lawlessness" as follows:

> They steal and kill. They smuggle goods off-world and they trade in stolen medicines; Mal happily accepts jobs from various crime boss types. The niceties of how the local planetary authorities or the Alliance would consider their actions seem mostly immaterial. In short SERENITY gives a rather good impression of being a pirate ship crewed by hardened criminals. Mal, Zoe and Jayne can easily be characterised as hired guns who "do the job" regardless of the legality or morality involved, and in aiding and abetting, the on-board support team of Kaylee and Wash seem equally culpable [2012: 286].

Yet, for all this, when Tranter refers to Whedon's genre play, he concentrates on the Western/space opera duality and never outright relates the outlaw intra-text to the crime film paradigm.

Serenity begins with two capers reminiscent of *Firefly* episodes such as "The Train Job" and "Ariel" (15 November 2002). The crew robs a railroad vault holding the payroll for the private security officers to whom the Alliance has subcontracted police powers on one of the outer planets; they barely escape with the loot and their lives when Reavers attack. Edited in parallel is a holographic record (or re-creation?) of Simon Tam (Sean Maher) infiltrating the Alliance lab where scientists are experimenting on his sister River (Summer Glau), freeing her, and escaping to a waiting space vessel whose crew he has hired to help him with the rescue; discounting the motives for the two "heists," these unseen mercenaries function for Simon as Mal and his team do for their twin gangster employers Mingo (Yan Feldman) and Fanty (Rafael Feldman). Caper films generally chronicle the bringing together of a team to pull off a robbery of a well-guarded, cash (or valuables)-rich institution like a bank, armored car, train, casino or race track. They rehearse the operation and then portray its execution, which generally does not go according to plan. John Huston's *The Asphalt Jungle* (1950) kicked off a cycle of such films both in Hollywood (*The Killing* [Stanley Kubrick, 1956], *The Thomas Crown Affair* [Norman Jewison, 1968]) and internationally (*Rififi* [Jules Dassin, 1955], *Topkapi* [Jules Dassin, 1964]). "The Train Job's" title nods toward *The Italian Job* (Peter Collinson, 1969), a British-Italian co-production in the sub-genre. The caper remains a reliable movie plot into the twenty-first century as exemplified by the success of the remake of *Ocean's 11* (Lewis Milestone, 1960) as *Ocean's Eleven* (Steven Soderbergh, 2001) and its sequels, *Ocean's Twelve* and *Thirteen*, also directed by Soderbergh in 2004 and 2007.

Nevertheless, these two capers are more shout outs to such crimes in *Firefly* than significant parts of *Serenity*'s narrative. The vault robbery occurs without showing the audience the planning for it and Simon's rescue operation is a flashback whose planning is also absent and whose fallout the television show has already documented. At most they alert spectators to the crime element and point to the sorts of tactical skills Mal will employ in escaping the Operative's trap at Inara's (Morena Baccarin) Teaching House, getting through the Reaver fleet to Miranda and then using them to delay the Alliance ships while he broadcasts the file that details what happened there. As soon as the Operative closes in on River, *Serenity* switches to the sub-genre of the political thriller.

Paul Cobley states that conspiracies play a large role in thrillers, conspiracies that are "a threat to both, at once, wider and local relations of equilibrium in thriller, and, more specifically, to the veneer of capitalist success" (2004: 318). If one were looking for the structure that facilitates this view, he adds, "it is likely that the word 'paranoia' would reside at the forefront of the search" (2004: 329). Pablo Castrillo and Pablo Ekhart define films in the sub-genre as "at their core investigative narratives in which the protagonist must face physical and moral threats so as to retrieve a hidden truth and hand it over to the people. Accordingly, the villain or antagonist of the political thriller must always seek to hide the truth and conceal it" (2015: 114). They thus agree with Cobley's notion that "the power of an almost omnipresent genre is to be found in its broad searching nature, an anxious quest for knowledge which not only underpins the notion of science but which might be the basis of human subjectivity itself" (2004: 332). Paranoid conspiracy political thrillers thus emphasize the gaining of knowledge and the dissemination of it to the populace at large. *Serenity* follows this rubric to the letter, as the crew struggles to determine what River knows that has made re-taking or silencing her so important to the Alliance, all the while evading the Operative and his deadly forces until they discover the horrors on Miranda, the Alliance's complicity in causing them, and succeed in making it known throughout the 'verse.

Political thrillers vary widely on the sorts of secrets being kept, who is doing the hiding, and for what purpose. These films tend to increase in number when nations or groups feel particularly threatened. Many times the fear is of subversive infiltration of government institutions by foreign actors and their agents. Thus the Cold War and Red Scare inspired thrillers such as *The Manchurian Candidate* (John Frankenheimer, 1962), in which the Communist Chinese brainwash an American POW as part of a plot to install their puppet as President of the United States. Usually these narratives about fear of the Other inspire counter-narratives about such fears empowering ultra-loyalists to attempt a coup from within because they chafe at the democratic constraints involved in going after such outside threats, as in *Seven Days in May*, also directed by Frankenheimer (1964). The 9/11 attacks brought the paranoid conspiracy thriller back to prominence, combining narratives about percolating Islamic extremist plots and moles within the intelligence services with those warning against government over-reach in using the surveillance state to violate the rights of innocent citizens in pursuit of safety, mirrored in the aims of the Miranda project that goes so horribly wrong. A year before *Serenity*'s release, Jonathan Demme remade *The Manchurian Candidate* (2004) with the villains changed to the U.S. military-industrial complex from the Communist Chinese. Serialized television shows of the post–9/11 era have also provided a good fit with paranoid political conspiracy plots. Many have sustained themselves for years on tales of both external subversion and internal corruption of government: *Alias* (2001–06), *24* (2001–10), *Homeland* (2011–), *Scandal* (2012–) and newcomer *Dedicated Survivor* (2016–).

If the Cold War provided the template for thrillers about infiltration and subversion, then the Watergate break-in and its ensuing cover-up made the 1970s the crucial era for those in which government or other American institutions are committing crimes against the values they claim to defend. Luis M. Garcia-Mainar asserts that during the 2000s the paranoid thriller, as well as the crime film generally, returned to the stylistic and thematic preoccupations of the decade (2016: 38–9). For *Serenity*, key films include *The Parallax View* (Alan J. Pakula, 1974), *Three Days of the Condor* (Sydney Pollack, 1975) and *All the President's Men* (Alan J. Pakula, 1976). *Condor* particularly shares story elements with Whedon's film: massacres of friends and allies of the protagonist on the run, Joseph Turner (Robert Redford); uncertainty about whom to trust among the authorities; a deadly pursuer who changes allegiance at the last moment to spare Turner's life and advise him on the dangers that lie ahead; and Turner's scoring at least a temporary victory by going to the media, in his case the *New York Times*, in Malcolm Reynolds' case Mr. Universe's signal. In both films, doubt remains as to whether going public with the government secrets will end the malfeasance or keep the protagonist safe from reprisals. Like River, Turner must figure out the nature of the secret he holds to understand why it threatens his pursuers. The same holds true for Joseph Frady (Warren Beatty) in *Parallax View*, frustrated that "I don't know what I know." This trope becomes increasingly popular in paranoid thrillers after 2000, with amnesiac protagonists, some of whom formerly were complicit in the actions others will kill them to conceal: *The Bourne Identity* (Doug Liman, 2002); *Unknown* (Jaume Collet-Saura, 2011) and the television series *Blindspot* (2015–).

The shift in *Serenity* from caper to conspiracy thriller parallels the shift J.P. Telotte discerns between the television series and the film in that the latter "seems far more intent on establishing a primary generic lineage in sf" (2012: 130). That is, train and bank robberies are more frequent crimes in Westerns than they are in science fiction, whereas paranoid thrillers are much more integral to science fiction than to Westerns. Science fiction, for example, often portrays such paranoia-inducing elements as omnipresent surveillance regimes and unstable identity formations (via cloning, android duplication, alien shapeshifters and scientific memory manipulation); *Invasion of the Body Snatchers* (Don Siegel, 1956) is one of the great paranoid films. These technologies are unavailable to the standard, non-Steampunk Western. To be sure, there are Western crime films that share as many plot points with *Serenity* as do paranoid thrillers like *Three Days of the Condor*. *The Wild Bunch* (Sam Peckinpah, 1969) takes place in a tamed frontier where, as Mal prophesies about his corner of the 'verse, "come a day there won't be room for naughty men like us to slip about at all"; involves an opening robbery that goes awry, an extended flight and pursuit of the outlaws by agents of the authorities; and culminates in the Bunch's being drawn into a cause larger than themselves in defense of one of their members. Like the Operative, the man leading the bounty hunters turns against them in the end. Yet these parallels omit the secrecy and crimes against the citizenry at large that the Alliance and their "meddlesome" biochemical experiments inject into Whedon's film.

Firefly, for all its space ships and new planets, is at its core a Western and *Serenity* must shake off that primary generic identity in order to tell its central story of a horrific Alliance-generated atrocity and its desperate cover-up. Although current genre theory—including his own later work (Altman, 1999)—looks beyond textual markers in determining how genres are constituted, Rick Altman's distinction between semantics and syntax (1984) serves well in disentangling the hybridity of *Firefly* and *Serenity*. Genre semantics refer to elements that recur in a given genre, including settings, character types, costumes, plot elements (singing, gunfights, the dead returning to life.) Syntax refers to the way these elements come together to form a narrative. Whedon's 'verse transports semantics from the nineteenth-century American West six hundred years into the future on terraformed planets, some of which look exactly like the dusty frontier towns of that distant time and place, down to patterns of speech, cowboy garb, and futuristic weapons that resemble traditional six-shooters and rifles. These semantics of the outer planets exist alongside the science fiction semantics of space ships, energy weapons, and high-tech environments on the core Alliance worlds.

If the semantic balance is more or less even, however, the Western dominates *Firefly*'s syntax. Its premise merely moves to outer space a frequent trope of that genre: a Confederate veteran, having lost everything in the Civil War, heads to the frontier to rebuild his life as best he can. The Browncoat Independents allegorize the gray-coated Johnny Rebs, at the same time rehabilitating their morally dubious support of racist chattel slavery; the war against Unification with the federal Alliance really is fought purely on the grounds of states'/planets' rights, as many Southern apologists erroneously claim for the Lost Cause. *Firefly* also eschews any science fiction syntaxes that do not overlap with those of the Western. Space is, as in the opening narration of *Star Trek*, the final frontier. Humans seek a new life elsewhere in the galaxy when "Earth-that-Was" cannot provide them with a sustainable existence. Although many sf narratives use aliens to stand in for the indigenous peoples whom settler colonialist societies battled, dispossessed, and oppressed, sometimes to the point of genocide, *Firefly* fills that role with the Reavers, fellow human colonists who have mysteriously turned savage. In other words, the outer space setting purges the ideological sins that have made Westerns rare in the twenty-first century while at the same time offering an ideal platform in which to replay classic Western tropes without guilt.

In addition to aliens of any sort, the television series takes off the table any explorations of the post human (cyborgs, robots, androids and other AIs); time travel; alternative universes; teleportation, and so forth. It does not, as Jeffrey Bussolini notes, portray "a technological utopianism seeming to offer a measure of deliverance from aspects of bodily life" (2008: 142; see also Jowett 2008: 108–11). This further reduces the sf syntaxes available to *Firefly* and locates its crime genre elements solely in the liminal areas between outlaw and lawman, wilderness and civilization. By taking on a narrative in which shadowy government entities manipulate the brains of non-consenting human subjects in order to eliminate dissent and create super-soldiers, *Serenity* moves into familiar sf territory in which the makers of the laws see themselves as exempt from their strictures, leading to governmental tyranny or corporate conspiracies, often working hand-in-hand.

The scientists who develop the Pax gas and drill into River's brain have obvious links to those working for the Weyland-Yutani corporation of the *Alien* films, the Cyberdyne corporation of the *Terminator* films, Omni Consumer Products of *RoboCop* (Paul Verhoeven, 1987) or the Tyrell corporation of *Blade Runner* (Ridley Scott, 1982). These futuristic "meddlers" in turn fit perfectly into the political thriller template, of which Castrillo and Echart remark:

> At the heart of the political thriller lies a conflict that confronts an individual with the system, the ordinary citizen against the institutions, the human being against the inhumanity of political and/or corporate power. Governments and companies are presented as forces bent on protecting their interests at any cost, to the extent of eliminating any opposition, even when such policy involves murder [2015: 120].

None of the crime lords that employ Serenity's crew, nor any of the banks, railroads and greedy landowners of the conventional Western, come anywhere close to unleashing the apocalyptic consequences of these nefarious sf organizations.

The frequency with which science fiction films have employed the syntax of the political thriller does not tend to override the generic primacy granted to their science fiction semantics. No more than with *Serenity* do commentators classify *Alien* (Ridley Scott, 1979) or *Terminator 2: Judgment Day* (James Cameron, 1991) as crime films, even if they share syntaxes associated with such paranoid conspiracy narratives. The futuristic settings of these films also militate against their reception as crime films, as do the nineteenth-century settings of Westerns. As Thomas Leitch points out:

> The most powerful generic claims are based on mise-en-scène. Crime-and-punishment tales like *Winchester 73* (1950) and *Rancho Notorious* (1952) are classified as westerns rather than crime films. Any movie set in outer space, from *Buck Rogers* (1939) to *Alien* (1979), becomes a science-fiction movie [2002: 9].

In addition, although many films depict crimes occurring in the past or projected into the future, presentness contributes to the likelihood of a film that depicts crime achieving generic status as first and foremost a crime film. Major sub-genres establish themselves within their contemporary eras. Gangster films multiply in the early 1930s as Prohibition increases the "business" opportunities for criminals. Film noir proliferates amid the uncertainties of American life after World War II until the beginning of the Cold War. In the nineteenth century, detective fiction arises just as police detectives emerge in law enforcement.

Political thrillers, as I have said, proliferated during twenty years of Communist infiltration fears, political assassinations, and government cover-ups. Castrillo and Echart, therefore, maintain that "political thrillers tend to avoid the construction of dystopian or fantasy story worlds" (2015: 117) and concentrate on a "world [that] remains, however, realistic, ordinary, and functioning according to the parameters of real life." Garcia-Mainar describes the style of the 70s thrillers as "a realist aesthetic that pervaded narratives, which adopted a blend of realism and pessimism" (2016, 41). Those paranoid thrillers based on actual crimes exposed by journalists or other investigators (*All the President's Men, Spotlight* [Tom McCarthy, 2015], *JFK* [Oliver Stone, 1991]) tend to have lower body counts than something like the nihilistic, fictional *The Parallax View*, in which the sinister assassins-for-hire conglomerate kills all who stumble onto its secrets and creates a false narrative endorsed by government and media. Yet it still seems like a plausible scenario taking place in the audience's here and now. *Serenity*'s temporal setting and action-movie style, on the other hand, obscure its identity as paranoid political thriller.

Nevertheless, considering how Whedon's film intersects with that crime sub-genre provides additional analytic tools for teasing out its themes. In the remainder of this essay I will read its text in this context to demonstrate its take on criminality and morality in a 'verse where the central government has created both River and the Reavers, a connection *Firefly* obscures yet also hints at through the slant rhyme of the two names. I ground this reading in a main thesis of Leitch's book, *Crime Films*, in which he argues that this genre and its sub-genres "insist on the distinctions among criminals, crime solvers, and victims, and that their obsessive focus is on the fluid and troubling boundaries among these categories" (2002:15).

Serenity's *Victim-Detective-Criminals*

Like the ever-morphing hybridity of its genre, *Serenity*'s characters slip and slide among Leitch's crime film character triad. River, her allies aboard Mal's ship, the Operative, the Reavers and the Alliance blend criminal and victim, or victim and detective, or criminal and detective, but in distinctive ways. The protagonists of political thrillers are usually either people who have been in the wrong place at the wrong time, acquiring knowledge that their pursuers would intimidate, kill or capture them to conceal, or curious observers who start pulling at threads when they come across facts that don't quite add up (Castrillo and Echart 2015: 114). This first type of protagonist occupies the victim role, the second the detective. River is this victim protagonist, her psychic powers having read jumbled images of the disaster on Miranda when top Alliance officials come to observe the result of its scientists' experiments aimed at enhancing her abilities to turn her into a weapon. More precisely, in this scenario, she is the victim of Alliance human behavior modification in a way that makes her a parallel to all those who died or transformed due to the Pax drug. Simon is the curious investigator who realizes that his sister is not simply a pupil at an exclusive academy and rescues her, making them both fugitives in their own tale of escape and pursuit. The knowledge she gleaned of the sinister Miranda experiment makes her the more typical "woman who knows too much" of Hitchcockian-style thrillers. It remains ambiguous in *Serenity* whether the Alliance pursuit would have been so relentless if she only held the secret of her own victimization and not also that of the victims she learned of second-hand.

Like many of these latter sorts of victims, River must unravel what she has unwittingly learned and assess why the Alliance will stop at nothing to silence her. Finally, the keyword "Miranda" surfaces into her consciousness and she can direct her allies to turn their search for answers toward the correct location, where she symbolically vomits up the poisonous horrors her brain has been repressing. More prominent than River's detective function, however, is her potential criminality. Like the brainwashed assassin of *The Manchurian Candidate*, whose trigger is a playing card, she violently takes out an entire bar full of patrons on Maidenhead when she sees an ad for a snack bar encoded with a subliminal on switch. Throughout *Firefly* and much of *Serenity*, River projects an aura of instability and danger. When she massacres the Reavers who have besieged her brother and crewmates, her deadly skills become crystal clear. Fortunately, at that point, she can control them and employ them in self-defense rather than at the behest of Alliance masters with dubious motives. By the end of the film, Mal trusts her to pilot the ship on the right course.

Mal takes over the detective role once River identifies the place where the mystery's solution resides. His identity as criminal, like hers as victim, has formed outside the parameters of *Serenity*'s conspiracy narrative. Two facets of that criminality are pertinent to his actions as investigator and avenger (of the massacre of Book's [Ron Glass] settlement) in that narrative, however. First of all, Mal has a flexible attitude toward what is legal but an inherent instinct for what is moral (see Magill 2008). Secondly, Mal takes on criminal jobs for a fee from the likes of the brutal Niska (Michael Fairman) or the "sad little king of a sad little hill" Badger (Mark A. Sheppard) but doesn't aspire to being a criminal boss himself. He and his crew are hired guns, in their best light like Shane (Alan Ladd, *Shane* [George Stevens, 1953]) or Paladin (Richard Boone, *Have Gun—Will Travel* [1957–63]), in their worst mere henchmen or mercenaries. Yet the ethical principles that often cause Mal to pull out of jobs contrast him with a pure mercenary like Jayne (Adam Baldwin.) As volunteers on the Independent side, Mal and Zoe (Gina Torres) also fought on the orders of superiors and found themselves betrayed among the dead and dying in Serenity Valley as the top commanders negotiated surrender terms. Mal's actions in pursuing the truth about Miranda and then broadcasting it, at great risk to himself and those he loves, show him on a self-directed mission, an advance from his habitual function as conflicted employee.

Were *Serenity* the opposite sort of political thriller, one in which a cop, soldier or spy seeks to uncover a plot against the government, the Operative would be its protagonist. His title suggests both Dashiell Hammett's Continental Op and the special forces members who carry out "black ops." The way he pursues his mission illuminates much about the Alliance. A nameless ideologue, he "believes hard" and with religious fervor in the ultimate good of what it represents: "a world without sin." His executions of opponents with his sword are ritualistic but there are no boundaries on whom he will kill to further the Alliance cause. He acknowledges his role as that of a monster who will be consigned to eternal darkness, like a much more malign Moses, leading his people to a Promised Land he may never himself enter. He regards his exclusion as a small price to pay for committing the sins that allow others to live without them. That other former or current Alliance agents who pursue its enemies, such as Shepherd Book and Jubal Early (Richard Brooks), also possess theological/philosophical worldviews illustrates the Alliance's fondness for a certain sort of intellectual zealotry that it perhaps only cynically endorses. (Whedon urges the audience to connect the three characters by casting them all with black actors.) Like Book, however, the Operative is not blind in his beliefs. After Mal compels him to watch the Miranda video, telling him "I'm going to show you a world without sin," he stops his soldiers from killing the Serenity crew and helps them to repair the ship. Declaring himself no longer the Alliance's man, in an act of self-abnegation he asserts that he will forever vanish from view. Bussolini remarks that the Operative goes counter to the anti-gnosticism of the 'verse in his wish "to escape from the human condition" and that his character arc reveals how "democracy and totalitarianism readily flow back and forth into one another" (2008: 152). Such oscillations thus rhyme with the fluidity among criminal, detective and victim Leitch sees in crime films generally and that *Serenity* foregrounds.

The Reavers represent the most extreme oscillation. As they descend upon the town at the beginning, Whedon, as he does throughout *Firefly*, reveals the well-founded panic and horror they evoke in all who encounter them, the supreme bogeymen of the 'verse. Calling them criminals almost seems beside the point, as they acknowledge no laws. They embody every fear of the savage Other colonialists project onto indigenous peoples (Rabb and Richardson 2008: 127–8). "The Reavers break every social taboo: self-mutilation, cannibalism, rape, and torture" says Magill (2008: 82). And yet the Reavers are not indigenous or alien; they are just fellow colonists whose turn to utter depravity no one in the 'verse can explain. For most of *Serenity* they seem unconnected to the political thriller mystery, mere threatening obstacles the crew must overcome to solve that mystery. The video found on

Miranda turns that notion on its head. The Reavers are central to the mystery—and not as perpetrators but as the most cruelly ironic of victims, the one tenth of one percent of the planet's population that the experimental Pax drug turned into "mindless aggressors" (Jowett 2008: 104).

The Alliance behind that experiment gone horribly wrong plays only one role, that of the Big Bad, as Whedon likes to call his featured villains. The Operative may protest that it "isn't some Evil Empire," but 30 million dead Miranda inhabitants is a casualty count the Death Star might envy. Still, the Alliance didn't intend mass murder. With a restive population that would soon after stage a wholesale insurrection, the government wanted to find some way to control rebellious impulses and produce social cohesion. Seeking to tamp down basic drives with the Pax, it overshoots the mark and, except for the tiny percentage it makes into Reavers, neutralizes even the drive to get up and drink a glass of water. The party line is that "we meant it for the best, to make people safer"; clearly the real goal is to enforce conformity to the dictates of an authoritarian state. The Pax pacifies, in the sense the military uses when it has bombed a hostile civilian population into submission.

Conclusion

Bussolini states that "'The Pax' is a clear analogue to Paxil, one of the major 'mood enhancing' drugs of recent pharmaceutical interventions" (2008: 145). This is certainly a reasonable assumption but its nickname should also alert viewers to its Latin meaning (and root of *pacify*), peace—especially in tandem with another word that is everywhere in the 'verse and metaverse: "serenity," as in Serenity Valley, the site of the bloody Battle that ended the War for Unification; in the ship Mal named after it; in the title of *Firefly*'s original pilot episode (20 December 2002) and of the film that followed three years later. Whedon uses both terms with irony. The Valley of carnage held no serenity and the Pax brought only the peace of the grave, of R.I.P. However, the film does not endorse them as goals in their straightforward sense either. To achieve peace and serenity is to abandon action and conflict, to be passive or to follow the dictates of others in order to escape pain. Even unironically, they stand too close to death. Book advises Mal to believe in something, and this behest may be what propels him to take the initiative to go to Miranda and then expose what happened there. But the Operative reveals the dangers of belief.

Whedon comes right out and says, through his characters, that positive emotion should take pride of place over peace and serenity. As the Operative studies the holographic images of Simon lifting up River to safety, the scientist Dr. Mathias (Michael Hitchcock) declares that Simon was mad to abandon his brilliant career and high social status to rescue his sister and make them both enemies of the government. The Operative insists that there is no madness on Simon's face, "It's love in point of fact—something far more dangerous." Mal also invokes love as the force that propels Serenity: "Love keeps her in the air when she ought to fall down, tells you she's hurting before she keels. Makes her a home." Love has to be reciprocal, requires active commitment to someone or something. In *Serenity* love is the only power in the 'verse that breaks the cycle of oscillation between criminal, victim, and punitive pursuer to create a community outside those triangulated points.

Jason Mittell points out that, because only some shared textual properties become markers of common genre memberships, "we need to look beyond the text as the locus for genre and instead locate genres within the complex interrelations among texts, industries, audiences, and historical contexts" (2001: 7) and to look first to discursive practices in assigning a particular film or television program to a particular genre. By the discursive practices rubric, *Serenity* is no crime film; as I have demonstrated, critics, scholars and marketers never discuss it as one. Yet discursive practices themselves are not static. To return to *The Great Train Robbery*, that seminal Western crime drama to which "The Train Job" nods, Leitch expresses the traditional view that "few viewers have called [it a] crime film" (2002: 5–6). Steve Neale, however, remarks that trade publications did classify it as a crime film, chase and railroad picture; no film was designated as a Western until 1912 (1990: 54). Neale then quotes Charles Musser's assertion that "Its success did not encourage other Westerns but other films of crime" (57). Perhaps, by demonstrating in this essay that *Serenity* is absolutely, among other things, a crime film, I can move the discursive needle a bit in that direction.

Works Cited

Altman, Rick. (1999). *Film/Genre*. London: British Film Institute.
_____ (1984). "A Semantic/Syntactic Approach to Film Genre," in *Cinema Journal* 23.3: 6–18.
Bussolini, Jeffrey. (2008). "A Geopolitical Interpretation of *Serenity*," in Rhonda V. Wilcox and Tanya R. Cochrane (eds.) *Investigating* Firefly *and* Serenity: *Science Fiction on the Frontier*. London: I.B. Tauris, 139–52.
Castrillo and Echart. (2015). "Towards A Narrative Definition of the American Political Thriller Film," in *Communication & Society*. 28.4: 109–23.
Cobley, Paul. (2004). "The Semiotics of Paranoia: The Thriller, Abduction, and the Self," in *Semiotica* 148.1: 317–36.
Funnell, Nick. (2005). "Serenity," in *Time Out*. Online. Available HTTP: https://www.timeout.com/london/film/serenity/ (3 June 2017).
García-Mainar, Luis M. (2016). *The Introspective Realist Crime Film*. London: Palgrave Macmillan.
Greydanus, Steven. (2005), "Serenity," in *DecentFilms*. Online. Available HTTP: http://www.decentfilms.com/reviews/serenity2005/ (3 June 2017).
Jowett, Lorna. (2008). "Back to the Future: Retrofuturism, Cyberpunk, and Humanity in *Firefly* and *Serenity*," in Rhonda V. Wilcox and Tanya R. Cochrane (eds.). *Investigating* Firefly *and* Serenity: *Science Fiction on the Frontier*. London: I.B. Tauris, 101–13.

Lane, Jim. (2005). "Serenity," in *Sacramento News and Review*. Online. Available HTTP: https://www.newsreview.com/sacramento/serenity/content?oid=44223/ (3 June 2017).

Leitch, Thomas. (2002). *Crime Films*. Cambridge: Cambridge UP.

Magill, David. (2008). "'I Aim to Misbehave': Masculinities in the 'Verse," in Rhonda V. Wilcox and Tanya R. Cochrane (eds.) *Investigating* Firefly *and* Serenity: *Science Fiction on the Frontier*. London: I.B. Tauris, 76–86.

Mittell, Jason. (2001). "A Cultural Approach to Genre Theory," in *Cinema Journal* 40.1: 3–24.

Musser, Charles. (1984). "The Travel Genre in 1903–04: Moving Toward Fictional Narratives," in *Iris* 2.1: 56–57.

Neale, Steve. (1990). "Questions of Genre," in *Steve Neale. Screen* 31.1: 45–66.

Rabb, J. Douglas, and J. Michael Richardson. (2008). "Reavers and Redskins: Creating the Frontier Savage," in Rhonda V. Wilcox and Tanya R. Cochrane (eds.) *Investigating* Firefly *and* Serenity: *Science Fiction on the Frontier*. London: I.B. Tauris, 127–38.

"Review: Serenity." (2005). Online. Available HTTP: https://www.rottentomatoes.com/m/serenity/ (3 June 2017).

Robinson, Tasha. (2005). "Serenity," in *AV Club*. Online. Available HTTP: https://www.rottentomatoes.com/m/serenity/ (3 June 2017).

Rocchi, James. (2005). "Serenity," in *Netflix*. Online. Available HTTP: https://www.rottentomatoes.com/m/serenity/ (3 June 2017).

"Serenity." (2005), in *Rotten Tomatoes*. Online. Available HTTP: https://www.rottentomatoes.com/m/serenity/ (3 June 2017).

Sutherland, Sharon, and Sarah Shaw. (2008). "'The Alliance Isn't Some Evil Empire': Dystopia in Joss Whedon's *Firefly/Serenity*," in Rhonda V. Wilcox and Tanya R. Cochrane (eds.) *Investigating* Firefly *and* Serenity: *Science Fiction on the Frontier*. London: I.B. Tauris, 89–100.

Telotte J.P. (2012). "Serenity, Genre, and Cinematization." J.P. Telotte and Gerald Duchovnay (eds.) *Science Fiction Film, Television, and Adaptation: Across the Screens*. London and New York: Routledge, 127–40.

Thomson, Desson. (2005). "'Serenity': A Wild Ride with Some New Space Cowboys," in *The Washington Post*. Online. Available HTTP: http://www.washingtonpost.com/wp-dyn/content/article/2005/09/29/AR2005092902146.html/(3 June 2017).

Tranter, K.M. (2012). "'Come a Day There Won't Be Room for Naughty Men Like Us to Slip About at All': The Multi-Media Outlaws of Serenity and the Possibilities of Post-Literate Justice," in *Law, Text, Culture* 16.1: 277–304.

Vice, Jeff. (2005). "Film Review: 'Serenity' a Bit Too Smart for Its Own Good," in *Deseret News*. Online. Available HTTP: http://www.deseretnews.com/article/700003979/Serenity-a-bit-too-smart-for-its-own-good.html/(3 June 2017).

Whedon, Joss (2005) Serenity: *The Official Visual Companion*. London: Titan Books.

Overconsumption, the Natural Environment and Lessons from Earth-That-Was

Eric Benson

In the opening sequence of *Serenity* (Joss Whedon, 2005), we see, for a few seconds, a peaceful image of twenty-sixth century Earth (formed in a transition from the Universal Pictures planet logo) that quickly changes from serene to perilous. Multiple white clouds of smoke rise from dangerous explosions on the planet's surface as spaceships race toward the viewer, fleeing the destruction at home. As the escape vessels grow closer, an aloof female narrator describes what happened to our planet: "Earth-That-Was could no longer sustain our numbers, we were so many. We found a new solar system. Dozens of planets and hundreds of moons. Each one terraformed, a process taking decades, to support human life. To be new Earths." She continues to describe how humanity formed the Alliance, but that not everyone was on board, and the savage outer planets rebelled, starting a devastating war. She ends her story proudly stating that the Alliance prevailed, creating a universe that is safe and peaceful. As the film switches away from these scenes in space, the narrator is revealed to be a teacher in a futuristic outdoor classroom sharing a history lesson on the Unification War. Students ask why the Independents fought the Alliance, and the teacher turns the question back on the class. One young girl responds, "We meddle. People don't like to be meddled with. We tell them what to do, what to think. Don't run, don't walk. We're in their homes and in their heads and we haven't the right. We're meddlesome." The teacher confidently walks over to the young girl, kneels down and grabs her stylus pen and says, "we're not telling people what to think. We're just trying to show them how." The teacher thrusts the stylus into the screaming young girl's forehead and the scene shifts to a blue-lit laboratory, where the same young girl (now older) sits yelling in a chair with a probe in her skull. Here, new audiences to "the 'Verse" are introduced to one of the most important characters in the film, River Tam (Summer Glau).

Many articles proceed from this point in the film to discuss *Serenity's* engagement with gender in science fiction, Westerns in space, faith, Libertarianism and politics, and philosophy. Instead, I will unpack three issues that have not been addressed in Whedon studies literature, but are prominent, if not central, in the opening sequence of the film: overconsumption, global warming, and environmentalism. This essay will explore what potentially caused "Earth-that-was" to become uninhabitable by analyzing the film's opening scene, settings on terraformed planets, hints in props and dialogue from the film and its tie-in comics, and existing dystopian tropes in science fiction. It will also hypothesize Joss Whedon's potential reasons for framing both the television series and the film as a cautionary story for the viewer.

Raison d'Être

To begin, Earth-that-was is the narrative starting-point for both *Firefly* and *Serenity* (outside of Joss Whedon, of course). Without leaving Earth, there are no space bandits, terraformed planets, Mr. Universe (David Krumholtz), River Tam, or the Alliance. The overconsumption of our natural resources, and most probably pollution and warming of the planet (I'll get to this later), created the eventual Alliance/Browncoat Unification War that lead to the escapades of Captain Malcolm Reynolds (Nathan Fillion) and the crew in both *Firefly* (2002–03) and the feature film *Serenity* (as well as in the comics that followed).

The opening narration of the film differs from that of the television series, but the two are equally vague about the problems that led to the evacuation of Earth-that-was. *Firefly* opened with (depending on the episode) either the Captain of the spaceship Serenity Malcolm Reynolds or the preacher Shepherd Book (Ron Glass) narrating "how it was." This brief voice-over before the opening credits explained the history of the crew and the premise of the show. Captain Reynolds's version goes like this:

> Here's how it is: Earth got used up, so we terraformed a whole new galaxy of Earths, some rich and flush with new technologies, some not so much. Central Planets, thems formed the Alliance, waged war to bring everyone under their rule; a few idiots tried to fight it, among them myself. I'm Malcolm Reynolds, captain of Serenity. She's a transport ship, Firefly class. Got a good crew: fighters, pilot, mechanic. We even picked up a preacher for some reason, and a bona fide companion. There's a

doctor, too, took his genius sister outta some Alliance camp, so they're keeping a low profile. You understand. You got a job, we can do it. Don't much care what it is.

We get different hints as to what happened to Earth-that-was in the varying opening monologues of *Firefly* and *Serenity*. While Malcolm Reynolds states, "Earth got used up" in *Firefly*, the Alliance teacher in *Serenity* says that "Earth-that-was could no longer sustain our numbers." Those two pieces of information combined tell us that humanity's population became too large and then over-consumed what little natural resources we had left. Each narration is from opposing sides of the Unification War, but essentially agree that humanity is guilty of screwing up the planet. Taken at face value, we, as moviegoers, could stop there, accept this as fact, and simply enjoy the rest of the action and witty dialogue in the film; but in doing so, we would miss Joss Whedon's subtle cautionary tale and critique of contemporary Western society (another topic for the last section in this essay). If we look a bit further, there is a lot more embedded in the film's opening sequence to unpack. When the opening monologue is put next to actual historical events in human history and small details within the sets of the film are more deeply analyzed, we can begin to see some of the deeper, environmental resonance of *Serenity*.

From Earth to Earth-That-Was

So what exactly did Joss Whedon imagine we had collectively done to create the end of our civilization on Earth in the twenty-sixth century? We can look to human history and the laws of nature to make some fairly educated guesses. We should begin by looking at our collective history to see where and when overpopulation and consequently overconsumption led to the collapse of civilizations. For this is exactly what must have happened to Malcolm Reynold's ancestors in *Serenity*; their way of life could no longer be sustained and they were forced to leave Earth, abandoning their homes.

There are a few cases in antiquity when a civilization collapsed as a result of high concentrations of people consuming more resources than their land could regenerate. The Maya, Anaszi, and Easter Islander civilizations are all sadly perfect examples of this, but I will focus on the Mayans in this section. The Mayans were a very sophisticated culture in their farming, architectural, and military achievements, but despite their prowess, they were forced eventually to hurriedly abandon their cities (without spaceships!) after a series of poorly strategized urban planning decisions. Scientist and author Jared Diamond, in his 2005 book *Collapse: How Societies Choose to Fail or Succeed*, theorized that the Mayans (with a quickly growing population) deforested too much of the surrounding landscape to build new structures and to farm more land to house and feed their new larger community. This sudden and significant lack of trees reduced water evaporation and increased land erosion. Combined with these mistakes, a prolonged drought eventually forced the Mayans to leave their homes to survive—leaving behind a once-great civilization in ruins. There are many other theories as to why the Mayans disappeared, but two recent studies, published in 2012 and 2010 by researchers at Arizona State University and Columbia University respectively, proved Diamond's hypothesis on the Mayans.

In the Arizona State study (Turner and Sabloff 2012: 109) the team analyzed archaeological data from the Yucatan Peninsula from the time of the Mayans to learn about their environmental conditions. They found a drastic drop in rainfall in the results of the research confirming a component of Diamond's theory. The team at Columbia University found similar results (Oglesby et al. 2010: 115) based on data from a computer model of deforestation (using numbers from the time of the Mayans) to determine the effect on overall rainfall in the same Yucatan Peninsula. They also found that the cleared land led to less water evaporation (and therefore less rain), which exacerbated the already increasing drought.

Diamond wrote in *Collapse* that the lesson learned from the collapse of the Mayans, "…is simple: maximum population, wealth, resource consumption, and waste production mean maximum environmental impact, approaching the limit where impact outstrips resources" (Diamond 2005: 509). In short, you cannot take more than there is. It is a basic natural law in ecology. For an ecological system to be balanced or sustainable, what is taken from that system must equal what is being put back in. The rapid deforestation of the land to build and farm, broke the natural balance of the ecosystem, causing it to fail.

A repeat of the Mayan downfall on a global scale is one possible explanation for what happened on Earth-that-was. However, as the Mayan example is isolated to a small region of the planet, we can extrapolate a more likely scenario by considering all the environmental catastrophes and human casualties connected to our current battle with global warming. Diamond is useful here again, as he proposes twelve different yet connected reasons why civilizations collapse. He theorizes that humans lose their way of life due to: deforestation and habitat destruction, soil problems (erosion, salinization, and soil fertility losses), water management problems, overhunting, overfishing, effects of introduced species on native species, overpopulation, increased per-capita impact of people, anthropogenic climate change, buildup of toxins in the environment, energy shortages, and/or full human use of the Earth's photosynthetic capacity. (2005: 7).

Civilization collapse from overhunting and/or overfishing (for example) will definitely occur when there is overpopulation, and that, in turn, will create deforestation and habitat destruction (and possibly more). Everything on our planet is connected, so one negative ripple in an ecosystem will have a domino affect on those tied to it. Environmental pioneer John Muir describes this concept: "When we try to pick out anything by itself we find that it is bound fast by a thousand invisible cords that cannot be broken, to everything in the universe." (Muir, 1911: 110). Our planet is one large system. As a case study, imagine a natural food chain from the world of ecology. As children, we learned that there are predators and prey where, typically, the larger stronger animal will eat the smaller weaker one. For instance, a red tailed hawk may seek nourishment from a rattlesnake, which in turn could prey on a grey squirrel that relies on the acorns that drop from a nearby oak tree. The oak tree maintains its own health from the fallen leaves, insects, and mushrooms that decompose into the soil around the roots to provide nutrients. These plants and animals are not only affected by each other but they are also affected by the climate, weather, humans, or other animals (Benson and Perullo 2016: 14–15). They are all interconnected, interdependent, and sustainable without negative human interaction like deforestation, urban sprawl, or pollution. However, throw in a possible cause for civilization collapse from Diamond, and things can spiral out of control.

In the Mayan example, once deforestation slows the possibility for normal rainfall causing the drought to worsen, the crops begin to fail. With less food available, the Tragedy of the Commons can occur. Here, when a community resource (corn for example) is in high demand but low supply, people can act in their own self-interest to take more than their fair share of the crop to survive (Hardin 1968: 162). This will leave less or none for those who are late to the fields or market, leading to starvation and potentially armed conflict. The possibility that using up the resources on Earth-that-was could lead to such conflict is not unlikely, supported by the explosions we saw in the beginning of the film. After consuming most of the natural resources on the planet, whatever was left was likely fought over, adding to the pressure and immediacy to leave and find new Earths.

The lyrics "Burn the land and boil the sea" from the *Firefly* theme song, written by Joss Whedon, also offer a fairly big clue that after Earth "was used up" and "couldn't sustain us," global warming made the planet uninhabitable. Combined with Diamond's list of twelve reasons for civilization collapse, it is easy to see how global warming could quickly escalate issues of habitat destruction, soil loss, energy shortages, and also an increased possibility of violence and war to protect one's land, water, and air for survival. "Burn the land and boil the sea," indeed!

Science tells us that burning coal for energy, or combusting gasoline in engines, releases greenhouse gases. These gases, like carbon dioxide and methane (for example), become trapped in the upper atmosphere of the planet. Visible light from the sun passes through these gases and warms the Earth. As the planet warms, it releases heat energy upwards that becomes trapped inside the upper atmosphere by these same greenhouse gases, making the planet hotter and hotter as the gases increase from the continued burning of fossil fuels. This very basic explanation of the "greenhouse effect," can help one understand the scientific concept of global warming. Current models from the IPCC (Intergovernmental Panel on Climate Change) predict that the negative effects of unchecked global warming by 2100 would cause the global temperature averages to exceed an increase of two degree Celsius (2014: 10) with, consequently, up to a one meter rise in ocean levels. This would cause coastal cities to flood from melting icebergs, millions of refugees fleeing lost sea-side homes, crop failure from extreme heat and inclement weather, natural resource loss, and a host of other horrible dystopian outcomes. Mind you *Serenity* takes place in the twenty-sixth century, some 400 years after these dire IPCC global climate predictions, so without proper greenhouse gas emission reductions, the situation would have been a lot worse by the time Malcolm Reynolds's ancestors fled Earth-that was as refugees.

In the present day, humanity can still do quite a lot to prevent the seemingly unbearable dystopian outcomes of global warming. Many of these initiatives are already underway. One of the most important policy decisions we can make as a society is to stop burning unsustainable fossil fuels and switch to renewable energy sources like solar, wind, tidal, or geothermal. According to the Solar Energy Industries Association, the U.S. solar market grew by 97 percent in 2016, while energy capacity is expected to triple by 2022 (SEIA 2016). This collective push for renewables helped the solar energy industry in the U.S. grow seventeen times faster than the entire American economy in 2016 (IRENA 2017). The American Wind Energy Association also had positive news in their 2016 annual report, stating that wind is now the number one renewable energy source in the U.S. with 81 gigawatts of wind powering 24 million homes (2016). Globally, renewables lead in all energy sectors for growth and the International Energy Agency predicts they will account for 700 gigawatts of energy production by 2020, which will be 26 percent of the energy created (2015). This is all very positive news, as I certainly wish to avoid the fate of Earth-that-was, despite wanting to join Captain Reynolds on adventures as a crewmember on Serenity.

What Was Life Like on Earth-That-Was?

We can be pretty sure that life was not very shiny on Earth-that-was in the lead-up to its evacuation. Extreme weather, flooded cities, poverty, and lack of clean air and water are just some of the horrors science tells us will happen in an overpopulated, warming planet, so it would be safe to assume that humanity faced such challenges. We can also look to other dystopian science fiction films for help in visualizing the conditions of Earth-that-was. Dystopian films are nothing new in Hollywood. One can easily find cynical commentary on our future through movies by quickly scanning the science fiction genre on any streaming film service. Cinematic dystopia spans nearly the entire span of film history, including classics like Fritz Lang's 1927 masterpiece *Metropolis*, along with more recent films and series like *The Handmaid's Tale* (2017–), *Snowpiercer* (Bong Joon Ho, 2013), *Wall-E* (Andrew Stanton, 2008), *The Matrix* (Lana and Lilly Wachowski, 1999), *Gattaca* (Andrew Niccol, 1997), *Waterworld* (Kevin Reynolds, 1995), *Blade Runner* (Ridley Scott, 1982), *Mad Max* (George Miller, 1979), and *Soylent Green* (Richard Fleisher, 1973). There are definitely thematic trends across these films and shows that tie them to *Serenity*'s opening scene. Overpopulation is a key element in *Blade Runner*, while the opposite is true in both *The Handmaid's Tale* and *Gattaca*. Energy shortages are definitely a large component of the *Mad Max* series, *The Matrix* trilogy, and *Snowpiercer*. *Wall-E* provides a dystopian commentary on overconsumption, while *Waterworld* and *Snowpiercer* both reflect fears of climate change.

Of all the films and television shows, however, *Serenity* seems to share aesthetic, thematic, and narrative features with *Blade Runner*, *The Matrix*, and *Mad Max*, making these obvious reference-points for what Earth-that-was may have looked like. Later texts like *Elysium* (Neill Blomkamp, 2013) and *Westworld* (2016–) could be productively considered alongside *Serenity*, though they certainly could not have influenced Whedon, whose series and film were released years ahead of them.

Throughout the film *Serenity*, we see further hints of what life might have been like on Earth-that-was. On the planet Beaumonde, where River Tam starts a brawl in the Maidenhead bar, we see a city under a dark foreboding sky, seemingly an apocalyptic version of a modern day Beijing or New York City. There are both English and Mandarin digital signs brightly illuminating the streets, full of flying cars, pedestrians, and bicyclists scurrying along. There are also food trucks and merchants, along with street lights that look like they came from Victorian London. Beaumonde is a mixture of high and low technologies, and the *Firefly* and *Serenity* Wiki further describes Beaumonde as a troubled industrial planet:

> Due to the high industrial output, pollution was a problem. Beaumonde's cities were covered in a perpetual haze. Weather control systems processed the worst of the pollution, but the science-minded believed the long-term effects may be more difficult to take care of. Every year more pollutants found their way into the water and the soil, causing many problems for those who lived off the land. Some people moved their homes and businesses underground to escape the air pollution [*Firefly-Serenity* Wiki 2006].

This information does not come up in the movie, but is instead noted in the 2005 *Serenity* Role Playing Game. These facts do, however, support my argument, articulated in the last section of this essay, that Joss Whedon was considering overconsumption, global warming, and environmentalism in the writing of the movie and television show. The aesthetic features of Beaumonde are also very similar to those in Ridley Scott's futuristic *Blade Runner,* where in an overpopulated and polluted Los Angeles, there are flying vehicles, neon signs, and a multicultural population of primarily Caucasian and Asian Americans.

So did Earth-that-was look like *Blade Runner*? *Blade Runner* takes place in 2019, while *Serenity* and *Firefly* take place in the twenty-sixth century—hundreds of years later. So, although Beaumonde looks eerily similar to 2019 L.A., life on twenty-sixth century Earth was probably much more polluted and inhospitable for safe and comfortable living. The films may take place in different narrative universes, but *Blade Runner*'s setting is still clearly habitable. It is more likely that Beaumonde (and places like it in the 'Verse) are what Earth-that-was looked like toward the end of the twenty-first century (and clearly the citizens on Beaumonde made and continue to make the same environmental mistakes they did on Earth, according to the Serenity RPG).

In the beginning of the *Mad Max* series, the world devolves into bedlam after all the coal and other fuel-powered generators stop working, leaving no electricity and unraveling the fabric of society. Food shortages and roving bands of bandits slowly take over control of what becomes "the Wasteland." As the series progresses, governments struggle over the last reserves of oil, and eventually start a nuclear war, creating a dry, radioactive and dangerous climate with very little water, food, or fuel. The series takes place in a future described as "a few years from now," but internet databases place its storyline between 1999/2000 and 2018 (*Mad Max* Wiki 2014) based on information gleaned from a movie prop from the first film.

Again, twenty-sixth-century Earth would be in worse shape than the dystopia seen in *Mad Max*. It is possible that Earth-that-was also suffered through a nuclear war at some point, and if so, that would have definitely exacerbated the threats to resources and the climate that the planet might have already been facing. While I would not count the possibility of a nuclear war out entirely, the opening scene is clear in its assertion that "Earth was used up," and not that wars forced populations to leave. I would employ Occam's Razor to support the theory that humanity faced a combination of overpopulation, overconsumption, and global warming in its last centuries on Earth. Jared Diamond would suggest here that it would be tough to avoid armed conflict when overpopulated areas struggle for resources. It is highly likely Earth-that-was had quite a few armed conflicts leading up to the twenty-sixth century, but not necessarily a nuclear war.

In the *Matrix* trilogy, powerful sentient machines take over humanity and the planet sometime in the twenty-first century, but the first film is set between 2199 and 2699, according to the character Morpheus (Laurence Fishburne). Earth itself is a dark dystopian wasteland, forcing those who survive underground, while others are subdued by the machines living in a simulated reality called the Matrix—or is everyone living in the Matrix? Perhaps a question for another book. In *The Matrix*, as in *Mad Max* and *Blade Runner*, life is bleak, and energy sources are at a premium. The important connection here for *Serenity* is the level of technology. To leave Earth at light speed and terraform planets in other galaxies, technology on Earth-that-was must have already been advanced, though the machines had certainly not become sentient.

Life on Earth-that-was in the twenty-sixth century was clearly under threat. Global warming, from the burning of fossil fuels, would have created unpredictable weather patterns, extreme temperatures, and crop failure. Scenes of dry arid lands like the sets in *Mad Max* would be the norm (perfect for a Western in space), but the technology would have to be significantly more advanced to send humanity into the black. Earth's technology may not have been sentient like in *The Matrix*, but the film's uninhabitable surface may be an accurate depiction of what *Serenity*'s space colonizers were fleeing.

Whedon's Cautionary Tale of Climate Fiction

So far my theory surrounding the collapse of human civilization on "Earth-that-was" has involved the interaction of many connected scenarios. Most likely, *Serenity*'s history is one in which the population of Earth continues to grow past its current 7.4 billion people (USCB 2017) to a point where we consume resources beyond the planet's carrying capacity. In the process we fail to curb global warming and its affects on us reach the point of catastrophe around the year 2517, leaving us no choice but to leave. This theory, so far, is based solely on the opening sequence of the film with some help from human history, the science of climate change, and other dystopian films and television programs. But, are there other clues from the rest of the film that can help support this theory? The short answer is yes. This section will explore the most important and yet subtle of these clues. These hints as to what happened to Earth-that-was are few, but they serve to bolster the monologue from the beginning of the film and support my larger theory.

The first interesting clue is offered on the planet Lilac, where the crew of Serenity lands to rob a bank near the beginning of the film. Here, we see a dry, arid planet similar to settings from the Old American West. This setting epitomizes the look of a good space Western. After landing on Lilac, most of the Serenity crew boards a yellow land speeder suitable for flying around a planet (an MF-813 Flying Mule) and heads into town for the heist. Along the way (and within the city limits) we see wind turbines, rainwater catchments, and solar panels. This is Whedon's vision of the new Old West. No longer do humans use coal-burning trains, but instead build clean energy sources to prevent what happened on Earth-that-was. The wind turbine is not an isolated image within the movie, however. Later in the film at the Maidenhead bar, we catch a quick glimpse of a newscast on an overhead screen showing installations of new wind turbines. The newscast leads into the Fruity Oaty Bar commercial that sets River off with the word "Miranda." The presence of these renewable energy sources in the film bodes well for the New Earth settings, but they are also a reminder to the audience that such technologies are the way of the future here on Old Earth. A subtle nudge by Joss Whedon, possibly.

Back on Lilac, while Mal and his crew are robbing the bank's Alliance money, a Reaver raiding party attacks the city. In their escape from the Reaver Land Stalker ship, we see another intriguing clue as to Whedon's message about energy sources. Throughout the film and television series we see Serenity produce beautiful shimmering golden lights from its main back engine. These special effects in the film help to add credence to the naming of Serenity as a Firefly class vessel. Fireflies (or lightning bugs), of course, glow from their lower abdomen producing a bioluminescence of yellow-green light. In comparison, the Reaver Land Stalker bellows copious amounts of putrid black smoke when it is in hot pursuit of the Serenity crew. The Mule, on the other hand, similar to Serenity, has glowing yellow-orange engine output. Whedon and his special effects staff are helping the viewers clearly understand through these visuals who to root for in the scene. The black smoke looks very similar to coal-powered trains from the Old American West, which also exhaled lung-cancer causing clouds of exhaust. This energy source is dated and depicted negatively through its connection to the Reavers. Later in the film, on the planet Haven, after finding their ex-crewmate Shepherd Book murdered by the Alliance Operative (Chiwetel Ejiofor) and his support team, Zoe calls the Captain's idea of strapping dead bodies to Serenity to pass as a Reaver ship an "abomination." Here, is another subtle connection to what we saw on Lilac with the Land Stalker as dated, barbaric, and (based on Zoe's adjective) an abomination. It stands in stark contrast to the apparently clean burning engines of Serenity, the Mule, and the shimmering wind turbines on the planet and in the newscast from the bar.

On Serenity herself, Kaylee paints leaves around the kitchen and dining room, while situated in the same area is a small coffee table made from a tree trunk. These are simple reminders of Earth-that-was, echoed in Wash's famous last words "I am a Leaf on the wind, watch how I soar." In the comic book follow-up to the film *Float Out*, we get another subtle reminder of the threat of global warming. *Float Out* takes place immediately after the film and focuses on the birth of Wash and Zoe's daughter, Emma, and flashbacks from three of Wash's former shipmates. In one of the flashbacks, Wash's friend Leland reminisces about their time as runners for PonyPacro on a ship called the Crazy Moon Madcap. His story mentions how difficult climate change made the trips to the planet: "Its weird spin and egg-yolk sun give it those turn-on-a-dime climate changes, one right on top of the other" (Oswalt 2010). The citizens of Earth-that-was likely faced a similar problem leading up to the twenty-sixth century.

These subtle choices in dialogue and set design, combined with more overt language in the opening monologue, also situate *Firefly* and *Serenity* within the realm of climate fiction (cli-fi)—a subset of dystopian science fiction that deals with global warming. This space Western franchise was written between 2002 and 2005 when very little was being done, policy-wise, by the American government, despite scientists and environmental organizations pushing for quick and decisive action to curb climate change. Whedon's writing and creative decisions are well thought out, intentional, and inspired. He is also no stranger to being involved and entangled in social and political movements. He and his fans fundraise for his favorite not-for-profit organization Equality Now, and more recently Whedon has called out politicians who deny climate change saying (in a Tweet) that "The climate IS changing—if we can't, that makes us dumber than weather #ClimateChangeIsReal," and that "Policy makers who deny basic scientific truth should also be denied penicillin, horseless carriages, [and] air time on the magic box of shadows," (Whedon 2015). These tweets have since been deleted. He also was active in the 2012 and 2016 elections calling Mitt Romney the right candidate to "put this country back on the path to the zombie apocalypse" (Whedon 2012) and describing now-President Donald Trump as "a racist, abusive coward who could permanently damage the fabric of our society" (Whedon 2016). It is not far-fetched to imagine that Whedon wanted to do something about global warming at the time and wrote a cautionary message into both *Firefly* and *Serenity*.

Despite the categorization of *Serenity* as science fiction, I argue it contains clear connections to the world of non-fiction. Overpopulation and over-consumption are not just isolated missteps in human history, but are also happening today on a mass scale. Currently we need four more Earths to keep up with our consumption levels (De Chant 2012) and global warming is causing flooding on American and other coastlines across the globe (Gillis 2016). In the ancient Mayan civilization example, a society fell due to rapid deforestation and a fast-growing population during a severe drought. In present day Guatemala, a similar scenario is playing out. In an attempt to expand sugarcane, palm oil, and cattle exports, Guatemala has cleared 40 percent of its National Forests (Foucart 2011) and now has the world's fastest rate of deforestation. Instead of drought, climate change has brought heavy rains that cause severe mudslides in the mountains since the trees have been cut down. The mudslides wipe out homes and cause more damage to the now delicate landscapes. Outside of Guatemala, Americans can look to their President as an example of current failures. Donald Trump does not believe in global warming and, in June of 2017, began the process of removing the United States from the Paris Climate Accords. If the process is successful, the U.S. will be one of three countries out of 195 that are not officially involved in positive climate action. Humanity may already be on the path that leads to Earth-that-was.

I believe it is both logical and vital for our civilization to heed the environmental warnings of our present day and past. *Serenity* is not a treatise on overconsumption, global warming, and environmentalism, but it does carry an important message about them all. Without quick collective action, we could be faced in the next few centuries with trying to live on Whedon's Earth-that-was—and potentially on the run from the Alliance somewhere "in the black."

Works Cited

American Wind Energy Association. (2016). *Wind Energy Facts at a Glance*. AWEA. Available HTTP: http://www.awea.org/wind-energy-facts-at-a-glance (30 May 2017).

Atkin, Emily. (2015). "Joss Whedon: Politicians Who Deny Climate Change 'Deny Basic Scientific Truth,'" *Think Progress*. Available HTTP: https://thinkprogress.org/joss-whedon-politicians-who-deny-climate-change-deny-basic-scientific-truth-db0cd13d609b (30 May 2017).

Benson, Eric, and Yvette Perullo. (2016). *Design to Renourish: Sustainable Graphic Design in Practice*. Boca Raton: CRC Press, 14–15.

De Chant, Tim. (2012.) "If the World's Population Lived Like…," *Per Square Mile*. Available HTTP: https://persquaremile.com/2012/08/08/if-the-worlds-population-lived-like/ (1 June 2017).

Diamond, Jared. (2005). *Collapse: How Societies Choose to Fail or Survive*. London: Penguin Books.

Firefly-Serenity Wiki. (2006). "Beaumonde." Available HTTP: http://firefly.wikia.com/wiki/Beaumonde (30 May 2017).

Foucart, Stéphane. (2011). "A Race for Land Is Destroying the Guatemalan Rainforest," *The Guardian*. Available HTTP: https://www.theguardian.com/environment/2011/jul/12/guatemala-rainforest-deforestation-farming-foucart (30 May 2017).

Gillis, Justin. (2016). "Flooding of Coast, Caused by Global Warming, Has Already Begun," *The New York Times*. Available HTTP: https://www.nytimes.com/2016/09/04/science/flooding-of-coast-caused-by-global-warming-has-already-begun.html (30 May 2017).

Hardin, Garrett. (1968). "The Tragedy of the Commons," in *Science* 162.3859: 1243–8.

Intergovernmental Panel on Climate Change. (2014). "Synthesis Report Summary for Policymakers." IPCC. Available HTTP: http://www.ipcc.ch/pdf/assessment-report/ar5/syr/AR5_SYR_FINAL_SPM.pdf (30 May 2017).

International Energy Agency. (2015). "Renewables to Lead World Power Market Growth to 2020." IEA. Available HTTP: https://www.iea.org/newsroom/news/2015/october/renewables-to-lead-world-power-market-growth-to-2020.html (30 May 2017).

International Renewable Energy Agency. (2017). "Renewable Energy Employs 9.8 Million People Worldwide, New IRENA Report Finds." IREA. Available HTTP: http://www.irena.org/News/Description.aspx?CatID=84&NType=A&News_ID=1490&PriMenuID=16&mnu=cat (30 May 2017).

Mad Max Wiki. (2014). "Timeline of Events (Original Trilogy." Available HTTP: http://madmax.wikia.com/wiki/Timeline_of_events_(original_trilogy) (30 May 2017).

The Matrix Wiki. (2010). "2199." Available HTTP: http://matrix.wikia.com/wiki/2199 (30 May 2017).

Muir, John. (1911). *My First Summer in the Sierra*. Boston: Houghton Mifflin.

Oglesby, Robert J., Thomas L. Sever, William Saturno, David J. Erickson III, and Jayanthi Srikishen. (2010). "Collapse of the Maya: Could Deforestation Have Contributed?" *Journal of Geophysical Research* 115.D12106: 1–10.

Oswalt, Patton. (2010). *Serenity: Float Out*. Milwaukie, OR: Dark Horse Comics.

Solar Energy Industries Association. (2016). "Solar Market Insight Report 2016 Year in Review." SEIA. Available HTTP: http://www.seia.org/research-resources/solar-market-insight-report-2016-year-review (14 July 2017).

Turner, B.L. II, and Jeremy A. Sabloff. (2012). "Classic Period Collapse of the Central Maya Lowlands: Insights About Human-Environment Relationships for Sustainability." *Proceedings of the National Academy of Sciences* (PNAS) 109: 13908–14.

United States Census Bureau. (2017). "U.S. and World Population Clock." Available HTTP: https://www.census.gov/popclock/ (30 May 2017).

Whedon, Joss. (2016). "Important." YouTube. Available HTTP: https://www.youtube.com/watch?v=nRp1CK_X_Yw (30 May 2017).

Whedon, Joss. (2012). "Whedon on Romney." YouTube. Available HTTP: https://www.youtube.com/watch?v=6TiXUF9xbTo (30 May 2017).

"Eat them all the time/ Let them blow your mind"
River and the Unacknowledged Corporate Hand in Serenity

ERIN GIANNINI

From the start of *Serenity* (Joss Whedon, 2005), the narrative makes it clear that, as was suggested in *Firefly* (2002), River Tam (Summer Glau) is a valuable asset to the Alliance government. Indeed, the film opens not with the main crew of Serenity (Mal [Nathan Fillion], Zoe [Gina Torres], Jayne [Adam Baldwin], Wash [Alan Tudyk], and Kaylee [Jewel Staite]), but with governmental agents such as Dr. Mathias (Michael Hitchcock) and the Operative (Chiwetel Ejiofor); the film's plot turns on River's knowledge of the Alliance government's tampering with the environment of the planet Miranda and the subsequent "blowback" (Bussolini 144–150) of their experiments (millions dead and the creation of the Reavers).

Serenity opens on an imagined classroom, in which a teacher (Tamara Taylor) provides her students, including a younger version of protagonist River Tam, with a particular version of planetary history, in which the Alliance government, run by a parliamentary system comprised of American and Chinese rule, has colonized a new solar system and attempted to bring all planets under "civilized" rule. The Alliances methods and the meaning of civilization itself are central concerns of the narrative. If a viewer enters the film having never seen the series, it may not be immediately clear that the teacher's version is heavy on alternative facts, glossing over the costs of such colonization and avoiding questions about precisely how stability was achieved. Even the question she asks the students implies the desired answer: she asks "why" the outer planets (aka "The Independents") would reject all the Alliance had to offer, rather than asking what the terms of such agreement might mean. Further, River's attempt to question such history ends with a needle shoved into her forehead, and the scene transitions into a medical lab, revealing River to be an experimental subject. The scene in the lab itself is then revealed to be a recording viewed by The Operative, an agent of the government tasked with reclaiming the escaped River.

This opening scene—a hallucination that transitions to a recording that transitions to the present day of the film itself—serves to set up the narrative trajectory of the film: the search for River Tam to silence what governmental secrets she may have in her head. What is of note is that the opening scene then transitions into the logo of the ship Serenity. At first seeming to float in space, the logo resolves into browns and yellows and a Chinese character, revealing itself to be painted on the side of a spaceship. The viewer goes through this logo inside of the ship itself where, in a five-minute unbroken tracking shot, the film introduces us to the crew and passengers of the ship Serenity.

It is the use of this logo to enter the literal world of Serenity (and *Serenity*) that is of interest here. In the months preceding the release of the film, the *Serenity* logo appeared on buttons passed out by fans, on key chains given to those who attended the film's pre-screening, as well as numerous fan sites across the Internet. The reduction of a film to a logo for the purposes of promotion is typical; as Naomi Klein indicates, the genesis of the brand as a metonym for a corporation's products is tied inextricably with the rise of the factory and mass-produced goods (2002: 5–6). That being said, having the logo serve as the visual entry point to the inside of the ship, I would argue, shows an awareness of the importance of this type of visual clue both for the promotion of the film itself and the direction of the film's narrative.

While the *Serenity* logo is very prominently featured in both the opening and closing of the film, the promotion and distribution of the film is not the central concern of this essay. Rather, it is what the logo can theoretically obscure: the inner workings of the corporation that produced the media product in question. I have previously written on the way in which River represents an "embodied culture jam"—that is, something that hijacks a corporation's brand to reveal its more nefarious activities (Giannini 2015)—in *Firefly*. Within *Firefly*, the antagonist was represented by the megacorporation Blue Sun, which produced a diverse array of goods and services, from food products to medical equipment, and frequently provoked fearful or violent reactions from River when she was faced with its logo. Blue Sun, however, is not directly referenced within *Serenity*. While my previous essay touched on the film, the seeming absence of Blue Sun as an antagonist within *Serenity* has not been explored. In the *Firefly* comics series *Those Left Behind* (Whedon and Matthews 2005), the final panels reveal that the Blue Sun agents chasing River have been killed, and the responsibility for retrieving River has fallen primarily to the Alliance Parliament, in the form of the Operative, suggesting a collusion between the corporation and the Alliance government. While the Operative and the Alliance operate as the central antagonists in the film, it is significant that what triggers River's assassin skills, and her memory of Miranda, is not only a commercial in which particular code has been embedded, but a commercial for a Blue Sun product, tying this particular moment of violence with those triggered in the series (tearing off Blue Sun labels in "Shindig" [1 November 2002]; slicing Jayne's chest, which was emblazoned with a Blue Sun logo in "Ariel" [15 November 2002]).

Much like the hidden code in the Fruity Oaty Bar commercials, corporate culture operates in the shadows of the film, from Mr. Universe's (David Krumholtz) endless media "puppet theater" with which he surrounds himself, to the unnamed pharmaceutical company that obviously produced the Pax compound responsible for Miranda's destruction. In this essay, I will examine the way in which the "invisible hand" of corporate culture operates within the narrative of the film, extending the critique evident within the series into the film's continuation of the narrative.

"They're everywhere": The Corporate Hand in Serenity

One of the many plotlines left unresolved in *Firefly*'s fourteen episodes was the role of two men known only as Hands of Blue (Jeff Ricketts and Dennis Cockrum). The mere suggestion of their presence, whether through memory ("The Train Job" [20 September 2002]) or proximity ("Ariel" 1.9), provokes such a strong reaction in River Tam throughout the series, but they remain altogether absent from the film. While the bridge-text comics between *Firefly* and *Serenity* provide some insight—they work for Blue Sun as contractors to the Alliance government—cancellation prevented the series from exploring this story to the same degree as Whedon's later series *Dollhouse* (2009–10) did with the Rossum corporation and its status as contractor to ("Stop-Loss" [18 December 2009]) and eventual puppet master of ("The Left Hand" [4 December 2009]; "Epitaph One" [11 August 2009]) the U.S. government. Nor was the particular arc referenced directly within *Serenity*. This, however, does not preclude a corporate presence within the film—a corporate presence is indeed featured in in both small and large ways.

Serenity belongs to a particular sub-genre of science fiction film that is highly susceptible to product placement; that is, texts which occur on Earth or a colonized human-compatible planet and are seemingly dominated by Western-style capitalism.[1] Films such as *Minority Report* (Steven Spielberg, 2002), *Total Recall* (Paul Verhoeven, 1990), *The Fifth Element* (Luc Besson,

1997), *Idiocracy* (Mike Judge, 2006), and *Demolition Man* (Marco Brambilla, 1993) all pre-suppose a future in which some form of capitalism is still active, made manifest through the proliferation of brands recognizable to the viewer: Pizza Hut, Coca-Cola, Starbucks; indeed, the satire *Idiocracy*, set in the same era as *Serenity* (the twenty-fifth century) features an Earth that has been so colonized by brands that even its residents are named after them, and their crops watered by a sports drink. That such texts are explicitly coded as dystopian is hardly surprising; as Klein writes, corporations, through the use of their brands, have been "attempting to free [them]selves from the corporeal world of commodities, manufacturing, and products to exist on another plane" (2002: 22), not unlike the fictional futures they inhabit. *Dollhouse*'s Rossum Corporation might claim that they prefer bodies over minds ("The Hollow Men" [15 January 2010]), but brands' desires reverse that: it is definitely the minds they require, to make a connection and ensure their own immorality.

This idea is made manifest in both *Firefly* and *Serenity*; it is River Tam's mind that the corporation invaded and the government wants. As I have written previously (Giannini 2015), neither *Firefly* nor *Serenity* overtly features recognizable brands within the diegesis of their respective texts; however, the fictional Blue Sun Corporation's logo makes several appearances within the series. On shipping containers in "Serenity" (20 December 2002); food products in "Shindig"; a t-shirt, videophone, and neuroimager in "Ariel"; and as a tattoo in "The Message" (28 July 2003). Less obvious are Blue Sun's appearances within *Serenity*; a blue sun graphic appears in the Fruity Oaty Bar commercial that triggers River, and as the crew debates what to do about the revelations regarding Miranda, Jayne Cobb drinks from a bottle with a Blue Sun label, which he passes to Simon Tam (Sean Maher).

It is the Fruity Oaty Bar commercial, however—and how its triggering effect on River ties in with the film's focus on media—that is of the greatest interest. It is difficult to argue with Jacob Clifton's assessment that the primary driver of the film is a critique of media (Clifton 203–215), particularly since, as Robert McChesney writes:

> Behind the lustrous glow of new technologies and electronic jargon, the media system has become increasingly concentrated and conglomerated into a relative handful of corporate hands. This concentration accentuates the core tendencies of a profit-driven, advertising-supported media system: hypercommercialism and denigration of journalism and public service. It is a poison pill for democracy [2000: 2].

McChesney's assertion recalls Mr. Universe's analysis of the media in *Serenity*; that is, he draws a distinction between the "truth of the signal"—what he sees, as a hacker with access to everything—and "the puppet theater the Parliament jesters foist on the somnambulant public." This is underscored in the scene in the Maidenhead bar, in which Mal and Jayne go to transact business. Over the noise of the bar, there is a video of a town destroyed by a Reaver attack (seen near the start of the film); however, the report goes on to say that the government has never affirmed the existence of Reavers, likely since they are responsible for creating them, as will be addressed below. In this respect, both the crew of Serenity and the viewer are aware of the lie, even if they are unaware of the particulars. Further, the fact that the news report merely repeats the government's line regarding the Reavers certainly points to a "denigration of journalism" in the sense McChesney meant.

Clifton asserts that:

> *Serenity* is a story about media, about the abuses of media that are possible, and more than probable in the current day, and the way those media can be used to subvert and question the very ways in which they are used to control the population, both within the story and without [2007: 204].

In that respect, the media (both corporate and otherwise) functions as both plot driver and critique at numerous intervals throughout the film, including the fact that freedom (both for River's mind and the crew of Serenity) is purchased through the release of a video, that River herself is triggered by a commercial, and that Mr. Universe's compound is defined by the numerous screens therein. That *Serenity* itself would likely not exist without *Firefly*'s fans understanding of how media corporations work (that is, buying numerous sets of the *Firefly* DVDs to proselytize the show to others [*Done the Impossible*, Tony Hadlock and Jason Heppler, 2006]) was acknowledged by Whedon during the preliminary screenings months before the official release and could arguably offer a subtextual reading of the film's simultaneous critique and valorization of media embodied in both the plot and the character of Mr. Universe. Indeed, Mr. Universe sells out the crew to the Operative: "Give me my 30 coin," he says—a reference, of course, to the 30 pieces of silver given to Judas Iscariot—indicating an awareness of his own betrayal. Despite this, before the Operative kills him, Mr. Universe is confident that regardless of either of their actions, the "signal" will not be stopped.

Thus, there is an added significance to the fact that the report regarding the Reaver attack is immediately followed by the commercial for Fruity Oaty Bars, done in anime style, full of bright colors (including a blue sun) and a peppy song. Like the aforementioned puppet theater, however, this advertisement hides its real purpose: to trigger a reaction in River Tam so she can be located and disposed of to prevent the release of information she has gleaned. The ability of the Alliance, through the use of the Operative, to tap into the commercial media for their own purposes suggests a further collusion between the corporate world (Blue Sun) and the Alliance that was indicated both in *Firefly* and in the comic series *Those Left Behind*. While Dr. Mathias, one of the doctors who experimented on River, claimed that any governmental secrets she may have gleaned would be "buried under layers of psychosis," the unintended consequences of the Operative's trigger is that it makes manifest in her mind the very secret the government (and corporation) wishes to keep. In this respect, both the government and the corporation have brought about the outcome they most wished to avoid. River's mental unearthing of the secrets of Miranda is an excellent example of "blowback," a governmental term for "the unintended consequences of intelligence, military, and diplomatic actions" (Bussolini 2008: 147), which I will address below. Viewed from that perspective, even the "puppet theater" media in *Serenity*, unintentional as it may be, can be said to have had a hand in the revelations regarding Miranda.

Brave New World: Corporate Pharmaceuticals and the Destruction of Miranda

In his analysis of the planet-wide genocide on the planet Miranda, the "truth that burned up River Tam's brain" in Mal's words, Jeffrey Bussolini succinctly argues that the Pax, the drug pumped into the planet's air processors to weed out aggression, offers a real-world analogue to the antidepressant Paxil. The side effects of Paxil can include weakness, loss of appetite, and loss of sex drive (among others) ("Paxil Side Effects"); however, in a small percentage of individuals (particularly younger users), it has been linked with violent behavior (Molero et al. 2015).

Both side effects—the lack of desire and the desire for violence—are seen in the outcome of the Alliance's meddling on Miranda. By attempting a pharmaceutical intervention to "weed out aggression,"[2] both the Alliance and the pharmaceutical corporation that developed the drug were unprepared for the consequences: the majority of the planet's residents lost all will to live and simply laid down and died. In a further turn, however, a small percentage had the opposite reaction: their aggressive responses "increased beyond madness" and manifested in excessively violent behavior, including murder, torture, and rape. This was the origin of the Reavers, the unseen terror of the galaxy in *Firefly* whose existence, as mentioned above, was unacknowledged by the government.

As Howard Kahm points out, the world of *Firefly*/*Serenity* exists in what he terms a "core-periphery relationship" in that the outer rim planets are those that are monetarily poor but resource-rich (Paradiso in "The Train Job" [20 September 2002] and Canton's Moon in "Jaynestown" [18 October 2002]) and the inner "core" planets (Ariel in "Ariel" [15 November 2002] and Bellephron in "Trash" [21 July 2003]) are those that reap the benefits of such resources (better healthcare, higher standards of living, etc.) (2015: 156–158). The existence of Miranda, however, complicates this dynamic; it is unclear where it fits in the core or rim, as it is positioned within an area known as "Reaver territory." This designation, however, only occurred after the afore-mentioned pharmaceutical genocide, and what is seen of Miranda in the film (populous, technologically enabled cities) does not fit in with what the series showed of the outer rim planets: rural, poor, and exploited. Further, while Mal says the he had heard Miranda was a "black rock, uninhabitable" (the version most likely released to the public), mechanic Kaylee indicates she remembers a call for workers to settle on Miranda years earlier; how then was such a planet-wide catastrophe covered up?

For the answer to that, it is instructive to look at the earlier claims by Mr. Universe, which suggest government (or corporate) management of the news. In the absence of an independent fourth estate, it is clearly easy, within the diegesis of *Serenity*, to either ignore or bury stories that challenge the dominant narrative. As the opening scene of the film indicates, the "lessons" that River Tam is given at the Academy offer an Alliance-friendly version of history, in which the planetary civil war between the Alliance and the "Independents" (the side with which Mal and Zoe were on the front lines) is framed as rejecting "the comfort and enlightenment of true civilization" rather than a desire not to be "meddled with" (*Serenity*), indicating a dystopian control of education (Sutherland and Swan 2008: 92–94).

Further, the use of pharmaceuticals to control the population on Miranda is a clear parallel to what was done with River; that is, the misuse of technology and pharmaceuticals to bring about outcomes desired by the sponsoring government and/or corporation, with little regard or allowance for negative consequences. Whedon's *Dollhouse*, which debuted four years after *Serenity*, extends this critique: the actions of a corporation, in collusion with the U.S. government, leads to the end of the world. Indeed, the plot around Priya Tsetsang (Dichen Lachman), who was forced into corporate service by an obsessed neurologist who responded to her rejection of him by misusing pharmaceuticals to simulate mental illness in her ("Belonging" [23 October 2009]), offers an analogue to the events on Miranda in *Serenity*. In both instances, the concept of consent was ignored, and the concept of "blow-back" unconsidered.[3]

In both *Serenity* and *Dollhouse*, it is not necessarily the technology itself, but the uses to which its creators or purchasers put it. As Bussolini writes, "there is an economic and power dimension" to *Serenity*'s narrative critique, in that "the companies that make these drugs are major vehicles for neo-liberal, U.S.-led domination in the world market" (2008: 145), particularly in that the "concern" is less about easing suffering, and more about profit share (146). Like *Serenity*'s Alliance, real-world governments and corporations rarely seem to account for potential negative consequences to their actions; while Bussolini uses the example of the U.S.'s investment in Saddam Hussein as an ally against Iran (148), there are numerous other examples of these types of interventions as short-term geopolitical solutions that create even greater problems.

While the film's narrative never makes clear what company is responsible for the creation of the Pax (given its prominence within *Firefly*, their connection with and search for River, and its diverse platform of products and services, Blue Sun is a likely candidate), the critique of the Alliance's actions within the narrative should be shared by the corporate actors that supplied the drug in the first place, particularly since, as Ken Wharton argues, the use of drugs and technology, both on River and on the planet Miranda, constitute a misuse of science and technology for profit rather than knowledge or care (2007: 149). These negative outcomes occur, regardless of intention, in many if not most of the series and films in Whedon's oeuvre, from the creation of Adam (George Hertzberg) by the government-funded Initiative in *Buffy the Vampire Slayer* ("The I in Team" [8 February 2000]), to the development of Ultron (James Spader) in a supposed peace-keeping capacity by Stark Industries in *Avengers: Age of Ultron* (Joss Whedon, 2015). This recurring theme seems to indicate that such consequences are a point Whedon seeks to emphasize. That the corporate actors in *Serenity* seemingly pay no consequences resonates with contemporary corporate actions; see, for example, the 2008 financial crisis, in which the banks and firms carrying a great deal of responsibility were well-shielded from the consequences suffered by the majority of the population (McLean and Nocera 2011). In a film about media, it is not surprising that what is unseen is often what is most difficult to fight.

Conclusion

While the corporate presence in *Serenity* is not as clear-cut as that seen in *Firefly* or *Those Left Behind*, it still manages to operate on a subtextual level throughout the film. That is, with *Serenity*'s implicit critique of managed, corporate media, the pharmaceutical basis of disaster on Miranda, and even the (fake) product placement of Blue Sun carried over from the series to the film, suggests that the Alliance government is not the only antagonist within the diegesis of *Serenity*. Mr. Universe's claim that the news/media the public sees is puppet theater not only implies that someone is pulling the strings, but also presages Whedon's screenplay for the later film *The Cabin in the Woods* (Drew Goddard, 2012). In *Cabin*, corporate actors more overtly stage-manage what is seen on both their own closed-circuit screens and the screens of the film's viewers, with the narrative's participants reduced to "externalities"

(Bakan 2004: 60–84). These notions are echoed in the use of "I've Got No Strings," from Disney's *Pinocchio* (Ben Sharpsteen et al., 1940), in *Age of Ultron* (a moment with additional resonance, given that Disney owns Marvel and employed Whedon). At the heart of these texts, from *Buffy* to *Ultron*, is the issue of control. In both *Firefly* and *Serenity*, the Alliance (and Blue Sun) seek to control River, as well as to control the population more generally through drug intervention. Yet the complacency sought through pharmaceuticals on Miranda is, the film suggests, already partially achieved through the media; hence Mr. Universe's denoting that the public is "somnambulant."

Yet the media that controls is also the media that saves, disallowing a straight reading of the film as either anti-media or anti-technology. As Mal says to his crew following their discovery of what happened on Miranda: "Sure as I know anything I know this, they will try again. Maybe on another world, maybe on this very ground swept clean. A year from now, ten, they'll swing back to the belief that they can make people … better." That they use a video that exposes Miranda's fate, as well as confirming the previously denied existence of the Reavers, suggests that the technology that hypnotizes can also be that which awakens.[4] In his analysis of what he terms the "Uprising of 2003" against shifts in the Federal Communications Commission's rules regarding media ownership, McChesney argues that one of the most important outcomes of the public's fight, which united such disparate entities as MoveOn and the National Rifle Association against allowing a greater degree of media concentration, was that it "convince[d] people that the media are political forces that can be shaped, not natural ones that must be endured. Once people grasp that … the possibilities for change and for democracy become much greater" (2004: 296–297). Of particular issue was the fact that the changes themselves had been largely written by and discussed with those same media conglomerates that would benefit from the rules changing, while ignoring or minimizing public discussion (including a media blackout of any dissenting opinions [252–297]): as clear an example of government/corporate collusion as the final panel of *Those Left Behind*.

The hard-won victories in that legislative and legal battle over the media also clearly indicated that neither viewers nor voters have to settle for the "puppet theater" that these entities foist upon the public. *Serenity* itself was released and distributed by the same media conglomerates that sought to strangle public discourse in favor of corporate profits, it still managed to make a cogent argument regarding the ways in which this same media can be used to educate, inform, and subvert the dominant narrative. That this dissemination cost the lives of Mr. Universe, pilot Wash, and Shepherd Book (Ron Glass) as well as the near-destruction of Serenity itself only underscores the film's central point about revealing the "truth of the signal" under the noise of either governmental or corporate interference.

Notes

1. This excludes *Star Wars* (George Lucas, 1977), to a great extent; that the *Star Wars* films became a product/brand in their own right—one of the first to exploit the toyetic potential of this genre of film, requires an analysis beyond the scope of this essay.

2. A similar plot appeared two years later on the series *Doctor Who*, in which a planet's population is killed by an emotion drug known as "Bliss" ("Gridlock" [14 April 2007]); this is not entirely surprising, as showrunner Russell T. Davies was inspired by Whedon's work, particularly the reliance on season-long arcs and "big bads," when rebooting the *Doctor Who* franchise (Aldridge and Murray 2009: 208).

3. It is an easy parallel to draw between *Dollhouse*'s "butchers"—i.e., those "programmed to kill anyone not programmed to kill" ("Epitaph One")—and the Reavers; both were created by mis-used technology wielded as a way of controlling the population.

4. This idea is brought to its fruition in *Dollhouse*; when programmer Topher Brink (Fran Kranz), who helped create and facilitate the technology that turned the planet into a wasteland ("Meet Jane Doe" [11 December 2009]; "The Hollow Men"), develops a similar technology that will return those affected to their original states ("Epitaph Two: Return" [29 January 2010]).

Works Cited

Aldridge, Mark, and Andy Murray. (2009). *T Is for Television: The Small Screen Adventures of Russell T. Davies*. Surrey, England: Reynolds & Hearn.

Bakan, Joel. (2004). *The Corporation: The Pathological Pursuit of Profit and Power*. New York: Free Press.

Bussolini, Jeffrey. (2008). "A Geopolitical Interpretation of *Serenity*," in Rhonda V. Wilcox and Tonya R. Cochran (eds.) *Investigating* Firefly *and* Serenity: *Science Fiction on the Frontier*. London: I.B. Tauris, 139–152.

Clifton, Jacob. (2007). "Signal to Noise: Media and Subversion in *Serenity*," in Jane Espenson and Leah Wilson (eds.) *Serenity Found: More Unauthorized Essays on Joss Whedon's* Firefly *Universe*. Dallas: Ben Bella Books, 203–215.

Giannini, Erin. (2015). "'It Doesn't Mean What You Think': River Tam as Embodied Culture Jam," in *Slayage: The Online International Journal of Whedon Studies* 13.2.

Hadlock, T., J. Heppler, J. Neish, J. Nelson, and B. Wiser (dir.) (2006) *Done the Impossible: The Fans' Tale of* Firefly *and* Serenity. Netflix. Done the Impossible [DTI].

Kahm, Howard. (2015). "'They Couldn't Let Us Profit—It Wouldn't Be Civilized': Economic Modalities and Core-Periphery Relationships in the Political Economy of *Firefly-Serenity*," in Michael Goodrum and Philip Smith (eds.) Firefly *Revisited: Essays on Joss Whedon's Classic Series*. Lanham, MD: Rowman and Littlefield, 155–170.

Klein, Naomi. (2002). *No Logo*. New York: Picador.

McChesney, Robert. (2004). *The Problem of the Media: U.S. Communication Politics in the 21st Century*. New York: Monthly Review Press.

_____. (2000). *Rich Media, Poor Democracy: Communication Politics in Dubious Times*. New York: New Press.

McLean, Bethany, and Joe Nocera. (2011). *All the Devils Are Here: The Hidden History of the Financial Crisis*. New York: Portfolio.

Molero, Yasmina, Paul Lichenstein, Johan Zetterqvist, Clara Hellner Gumpert, and Seena Fazel. (2015). "Selective Serotonin Reuptake Inhibitors and Violent Crime: A Cohort Study," in *PLOS Med.* 12.9. Available HTTP: http://journals.plos.org/plosmedicine/article?id=10.1371/journal.pmed.1001875 (15 May 2017).

"Paxil Side Effects." Drugs.com. Available HTTP: https://www.drugs.com/sfx/paxil-side-effects.html (14 May 2017).

Sutherland, Sharon, and Sarah Swan (2008). "'The Alliance Isn't Some Evil Empire': Dystopia in Joss Whedon's *Firefly/Serenity*," in Rhonda V. Wilcox and Tonya R. Cochran (eds.) *Investigating* Firefly *and* Serenity: *Science Fiction on the Frontier*. London: I.B. Tauris, 89–100.

Wharton, Ken. (2007). "The Alliance's War on Science," in Jane Espenson and Leah Wilson (eds.) *Serenity Found: More Unauthorized Essays on Joss Whedon's* Firefly *Universe.* Dallas: Ben Bella Books, 141–150.
Whedon, Joss, and Brett Matthews. (2005). *Those Left Behind: Issues 1–3.* Milwaukie, OR: Dark Horse Comics.

Failed Experiment
Miranda and the Critique
of Social Engineering

ANDREW HOWE

In *Serenity* (Joss Whedon, 2005), the planet Miranda is a pivotal destination in the journey undertaken by Mal and his shipmates, but it also holds the answer to the origins of the Reavers. Above and beyond these aspects of plot and character, Miranda serves to highlight a few of Joss Whedon's more philosophical concerns. At its core, the fate of the planet underscores Malcolm Reynolds (Nathan Fillion) and his resistance to a centralized authority invested in a vertical program of control over the daily lives of those existing within the 'verse. Miranda represents a failed experiment, highlighting the dangers of social engineering, in this case at the intersection of scientific research and population dynamics. The utter control of media is also a key component of the planet's history, pursuant to the failure of the experiment. Although not necessarily reflecting a purely libertarian ideal, Mal's suspicion of authority and its vested agents—who prove willing to employ coercion and violence in their agenda of ensuring conformity—nevertheless reveals a spirit of self-determination and fluidity of identity.

Throughout *Serenity*, Miranda is contrasted with several other micro-societies predicated upon governance structures that develop naturally and largely exist without coercive, top-down practices. This essay examines Miranda and the contrasts evident with the following communities, with the goal of getting at the core of Whedon's critique of authority: Haven, a location about which little is known but in which equality and acceptance are clearly present; Mr. Universe (David Krumholtz), in one sense a micro-society of a single individual, but in another frame the complete and horizontal interconnectedness of the entire 'verse; and Serenity, a ship with a captain and division of labor, but in which mutual respect is shown even within vertical relationships. Mal and the Operative (Chiwetel Ejiofor) will also be examined as reflective of two very different ideologies.

The opening of the film is brilliant, on several levels. A shot of the Earth from space shows several flashes that, momentarily, call to mind nuclear explosions. Quickly, due to the accompanying narration and the fact that space ships are in short order seen leaving the atmosphere, it is clear that these flashes of light do not involve war but instead exploration. However, the association has been made, indicating something fundamental about such journeys: striking out into new territory often follows conflict or devastation, whether it be from war, over-population, environmental degradation, or political oppression. The voice-over narration, at first blush, seems like a neutral cataloguing of history, something audiences are often conditioned to expect at the beginning of a narrative. However, after a few sentences it becomes clear that this narration is pushing a specific, pro-Alliance agenda, the verbiage quickly slipping into propaganda:

> Earth that was could no longer sustain our numbers, we were so many. We found a new solar system, dozens of planets and hundreds of moons. Each one terra-formed, a process taking decades to support human life, to be new Earths. The central planets formed the Alliance. Ruled by an inter-planetary parliament, the Alliance was a beacon of civilization. The savage outer planets were not so enlightened and refused Alliance control. The war was devastating. But the Alliance's victory over the independents ensured a safer universe. And now everyone can enjoy the comfort and enlightenment of true civilization.

So much is elided in this statement, including how many generations this process took, how many perished in the initial stage of exploration, and how the Alliance consolidated power initially on and amongst the core planets before vanquishing, and dictating terms to, the outer planets. Empire building is neither quick nor clean, although the opening narration boils it down to a single paragraph. With its focus upon a centralized authority and its attempts to dictate to a frontier where pockets of resistance are able to survive, *Serenity* is part of a tradition of Sci-fi that includes such texts as *Star Wars* (George Lucas, 1977) and Suzanne Collins's *The Hunger Games*. Historical parallels can be found in the Roman empire, the propaganda machines of which established all of those living in the provenances as "savages," and in the American West, where the further west one progressed, the freer they generally were from dominant social conventions and political restrictions.

As the narration concludes, the scene transitions to a classroom. The agenda-based message has not just been for our benefit, but is instead propaganda directed at a small group of students, one of which we soon find out is River Tam (Summer Glau). River gives the film's thesis in response to the teacher's speech: "People don't like to be meddled with. We tell them what to do, what to think. Don't run, don't walk. We're in their homes and in their heads and we haven't the right. We're meddlesome." It is ironic that River, who is the one character throughout the narrative who, literally, is in people's heads, is the one to offer this critique, although, in all fairness, she was weaponized by the Alliance against her will. The teacher's response—"We're not telling people what to think, we're just trying to show them how"—completes Whedon's accusation about the abuse of power. The Alliance's scientific and military endeavors are supported by the media and a state-run educational apparatus, an unholy combination that seeks to disenfranchise its citizens on every level. Fueled by the imperative of "maintaining civilization," the Alliance is willing to participate in horrific acts of coercion and violence, a truth that becomes evident in the following scene when Simon Tam (Sean Maher) breaks his sister out of a maximum-security medical facility at the Academy, where intellectually gifted children are being subjected to experiments. Due to experiments conducted upon her brain, River has devolved from an intelligent and clearly functional girl to a nearly catatonic young woman. Symbolically, however, her transformation is evocative of the media's conditioning of its citizens. The cold sterility of The Academy anticipates the city on Miranda, a reminder that it is not just a select group of highly talented schoolchildren whose lives were destroyed by the Alliance.

The tragedy of River Tam personalizes this tale of the abuses of power that accompany entrenched, institutionalized authority. However, the planet Miranda and its 30 million residents constitute the largest casualty, as Mal and company discover toward the end of the film. The seeds for the mystery are sown on Beaumonde, when River begins attacking strangers in the Maidenhead bar. Rhonda Wilcox suggests that these two names were chosen purposefully, "beau monde" meaning "beautiful world" in French and "maidenhead" representative of virginity (2008: 162). In William Shakespeare's *The Tempest*, Miranda is virginal, naïve, and at the beginning of the play reliant upon her father Prospero, an accomplished magician. The parallels to an Alliance that is willing to use illusion and subterfuge to obfuscate reality for its citizens is clear: River is the naïve innocent, although in this case the consequences are much more severe, and she bears the physical and, most damagingly, psychological scars to prove it. The scene where Miranda is first referenced, when River whispers the word before destroying the bar (and most of its patrons), indicates something powerful about the lengths to which the Alliance is willing to go in order to reclaim her. In order to trigger River, the Alliance hides a subliminal message in an advertisement for Fruity Oaty Bars, willing to transmit an activation order to millions of children with the hopes that it will elicit a response in only a single person, and also not caring about the damage inflicted on those who happen to be present for River's subsequent rampage.

Eventually, Mal and the crew discover that Miranda is a planet, erased from history, and they endeavor to travel to it, despite having to maneuver through Reaver space. After doctoring up Serenity to make it appear to be a Reaver ship, they move through an asteroid field filled with space junk, with ships being pulled apart and a bright light being shone into the cockpit. Miranda, a bright blue planet, is visible in the distance, a seeming beacon of safety from the violence of Reaver space. As Mal and company are about to find out, however, that safety is illusory. The "civilization" of the frontier following eras of exploration may bring with it safety, but it also brings a loss of empowerment and, often, coercion. The planet itself is very bright and sunny, almost sterile in its over-exposure and its light color palette. Between this and the shot of a bright blue Miranda beyond the asteroid belt, Whedon is telling a visual story. Even before they discover the first dead body, Mal and his crew are visibly unsettled, as the world is too bright, resonant with the notion that too much of a good thing can be a problem. Even before they make it into the science facility, it is clear that Miranda is a failed utopia, each dead body grislier than the last but none of them indicating that they were the victims of physical violence.

The truth, when it comes, is shocking: the Reavers, a force more destructive than even the Alliance, were accidentally created by that very entity. And out of an attempt to do good! Mal activates a recording that chronicles the use of G-23 Paxilon Hydroclorate, or the "Pax," on Miranda's population. A chemical compound designed to inhibit aggression and induce peace, the Pax had unintended consequences. Most of the planet's citizens did become peaceful, but so relaxed that they lost the will to live, dying from starvation as a consequence. However, according to the scientist on the recording—Dr. Caron (Sarah Paulson)—0.1 percent of the population became hyper-aggressive, hyper-sexualized, and cannibalistic. Being denoted as Reavers was a subsequent mythologizing act by those who did not know their true origins and presumably with the encouragement of the Alliance propaganda engines. There are three historical antecedents that resonate with this plot development. The first is Paxil, which some have noted as the model for G-23 Paxilon Hydroclorate (Richardson & Rabb 2007: 145). An anti-depressant that made its debut in 1992, Paxil is now most well known as the drug that was marketed to teens when it was known to increase the risk of suicide in this group. Miranda is not the only world in which drugs are known to have effects opposite to those intended, although in this case over-medication occurred without the populace's knowledge. Secondly, the use of the word Pax in the context of empire building brings to mind the Pax Romana (or Britannica or Americana), when, in the name of civilization, empires were built and individual rights curtailed.

The final historical antecedent involves neither the role of drugs nor the process of empire building, but instead animal nature. Although there is no evidence that such behavioral tendencies exist in humans, in the late 1950s John B. Calhoun's experiments on Norway Rats did indicate that, at least with this rodent species, having all of one's needs taken care of can result in the failure of a community. In his study, providing all of the resources a rat colony might need resulted in a population explosion and then precipitous decline to colony extinction, with rats either becoming completely withdrawn or hyper-aggressive and—despite ample food sources—cannibalistic. Jacob Clifton also notes how such a dichotomy between passive acquiescence and active rage represents a metaphor for media and its role in propaganda (2007: 211), a distinction perhaps truer than ever in the current political climate of the early Trump presidency. Personal motivation is key when it comes to resisting propaganda. Serenity's crew represents a counterpoint to the passivity displayed by 99.9 percent of Miranda's population, both in choosing to risk their lives in getting out the message and in surviving when they are surrounded and hopelessly outnumbered by Reavers. Although it appears in the narrative as a joke, Kaylee (Jewel Staite) and her renewed drive to live so that she can have sex with Simon indicates something fundamental about humans. True, the crew commits to protect one another out of high-minded ideals—mutual love and respect, as well as the knowledge that the 'verse deserves to hear the truth about Miranda—but also out of basic emotion such as Kaylee and her desire for Simon, and Zoe (Gina Torres) and her need to avenge her husband. Both sides of the human mind, the ethos and the pathos, are important when it comes to being actualized as a person.

The Alliance is accountable for the deaths of 30 million people. By abstraction, all centralized authorities that privilege conformity over freedom of determination from their citizens are implicated. Out of all of the characters in both *Firefly* (2002–03) and *Serenity*, River is of course the one upon which this message is written most clearly. The Alliance's crimes on Miranda are similar to those enacted upon River, but they are de-personalized, implicating almost everyone in the 'verse as a victim. The drama that took place on the planet is later personalized in a brief, but very effective, turn by Sarah Paulson, whose Dr. Caron risks everything in order to document what transpired, waiting just a fraction of a second too long to attempt suicide. As Sarah Sutherland reminds us: "The horror of mass and behavioral control like that attempted by the Alliance on Miranda and individual mind control as attempted on River are important themes in countless dystopias" (2008: 93–94). The abridgement of free will at the level of thought or emotion through a specific mechanism of control appears in *Brave New World* (drugs), *A Clockwork Orange* (conditioning), *1984* (media), and *Brazil* (torture). The recording is twelve years old; it is too late to do anything about the Reavers, who we find out in other parts of the narrative are pushing out annually into space they haven't previously controlled. No one was safe on Miranda, not even Dr. Caron barricaded in the control center. And no one is safe in the 'verse, not even those on the core planets who, although in the here and now live far away from Reaver-controlled space, may not be able to do so forever. This is the essence of "blowback," the unseen consequences that often attend actions predicated on short-term expediencies. Blowback is often associated with entities that are not moderated by robust checks and balances. In this case, the Reavers are the result of an Alliance that is emboldened in their agenda of creating civilization on the outer planets (Bussolini 2008: 147–150). As Dr. Caron states: "We meant it for the best, to make people safer." This distinction is lost on those who starve to death due to their inaction, as well as the Reavers who eat her alive, fortunately off-camera but with animalistic feeding sounds that turn even Jayne's (Adam Baldwin) stomach.

The Reavers themselves deserve a bit of analysis. Shepherd Book (Ron Glass) believes that they are men who went mad when they reached the edge of space. People do need structure, although clearly this explanation makes no sense, even before Serenity reaches Miranda and the crew finds out the truth. There are plenty of characters throughout the narrative who exist on the outskirts of known space and who thrive on such an existence without going mad. The Reavers themselves are a bit of an enigma, somewhat disappointing in that the purest evil in the 'verse (*Firefly*'s Adelai Niska [Michael Fairman] notwithstanding) is shown to have a biological genesis. Throughout the entire narrative (television show, film, and comic books), the Reavers are portrayed as solely about self-satisfying instinct, although clearly they have some capacity for planning, as can be seen in their attack on the outpost at the beginning of *Serenity*. In this attack, they are portrayed as animalistic, but also coordinated. They descend from their spacecraft on zip-lines, like soldiers. One leaps on all fours like some sort of cat while another drags of an unfortunate victim. The camera lingers on another's heavy boots, often employed in film as a symbol of authoritarianism. In scenes such as this one, the Reavers are clearly governed by selfish impulses.

What is not clear is how their governance structure works, e.g., what form of vertical hierarchy is required in order to run their ships. Sean Cubitt sees them as:

> the rubbish that is left when men (and they are portrayed as male) lose their humanity. Reavers are revealed as the cannibalistic post-human consequences of Alliance plans to produce a perfectly subjugated population, their savagery not "native" but generated [2016: 55].

Cubitt is correct that the Reavers are as much employed for their philosophical underpinnings as they are for their efficacy to the plot. They not only resonate with the political concept of blowback, but also with the project of nineteenth century nation building on the American frontier. Many critics have noted that, given the show's genre bona fides as a Western, the Reavers are equivalent to the Indians of Hollywood cinema. Whedon has come under fire for such a representation, although some critics, such as J. Michael Richardson and J. Douglas Rabb, have noted that Whedon actually deconstructs frontier Indian savagery as it appeared in classical Hollywood (2008: 127).

Lorna Jowett notes that in the Alliance's attempts to spread its influence as far as possible—Miranda is noted as the furthest planet from the core—and in the subsequent devastation caused by such a project, Manifest Destiny is called to mind. As Jowett reminds us, the Alliance's drive to socially engineer the frontier is a high tech version of this civilizing impulse (2008: 104). The truth behind the Reavers' origins, however, takes the critique of Manifest Destiny just a bit further. The institution is completely undermined in *Serenity*, as Reavers are both reminiscent of the frontier "savagery" that resulted in scalping and other forms of torture, and, symbolically and on a deeper level, the runaway appetites for consumption that accompanied wave after wave of European settlers. Those who did not die on Miranda became the ultimate consumers seeking to take over space. The narrative, incidentally, is silent on the procreative possibilities of the Reavers. One can only hope that they will die out after a generation; Whedon wisely avoids delving too deeply into these specifics, most likely in that such concerns would be a distraction from the story at hand. Providing commentary on their origins but not their functionality, however, also serves to keep open both the possibility that this is a problem that can be solved or, conversely, that the problem is systemic and will never go away.

The Reavers, in many ways, are the perfect counterpoint to the Alliance, although both are about consumption, in one case of a brutish, corporeal variety, and in the other of physical space and personal freedoms. In both cases, personal rights are obliterated, although it is with the Alliance that most critical works have perceived the focus of Whedon's thesis. As Jeffrey Bussolini notes:

> River's fundamental human rights count for naught next to the state imperative of developing a human weapon (probably to try to counter the blowback from an earlier failed experiment in bioengineering). The rights and memories of the Miranda settlers were similarly quashed in the search for better regulations of biological life [2008: 151].

P. Gardner Goldsmith goes even further, noting that the film's goal was to: "tear the façade off the government utopia and show what hides beneath: experimentation, mass murder, and the creation of horrific human monsters" (2007: 63). Some have analyzed Whedon's critique of the Alliance through the notion of social contracts and the seventeenth century English philosophers Thomas Hobbes and John Locke. James J. Foy, perceptively, denotes the Reavers as indicative of Whedon's suspicion of a Hobbesian state of nature, a system of governance with no fetters whatsoever, contrasted with a Lockean form of social contract that does encumber a loss of power (2011: 48).

In their analysis of power and governance in *Serenity*, Susanne E. Foster and James B. South focus upon a specific aspect of such social contracts: the ceding of freedom in order to gain security:

> One way of understanding why the government's interference with the people on Miranda is wrong is provided by *contractarian theory*. On this view, individuals surrender their right to respond to aggression (beyond the point of self protection) in exchange for protection from the state. Any activity of the state beyond protecting its citizens is thereby an infringement of their freedom since the activity transgresses the bounds of the agreement.… Even something as apparently benign as a teacher trying to correct a disruptive student by the intellectual enforcement of a political ideology is shown to be a grave violation of River's personal integrity by its visual juxtaposition with a scene of intrusive bodily violence [2013: 153].

As the narrative unfolds, it is clear that security is not available to all Alliance citizens equitably. Furthermore, amidst the show's specific critique of the Alliance and general indictment of power structures, ambivalence is also evident. As Lorna Jowett notes, although progress and technology in *Serenity* are often positioned as damaging to personal freedoms, the very outer worlds upon which anti–Alliance living is able to occur were themselves built upon terraforming (2008: 107). Bad as the Alliance may be, living in forced conformity is preferable to rape and cannibalization, a complete lack of order even more dangerous than governmental omnipresence. The following list of plot elements we see in *Firefly*—slavery in "Shindig" (1 November 2002), feudal labor in "Jaynestown" (18 October 2002), women as property in "Our Mrs. Reynolds" (4 October 2002), public sexual assault in "Heart of Gold" (4 August 2003)—all happen on the frontier, making one wonder about the efficacy of living free on the outer planets.

The implied message in *Serenity* is that there are no places of safety, something that will be explored shortly with brief analyses of Haven and Mr. Universe. Most who have written about the Whedonverse have focused upon a critique of dystopia that fits within the model of *Brave New World* and *1984*. Whedon, however, is more nuanced in his fictional world, also fitting into the *Mad Max* and *Escape from New York* meta-narrative in being equally suspicious of the might makes right/survival of the fittest form of dystopia. Whedon says as much in an interview with Mike Russell for CulturePulp. After noting that the Alliance is "not really the evil empire" and that Mal's politics are not necessarily his own, Whedon indicated that *Serenity* was more about having a freedom of choice, even if none of the choices will result in a perfect society: "if the movie's about anything, it's about the right to be wrong. It's about the messiness of people. And if you try to eradicate that, you eradicate them" (2011: 110). Whedon continues by denoting the harm in dichotomies: "I would say about the movie that it is very political, but it's not *partisan.* And I think the curse, right now, of the politics of our nation is that a line has been drawn down the middle of our country—and that's not actually how the human mind works" (2011: 112). Whedon presents a spectrum of political structures, with the Reavers and the Alliance at the two opposite poles. In *Firefly: The Official Companion,* Whedon indicates that the revelation of failed social engineering on Miranda would not have led to the downfall of the Alliance, instead serving as the impetus for River's continued transformation (2006: 11). There is no perfect situation; hierarchy and competition will always undergird any society, no matter how small, and even those rare micro-societies that do manage complete freedom for their citizens are vulnerable from outside influence.

Haven and Mr. Universe represent two such communities. We are given very little information about Haven, either in *Serenity* or in the Dark Horse Comics. The moon does, however, seem to be true to its name in that the crew finds refuge there. A child runs up to give Kaylee a hug; even Jayne appears to have a close friend. However, there are signs that such a place of safety is vulnerable to discovery, either by the Alliance or some other group that might seek to take advantage of the community. Wash (Alan Tudyk) has to take Serenity below the surface, presumably away from prying eyes. Markings on the side of a mine shaft indicate that this is well below ground, and one wonders if Haven is either an abandoned mining colony where the miners stayed on, or perhaps if they staged a rebellion against their overseers and took control. Regardless, Haven does not end up being a harbor of safety, as Mal discovers upon returning to find the community destroyed. Kaylee finds the dead body of the child who greeted her and Mal finds Book, who survived the initial attack by shooting down the gunship attacking them.

It was Book who, ironically, forecast his own death, telling Mal that his pursuer would "come at you sideways." As the Operative later states, matter-of-factly: "If your quarry goes to ground, leave no ground to go to." As a micro-society, Haven has no way of defending itself against the Alliance. Once discovered, it is dispatched by a single gunship, leaving Book able to survive only long enough to give Mal one final piece of advice: "I don't care what you believe, just believe it." As Sean Cubitt notes: "It is the openness of the frontier that provides the terrain of hope in *Serenity,* a place undefined by plans, other than the tactics required to escape from any given narrative scrape" (2016: 52). It is difficult to escape, however, when you are rooted in one place, a liability that eventually leads to Haven's destruction.

Like the residents of Haven, Mr. Universe is restricted to a small moon. However, he enjoys a greater freedom in the digital fluidity that he is afforded through his technological skill. His moon is surrounded by a swirling blue cloud of gas with currents of electricity, suggesting that this is a location bursting with energy. True, Mr. Universe is able to, ethereally, exist in many places at once, extending his digital tendrils into numerous worlds. There is the implication that his footprint is greater on the core planets, however, as he has not yet seen the footage of River laying waste to the Maidenhead until Mal sends it to him. Additionally, there are warning signs that this micro-society is not healthy and is doomed to failure. As he watches the bar fight, Mr. Universe declares: "You guys always bring me the very best violence." Along with his lovebot, Lenore, visible in the background, the fight footage suggests that the twin occupations of sex and violence are part of any society, no matter how small.

The fact that Mr. Universe appears to live alone, with only Lenore as a companion, is problematic (if not unrealistic). What use is a micro-society fully free from the dominance of the Alliance if it is a society of one? Furthermore, the fact that the Alliance was able to reach River through the Fruity Oaty Bar commercial indicates that they have their own technological wizards. Sure enough, Mr. Universe's location is divined and he is forced to work with the Alliance in luring Mal. He is subsequently murdered by the Operative, although not before demonstrating his abilities one last time in recording a message for Mal through Lenore. Mike Russell notes that Mr. Universe stands in for the fans (2011: 121), which is certainly seen in the incorporation of the motto "Can't stop the signal" by the Browncoats, a key *Serenity* fan base that, among other actions, lobbied Universal Pictures to make the film. Mr. Universe is also emblematic, however, of the ability of the media to speak truth to power. In this case, the truth does indeed come out, although we do not know the full impact it has upon the 'verse, and it comes at a price. This micro-society, much like Haven, is destroyed, but not before Mr. Universe aids Mal in spreading his message about the Alliance and its failures in social engineering.

That only leaves one final hope for a community where power does not corrupt, disenfranchise, or destroy: Serenity. Both the television series and the film went to great lengths to contrast the ship with the various institutions of the Alliance. Everything about the Alliance is sanitized, from its ships to its scientific facilities to its uniforms. The same color pallet, not coincidentally, is employed in depicting Miranda: bright, colorless, and over-exposed. Even though Mal is the captain and there is a clear chain of command, Serenity is a micro-society filled with individuals who, despite their differing roles and petty quarrels, have mutual respect for one another. The bonds of friendship and fidelity are tested but strong enough to withstand this conflict from within during times of stress induced by Reavers, the Alliance, and other external forces.

Most of the criticism that has focused upon Serenity and its crew has involved the utopian elements of the ship's equitable power structure. In discussing negative liberty, a freedom from external constraints, Amy Sturgis states that

> Joss Whedon … implies that people are capable of living together in cooperation and community, of exercising individual liberty in moral and meaningful ways…. Whedon seems to say that, left to their own devices, diverse people have the ability to come together to create family and build cooperative and compassionate lives together—by choice and without coercion [2011: 33].

Whereas this statement is largely true, it should be noted that Mal and his crew are thieves, routinely abridging the rights of others. Yes, they often end up doing the right thing, such as giving back the medicine they stole in "The Train Job" (20 September 2002). However, thievery is a way of life for this crew, and at the beginning of *Serenity* they do steal a payroll from a mining outpost. True, the monies are earmarked for a security firm working for the Alliance. However, clearly in such situations there will be consequences for the community and the miners who call it home. Surely, there will be a trickle down effect in their wages for the lost payroll. Mal and his crew are not just stealing from the Alliance. Of course, it does not ultimately matter in this case due to the Reaver attack, but it does introduce a tension into the film when Zoe questions Mal's decision to, instead of ditching the money, throw a man off of their vehicle and to his death so that they can escape. The fact that one Reaver makes it into the cargo hold before Serenity takes off suggests that one is never safe, that the ill effects of power will leave their mark upon any society, no matter how limited or hermetically sealed.

P. Gardner Goldsmith sees Mal as one of few pure fictional examples of "negative reciprocity," a libertarian notion that involves the rights of two parties to be left alone by one another (2007: 56). However, as with Sturgis, this assertion ignores the fact that Mal is, at his core, a criminal, a hero only in that he is the focus of the narrative and a foil to the Alliance (a brutalizing force that conducts medical experiments on children) and the Reavers (who eat people alive). At the beginning of *Serenity*, Mal is willing to steal from strangers and even consign them to death in order to advance his own interests. Richardson and Rabb go a step further in this identification, noting that in a twisted sort of way Mal's smuggling activities serve Alliance interests:

> The Alliance's resources are stretched far too thinly to provide adequate services to the outer planets, so the Alliance is quite happy to allow smugglers like Reynolds to keep the populations somewhat contented by moving required goods such as food and medical supplies illegally. Malcolm Reynolds is unwittingly helping the Alliance govern the outer planets, or at least preventing their populations from rebelling. Mal thinks he is free, and the Alliance is more than willing to let him persist in this delusion, since he and those like him are performing a useful service for their imperial administration [2007: 139].

Richardson and Rabb are correct in their assessment. Mal and others like him allow a series of black markets to exist and serve as pressure release valves keeping the populations from rebellion. So what is it that sets Mal apart and, despite his flaws, allows him to distinguish himself from the Alliance?

Sean Cubitt contrasts the rigidity of the Alliance and their long-term planning with Mal's fluidity and adaptation (2016: 53). There is something to this analysis, especially when the example of Miranda as a site of focused social engineering is contrasted with the natural and unstructured manner in which Mal comes to acquire his crew, as seen in "Out of Gas" (25 October 2002). However, what Cubitt and Sturgis and others largely omit from their analyses is that Mal is often autocratic in his dealings with his crew. In forcing River to accompany himself, Zoe, and Jayne on the payroll raid, Mal admits that he is putting her in harm's way for a utilitarian advantage, noting that due to her psychic abilities she "might see trouble before it's coming, which is of use to me." Mal's dictatorial streak continues following his confrontation with Simon over putting River at risk. He plans to cut the siblings loose on Beaumonde, even though he knows they will never survive without his help. His "my ship, my rules" mentality continues with his unilateral decision that they will voyage to Miranda, and it peaks following the carnage on Haven, when after shooting an Alliance soldier who survived the fight says he'll do it to any member of his own crew who gets in his way. All of these moments of asserted authority, as well as the numerous ones that appear throughout the show, should not be ignored, as they demonstrate that Mal is not a saint but instead a person who struggles daily with finding the right balance between asserting his power in making the critical decisions that ensure survival during times of danger and in maintaining a community of peers where empowerment is facilitated and freedom is assured.

Ultimately, Mal realizes that "Serenity" is neither just a valley where a transformative battle took place nor a ship that gives him freedom of mobility, but is instead a philosophy that allows him to create a community founded upon mutual respect. Abandoning his previous stance of "I look out for me and mine" and his tendency towards autocratic decision-making, Mal makes a speech about the need to risk getting out the word on Miranda as the Alliance will inevitably try, once again, to "make people better." During what is Mal's equivalent of a St. Crispin's Day Speech, he is illuminated by a light, signaling his transformation. He does not dictate, instead asking for their help: "You all got on this boat for different reasons, but you all come to the same place. So now I'm asking more of you than I have before. Maybe all." Mal has evolved from coercively risking River's life and consigning a stranger at the outpost to death to asking his crew to join him in risking their safety in order to pass along information to people he does not know and will never meet. The plight of Miranda and the failed project of social engineering is the narrative device that forces Malcolm Reynolds, once and for all, to decide what type of captain he will be.

The confrontation between Mal and the Operative, which plays out over the course of the film, is the final indicator of the contrasts between Mal and the way he operates and the Alliance and their agenda of total control. When we first see the Operative, he walks through a hologram of River's escape from the Academy, his flesh-and-blood face coming directly through her holographic one. Like her, he has been engineered to be a weapon; the only difference being that with him, the propaganda took hold (Wilcox 2008: 159). He lives and breathes his fidelity to the Alliance, leading him to all manner of atrocities. He is coercive, although unlike Mal the implications are not just in making decisions for others but instead in acts such as murder, as the scientist at The Academy discovers to his detriment. As the man slowly dies, the Operative tells him: "This is a good death. There is no shame in this... We're making a better world." This statement not only crystallizes the Alliance philosophy that resulted in Miranda, but also establishes a contrast with Mal and his views of negative reciprocity.

As Eric Greene notes: "The Alliance and its Operative, unlike Mal, act almost exclusively in the name of abstractions like order, law, and morality. Yet these ideals have been severed from the true values that arise from lived human experience: the need for self-determination, the importance of dissent" (2007: 86). The utilitarian notion of "the greater good," espoused by figures as disparate as Jeremy Bentham and Spock, is what, in its extreme form, leads the Operative to admit to killing children at Haven and destroying threats like Mr. Universe, all in the pursuit of "a world without sin." The fact that the Operative is played as rational, intelligent, and calm makes his actions all the more horrible, with a string of dead people left in his wake, many of them innocents with no part in the play other than in their connection to someone else.

The final showdown between Mal and the Operative, in the bowels of Mr. Universe's super computer, showcases the differing philosophies and crystallizes the essence of the film and the failed experiment of Miranda as exemplar of power allowed to run unchecked. In the midst of their confrontation, Mal and the Operative find the time to talk about sin. Mal professes the usefulness of sin, specifically wrath, an example of justifiable "sinning" that was taken away from the residents of Miranda by the Alliance and its use of the Pax. Mal's expression of emotion stands in contrast to the Operative, who after gaining the upper hand compliments Mal before initiating the death-blow. It is chilling to see someone admire another so clearly yet be willing to kill him without hesitation or any remorse whatsoever. In the end, the Operative fails because he relies upon corporate, universal knowledge in stunning

Mal with a blow to a nerve cluster, whereas individual differences are key in life, in this case the fact that Mal lacks the nerve cluster in question. Mal incapacitates the Operative and shows him, and the rest of the 'verse, the truth about Miranda and "a world without sin."

Jacob Clifton, in comparing the Operative to River, notes that the sudden removal of structure and a narrative in which to believe leaves some bereft:

> The purification which was River's redemption has an equal but opposite effect on the Operative. The removal of the Alliance's influence left her with the universe as it truly is, whereas left without the infallible Alliance's help to comprehend the system, the Operative finds he has nothing left [2007: 213].

Desirée de Jesus takes this analysis a step further, noting that a more powerful transformation takes place with the Operative in that he comes to embrace Mal's view that people cannot be made better due to the ministrations of social engineering (2013: 93). On Miranda, 30 million people lost their lives, and the Reavers were created. However, due to the effort and the sacrifices of Malcolm Reynolds and his crew, the excesses of the Alliance's social engineering program will come to light. It is a small victory, to be sure, as the Operative himself indicates. However, if even the most hardcore supporter of the Alliance is, in his own words, "no longer their man," there is hope that others may also begin to question the power structure and its programs of social engineering, and that the example of Miranda will eventually lead to a better 'verse, where communities develop naturally and without interference from above.

Works Cited

Bussolini, Jeffrey. (2008). "A Geopolitical Interpretation of *Serenity*," in Rhonda V. Wilcox and Tanya R. Cochran (eds.) *Investigating* Firefly *and* Serenity: *Science Fiction on the Frontier*. New York: Palgrave MacMillan, 139–52.

Clifton, Jacob. (2007). "Signal to Noise: Media and Subversion in *Serenity*," in Jane Espenson (ed.) *Serenity Found: More Unauthorized Essays on Joss Whedon's* Firefly *Universe*. Dallas: BenBella Books, 203–15.

Cubitt, Sean. (2016). "Hope in *Children of Men* and *Firefly/Serenity*," in Sean Redmond and Leon Marvell (eds.) *Endangering Science Fiction Film*. New York: Routledge, 51–65.

de Jesus, Desirée. (2013). "Who's Afraid of the Big Black Wolf?: Racial Identity and the Irrationality of Religious Belief in *Firefly* and *Serenity*," in Anthony R. Mills, John W. Morehead, and J. Ryan Parker (eds.) *Joss Whedon and Religion: Essays on an Angry Atheist's Explorations of the Sacred*. Jefferson, NC: McFarland, 83–101.

Foster, Susanne E., and James B. South. (2013). "'There's No Place I Can Be': Whedon, Augustine and the Earthly City," in Anthony R. Mills, John W. Morehead, and J. Ryan Parker (eds.) *Joss Whedon and Religion: Essays on an Angry Atheist's Explorations of the Sacred*. Jefferson, NC: McFarland, 83–101.

Foy, Joseph J. (2011). "The State of Nature and Social Contracts on Spaceship *Serenity*," in Dean A. Kowalski and S. Evan Kreider (eds.) *The Philosophy of Joss Whedon*. Lexington: University of Kentucky Press, 39–54.

Goldsmith, P. Gardner. (2007). "Freedom in an Unfree World," in Jane Espenson (ed.) *Serenity Found: More Unauthorized Essays on Joss Whedon's* Firefly *Universe*. Dallas: BenBella Books, 55–65.

Greene, Eric. (2007). "The Good Book," in Jane Espenson (ed.) *Serenity Found: More Unauthorized Essays on Joss Whedon's* Firefly *Universe*. Dallas: BenBella Books, 79–94.

Jowett, Lorna. (2008). "Back to the Future: Retrofuturism, Cyberpunk, and Humanity in *Firefly* and *Serenity*," in Rhonda V. Wilcox and Tanya R. Cochran (eds.) *Investigating* Firefly *and* Serenity: *Science Fiction on the Frontier*. New York: Palgrave MacMillan, 101–13.

Richardson, J. Michael, and J. Douglas Rabb. (2007). *The Existential Joss Whedon: Evil and Human Freedom in* Buffy the Vampire Slayer, Angel, Firefly *and* Serenity. Jefferson, NC: McFarland.

______. (2008). "Reavers and Redskins: Creating the Frontier Savage," in Rhonda V. Wilcox and Tanya R. Cochran (eds.) *Investigating* Firefly *and* Serenity: *Science Fiction on the Frontier*. New York: Palgrave MacMillan, 127–38.

Russell, Mike. (2011). "The CulturePulp Q&A: Joss Whedon," in David Lavery and Cynthia Burkhead (eds.) *Joss Whedon: Conversations*. Jackson: University of Mississippi Press, 107–28.

Sturgis, Amy. (2011). "'Just Get Us a Little Further': Liberty and the Frontier in *Firefly* and *Serenity*," in Dean A. Kowalski and S. Evan Kreider (eds.) *The Philosophy of Joss Whedon*. Lexington: University of Kentucky Press, 24–38.

Sutherland, Sharon, and Sarah Swan. (2008). "The Alliance Isn't Some Evil Empire: Dystopia in Joss Whedon's *Firefly/Serenity*," in Rhonda V. Wilcox and Tanya R. Cochran (eds.) *Investigating* Firefly *and* Serenity: *Science Fiction on the Frontier*. New York: Palgrave MacMillan, 89–100.

Whedon, Joss. (2007). Firefly: *The Official Companion, Volume Two*. London: Titan Books.

Wilcox, Rhonda V. (2008). "'I Do Not Hold to That': Joss Whedon and Original Sin," in Rhonda V. Wilcox and Tanya R. Cochran (eds.) *Investigating* Firefly *and* Serenity: *Science Fiction on the Frontier*. New York: Palgrave MacMillan, 155–66.

Miranda

*Conflicting Anxieties, Ableism
and Population Health*

Max Ferguson

Introduction

Firefly (2002–03) and its follow-up *Serenity* (Joss Whedon, 2005) both wonderfully depict the humanity, bravery, and scrappiness of a small group of people against an unfair and unjust authoritarian government. In *Serenity,* the true evil and hubris of the Alliance is shown through the extermination of an entire world's population resulting from the Alliance's desire to control its subjects. The film strongly reflects both the health care climate and widespread public attitudes towards mental health contemporaneous to its release. The film was created at a turning point in public health history—the Severe Acute Respiratory Syndrome (or SARS) outbreak had upped the fear of pandemic in our social psyche as well as triggering governmental emergency epidemic health systems. Following the wave of SARS came eddies of fear around governmental intervention in individual health and debates over individual versus collective rights.

Serenity comments on these discourses using its own fictional disease—but what exactly is the nature of the illness transmitted in the film? A discussion of mental illness as infectious disease will be enlightening, as will a broader critique of the treatment of mental illness in the film. The plot of *Serenity* revolves around fear of disease and overt governmental control of health, yet the disease featured in the film takes the form of mental illness, which renders its victims not only incurable but also, quite problematically, undeserving of humane treatment. By exploring these representations through a lens of real-world public health strategies, I argue that the film's engagement with fears of pandemic is as illuminating as it is troubling.

SARS

In *Serenity,* the crew of the titular Firefly-class vessel makes a grisly discovery—on the furthest planet in the 'verse, Miranda, the authoritarian Alliance government has released an agent called the Pax into the air, with the goal of calming the population. While most of the population died from simply ceasing to function, there was a small subset of the population that lost its humanity, the Pax making these few colonists unspeakably violent— they became the Reavers, legendary bogeymen who roam through space and attack whatever unsuspecting ships cross their paths.

This is naturally terrifying to the audience. A pandemic is an epidemic that spreads worldwide, and this pandemic either killed or irrevocably changed all the inhabitants of Miranda. While Miranda is one of many inhabited worlds in the 'verse, we as the audience only have our one habitable planet as a reference point.[1] The thought of the entire world's population succumbing to a single pandemic is horrifying. But why did *Serenity* tell the story of a pandemic that was previously wholly unexplored in *Firefly*? The film's departure from the series into the genre of horror was abrupt after the mostly playful tone of *Firefly*. The years between the series and the film had seen the world react to the SARS epidemic, making it narratively compelling and quite timely for the film to refocus its underlying messaging on governmental overstep onto the realm of health and biopower in such a way.

The global response to the SARS epidemic is reflected in the tone and premise of the film, which was released just three years after the first cases of SARS were reported. Yet while much of the narrative points to SARS, a respiratory illness that prompted extreme flu-like symptoms and fever, the illness transferred through the Pax primarily affected mental health. Despite this, *Serenity* can be put in direct discussion with the 2002 and 2003 SARS epidemic. Clusters of SARS surfaced in China, Hong Kong, Vietnam, Singapore, Taiwan, and Canada (Lingappa, McDonald, Simone, and Parashar 2004). The epidemic caused an estimated 8,098 cases and 774 deaths worldwide (Lingappa et al. 2004). Public health authorities faced an international epidemic without knowing the agent that caused the illness, nor how it was transmitted, or how to prevent its spread (Lingappa et al. 2004).

Extreme measures were instituted to help contain the spread of the illness—to the point of infringing on human rights. Public health authorities instituted 10-day periods of quarantine for those exposed to SARS, yet what was to be done with hospitals was a difficult question and posed problems for public health clinicians (Gensini, Yacoub, and Conti 2004). The *New York Times* reported that in Taiwan thousands of people were placed in quarantine—some as part of large-scale hospital-wide quarantines that included staff, service users, and visitors (Barbisch, Koenig, and Shih 2015 and McNeil

2003). Following the quarantine things went a step further: citing security issues, authorities subsequently cut telephone and television lines in certain hospital-wide quarantines (Barbisch et al. 2015). This measure was widely regarded as an overstep, and endangered those who had not been exposed by locking them in with people with active SARS infections.

Two years later *Serenity* was released. Worldwide, fear of pandemics was ubiquitous and the morality of such quarantining practices was still under public discussion. *Serenity* channels both the fear of disease and the fear of government intervention into the arena of public health, combining the two into a single threat.

The Pax

In a chilling scene, Dr. Caron (Sarah Paulson) explains what wiped out the population of Miranda:

> It's the Pax, the G-23 Paxilon Hydrochloric that we added to the air processors. It was supposed to calm the population and weed out aggression. Well, it works. The people here stopped fighting, and then they stopped everything else…. There's 30 million people here, and they just let themselves die … we meant it for the best, to make people safer.

The name of the agent which causes the demise of so much of Miranda's population has some interestingly suggestive etymology. The Latin word "pax" means "peace," which fits with the drug's intended use, as described by Caron—the government wanted to artificially create peace by controlling the population via the agent Pax. Perhaps it was also the Latin meaning that inspired the pharmaceutical company GlaxoSmithKline to name their branded version of the antidepressant paroxetine "Paxil." Paxil is also a fabricated agent, and was ostensibly designed to "improve" on human nature by relieving people of depressive symptoms.

The name also quite clearly invokes "vaccine" or "vax," as in the anti-vax movement, and common pharmaceutical naming conventions such as Twinrix—a vaccine for hepatitis. Regardless of the etymological origin, the Pax is a clear disparagement of unethical pharmaceutical companies and their alignment and influence over governmental policies, as has been observed by Bussolini (2008).

In a moment of expository foreshadowing at the beginning of the film, River (Summer Glau), hallucinates herself as a child responding to a teacher's (Tamara Taylor) question in class: "With all the social and medical advancements we can bring to the independents, why would they fight so hard against us?" the teacher asks. River's answer points to the later government overreach on Miranda: "People don't like to be meddled with. We tell them what to do, what to think, don't run, don't walk. We're in their homes and in their heads, and we haven't the right. We're meddlesome." River is understood to be a truth-teller in this moment, directing the audience to what they *ought to* think.

In this scene, nuanced messaging is boiled down to "the government should not meddle in individuals' business" generally rather than looking specifically at any particular issue. While libertarianism has always been an undercurrent of the *Firefly/Serenity* universe, *Serenity* directly focuses its libertarianism on population health, but not necessarily on ethical administration of public health. This attitude is somewhat reminiscent of the contemporary anti-vax movements. River's attitude invites further discussion on the meaning behind the Pax by foregrounding the politics of *Serenity*.

The Pax as Infectious Disease

The Pax is presented as functioning, in some ways, like an infectious illness. In the *Firefly* episode "Bushwhacked" (27 September 2002) we see a character (Branden Morgan) contract whatever makes the Reavers act as they do. When the boy begins to "turn," Mal (Nathan Fillion) states that

> that poor bastard that you took off my ship, he looked right into the face of it and was made to stare ... a darkness, a kind of darkness that you can't even imagine, blacker than the space it moves through.... They made him watch. He probably tried to turn away and they wouldn't let him. You call him a survivor, he's not. A man comes up against that kind of will, the only way to deal with it, I suspect, is to become it. He's following the only course left to him. First, he'll try to make himself look like one: cut on himself, desecrate his flesh, and then he'll start acting like one."

The Reaver-ness, according to this explanation, has infected the boy, and what is more, this does not surprise Mal—he guesses what happened after only hearing hints of the situation, and delivers his explanation without skipping a beat. Has this happened in the past?

There are other clues to an infection-like presentation of the Pax. The boy is the only person we know of to come into prolonged, direct physical contact with the Reavers, as they force him to watch their brutality (though how Mal could be so sure of this detail remains a mystery). Beyond this detail, the Pax is put into the air supply on Miranda, yet most of the Reavers are away from that air supply but continue to act like Reavers. While there are many different possible interpretations of the specific nature of the Pax, a mental-illness-as-infectious-disease explanation fits what we know of the agent.

Mental Illness in the 'Verse

Mental illness is depicted as something unnatural, violent, and incurable both in the Reavers and in River Tam, who is deeply connected to the Reavers in both her lack of mental health and her psychic visions. We realize that both the Reavers and River share a lack of health that has been manufactured—yet no conclusions are drawn on the shared nature of their humanity. The movie ends with the audience invited to accept that the Reavers are sub humans that should be killed, while River is merely abnormal and needs to be cured. The crew prioritize their libertarian struggle against the government over any reflection on what the implications of their discovery of the Pax might mean for the Reavers, who they do not hesitate to kill.

The Reavers and Unnatural Mental Illness

A break in the narrative logic occurs when we look at the nature of what the Pax has caused and how its victims are treated. While what destroyed the population of Miranda can be seen to maybe be an infectious illness, the symptoms discussed are strictly those of mental illness. The question "then what?" is never really asked or answered as it relates to the Reavers. We understand that these individuals have a manufactured illness, yet they are not treated like ill individuals so much as monsters.

In a playful Halloween seminar on the public health science behind the zombie apocalypse hosted by the University of British Columbia, Dr. David Patrick memorably commented that

> If we've learned anything from AIDS and the fentanyl crisis, we can't stigmatize the victims of an infection. We may or may not need to use humane isolation and infection control to protect others, but the Hollywood solution of shooting people with Zombie infection is not how we do medicine or public health [2016].

And herein lies the problem with the representation of the Reavers: what the hell is going on with the crew? Why does it not occur to one single person that there may be a way to reverse this manufactured illness? Mal delivers a rousing speech, championing the victims on Miranda. "Somebody needs to speak for these people," he says. And he condemns the Alliance for its treatment of human subjects: "as sure as I know anything, I know this: they will try again. Maybe on another world, maybe on this ground swept clean. Maybe a year from now. Maybe ten." But why does *no one* think of the living victims of Miranda?

Dr. Caron, one of the people who initially released the agent on Miranda, states that "About a tenth of a percent of the population had the opposite reaction to the Pax. Their aggressor response increased beyond madness." Why are we so willing to dispose of 30,000 people? There is a flavor of AIDS crisis victim blaming; was there some aspect of these peoples' characters which predisposed them to becoming the violent monsters that we see in *Serenity*? If that is the crew's assumption, how could they possibly have drawn it? If this assumption is not present, how can they dismiss and kill the Reavers so easily?

In the 'verse, the Reavers are explicitly inhuman—the Operative (Chiwetel Ejiofor) says, "You're not a Reaver, Mal, you're a human man." The Reavers are introduced at the beginning of the film, in River's hallucination/memory, wherein students in a class argue about whether Reavers truly exist, one stating that the Reavers will "kill them, wear their skins, and rape them for hours and hours and hours." The Reavers are perfect villains—they senselessly and brutally kill. Yet, there is an inherent contradiction in how they are depicted. They are compelled to murder, torture, and rape—this is their fundamental character, as they are depicted as operating purely on instinct— but somehow they manage to find and launch space ships, keep ships functioning, and plan rather complex raids and ambushes.

Instead of being "Indians" to rival the "cowboys" (while absolutely not creating enough distance from that racist trope [see Rabb and Richardson 2008]), the Reavers are explicitly people who have gone "mad." Kaylee (Jewel Staite) states, "Shepherd Book says they was men who just reached the edge of space, saw a vasty nothingness, and went bibbledy over it."[2] Likewise, Dr. Caron describes the Reavers as being aggressive "past madness."

Some of the illogic of the plot rests on the contradiction at the heart of the Reavers, beings reduced to senseless monsters yet who are shown to have strategic cognitive function. This contradiction is mirrored in how we socially represent mental illness—people with poor mental health (especially those with psychosis) are viewed as intrinsically violent and incapable, yet we overlook their strengths and abilities. We see the same contradiction in how the Reavers and mental illness inter-relate specifically with regards to how characters deal with trauma—only Mal and Zoe (Gina Torres), as the heroes of *Serenity*, can escape being destroyed by the mental stressors that they experience.

In the episode "Bushwhacked" Mal states that he believes that the trauma of seeing the Reavers torture and kill friends and family turns a boy into a Reaver. This is a strange attitude coming from a veteran who cannot bite into an apple because of traumatic memories of bombs hidden in food, as seen in the *Firefly* episode "War Stories" (6 December 2002). Both Mal and Zoe are understood to have incredibly traumatic backgrounds, yet according to Mal, the only response to extreme levels of trauma is to become a monster. This boy is the only character in the 'verse that we know about who has had prolonged contact with living Reavers, yet Mal appears to think this response—to lose one's personhood—is inevitable.

Interestingly, at the film's conclusion, Zoe and Mal have a conversation about the ship, wherein Mal inquires, albeit in a roundabout way, about how she is faring after the death of her husband Wash (Alan Tudyk). She, infinitely repairable like the ship, prevails through trauma, yet the boy who became a Reaver is never afforded such strength.[3]

Zoe and Mal exhibit stoicism in the face of trauma in stark opposition to the boy from "Bushwhacked" or to River. The trauma that Zoe and Mal have experienced, as well as how they live with mental illness, is presented in a stereotypically masculine way. They have lived through war and have watched friends—and in Zoe's case a spouse—die. Both the boy from "Bush-whacked" and River lose their bodily autonomy and are psychologically tor-mented—stereotypically feminized experiences of trauma. In the boy's case, he is forced to watch as his loved ones are raped, tortured, and killed, while River's ability to regulate her emotions is stripped in invasive medical pro-cedures, as she is given brain surgery without anesthesia. Both characters are debilitated by their trauma and are shown as "hysterical": the boy is unintel-ligible in his fear, and River is scared by nothing at all on a regular basis. Both are later dehumanized: the boy as a Reaver, and River as a weapon.

Race and mental illness problematically intersect in the portrayal of the Reavers. The Reavers are racialized, with disproportionately large numbers of them depicted as people of color, and the majority with their hair in locks, yet when Miranda is shown, the people who "just laid down" and died pas-sively are largely white and seemingly wealthy. Mal's earlier description of the Reavers is also suggestive: "The darkness. Kinda darkness you can't even imagine. Blacker than the space it moves in." People of color—specifically black people—are often portrayed as violent and unpredictable, as are people living with mental illness (Perry 2017). The depiction of this intersection of identities as monsters is especially problematic considering the rate of mur-ders of disabled people of color (Perry 2017). The film racializes madness in a way that plays off of the ablest and racist fears of its audience.

While I do not believe it is the film's intention, racialized madness con-nects to the history of public health abuse in the United States—specifically the Tuskegee medical trials. Well before the SARS epidemic, North American governmental agencies had earned the distrust of the public through a hor-rifying and systemic devaluing of non-white lives in research.

From 1932 to 1972 a research team monitored the health of 399 black men living in poverty in Alabama who had been diagnosed with syphilis (Northington Gamble 1997). When the Tuskegee trials started, there was no cure for syphilis, yet when penicillin was introduced as the standard treatment in 1947, it was withheld from the study's participants in order to observe the natural course of the disease (Northington Gamble 1997). Especially pertinent to the film were the neurological symptoms inflicted on this group of men—end stage syphilis causes tumors, blindness, paralyses and neurological effects (Anon. n.d. and Marra 2015). The neurological effects of syphilis are referred to as neurosyphilis and start with personality changes and can present as mania, depression, or psychosis (Marra 2015).

This research trial is now understood to be an act of genocide (Northington Gamble 1997). The Tuskegee trials, as well as a history of medical experiments on people of color, has had resonating effects on how black people and people of color trust, and in turn engage with, health care at large and public health authorities (Northington Gamble 1997). This distrust had fatal repercussions during the AIDS crises as many people were afraid of the testing and treatment that governmental public health agencies were so vehemently pushing (Northington Gamble 1997).

That the racialized Reavers have been made mentally ill and violent harkens back to America's history of abusive medical trials. If this parallel is accepted, the crew's apathy towards the Reavers becomes especially troubling.

River and the Reavers

River's character is inextricably linked to the Reavers, both through her psychic visions and through her deteriorated mental health, brought on by Alliance intervention. River has nightmares about Miranda, and memories of Miranda accompany her altered states when her conditioning is triggered. River is said to have psychically read the mind of an official who knew of the Reavers, but her connection to them is clearly less a passing knowledge and more a visceral fear-based understanding of and connection to them. Her visions depict the Reavers attacking in a blur. Due to these ongoing visions, River eventually leads the crew to the planet Miranda.

In the *Firefly* episode "Safe" (8 November 2002), River's brother Simon (Sean Maher), a doctor, explicitly labels her condition an artificially triggered case of what is essentially "paranoid schizophrenia." In *Serenity*, Dr. Mathias (Michael Hitchcock), the government official who is destroying River's brain to weaponize her, states, "obviously, she's unstable. The neuro-stripping does tend to fragment their own reality matrix. It manifests as borderline schizophr—" before he is interrupted. She has been made into a psychic but is also mentally destabilized by the process. It is strange that she is so explicitly given a diagnosis of schizophrenia. This is solely for the audience's benefit; in the *Diagnostic and Statistical Manual of Mental Disorders* a diagnosis of schizophrenia is explicitly made when symptoms occur and cannot be attributed to a substance such as drugs or medications or another medical condition (Tandon et al. 2013). River believes that the Alliance government is coming to get her—a not uncommon paranoid delusion—but, in her case, the government is *very much* coming to get her, which begs the question: why is she labeled as having paranoid schizophrenia? Simon states in "Ariel" (15 November 2002) that

> they stripped her amygdala…. You know, uh, you know how you get … scared, or, or worried or nervous when you don't want to be scared or worried or nervous; you push it to the back of your mind, you try not to think about it. Your amygdala is what lets you do that. It's like a, a filter in your brain that keeps your feelings in check … She feels everything; she can't not.

This is compelling for the narrative but does not match schizophrenia's pathophysiology. Our current neurobiological understanding of schizophrenia is that symptoms are caused by unbalanced levels of neurotransmitters (to simplify a very complicated pathophysiological process) (Kahn & Sommer 2014). River does not have schizophrenia (as Simon and the Alliance medical officer would certainly know) yet our negative stereotypes of the mental illness are used to leverage a picture of her as violent, unpredictable, and a little wacky. Where River does reflect the stereotype of schizophrenia is her presentation—she is disheveled and erratic.

Similar to the stigma that people living with schizophrenia face, River is infantilized throughout *Firefly* and *Serenity*, despite being seventeen years old in the film. The Operative, sent to hunt down River, chillingly calls "Where are you hiding, little girl?" and she berates Simon in "Safe" stating, "Stupid son of a bitch, dress me up like a gorram doll!" about the childish clothing that she wears throughout the show and the film, presumably provided by Simon. The only way that her brother, Simon, knows how to handle River is to medicate her (Corsie 2015). While Simon loves River very much, he cannot see her other than as the child that he knew; he does not treat her as a young adult. This infantalization occurs even within the context of River having tremendous abilities, such as in dance, math, ship mechanics, fighting, not to mention the fact that she is psychic. Our sympathy for River is largely based on her "wasted" intelligence and potential, and the understanding that her illness is not her fault but was imposed on her. The audience rarely gets to see how competent River is despite her odd behavior.

Conclusion

A tension exists in the anxieties at the center of *Serenity*'s narrative: the government's intervention into mental health both creates monsters and is, in of itself, monstrous. The film's antagonists are not only the authoritative government but also those who are mentally ill. How the film turns on the victims of governmental intervention—and on River—is deeply ablest and creates dissonance in the plot. How can we sympathize with the crew when they exhibit such apathy?

While the movie sends an important message about the need for governments to respect the autonomy of their people, it delivers that message in a way hostile to many people living with mental illness. *Serenity* paints people who have ill mental health as out of control, violent, and unnatural, and in such depictions, it loses its strength and its moral high ground. If informing the 'verse about the Alliance's crimes is paramount—and indeed the task is enough for Mal to finally take up arms in earnest against the government— then what do we make of our heroes' wanton disregard for the surviving victims of said crimes? One hopes that when human subjectivity is denied by governments, those who fight for justice will be less ambivalent, or worse hostile, to those trod upon by the forces of oppression. Otherwise what are we fighting for?

Notes

1. One could argue that the entire 'verse stands in for Earth, with each planet functioning as one country or city in a larger whole, but Miranda is discussed as an entire "world" in its own right by Mal and the crew, amplifying the horrors of the Pax and making the language of pandemic more useful to this discussion.

2. Jayne's (Adam Baldwin) response that he has also been to the edge without such negative repercussions already hints that this explanation is lacking in substance as a cause for widespread ill mental health.

3. While the boy's Reaver "infection" can certainly be read as metaphorical, a way to cope with trauma rather than a literal response to contagion, this seeming inability to recognize PTSD by two war veterans supports a more literal reading of the boy's transformation into a Reaver after contact.

Works Cited

Anon. (n.d.). "What Are the Symptoms of Syphilis," in Planned Parenthood. On-line. Available HTTP: https://www.plannedparenthood.org/learn/stds-hiv-safer-sex/syphilis/what-are-the-symptoms-of-syphilis (11 September 2017).

Barbisch, Donna, Koenig, Kristi L., and Shih, Fuh-Yuan. (2015). "Is There a Case for Quarantine? Perspectives from SARS to Ebola," in *Disaster Medicine and Public Health Preparedness* 9.5: 547–53.

Bussolini, Jeffery. (2008). "A Geopolitical Interpretation of *Serenity*," in Rhonda V. Wilcox and Tanya. R. Cochran (eds.) *Investigating* Firefly *and* Serenity: *Science Fiction on the Frontier*. London: I.B. Tauris, 139–52.

Corsie, Sarah. (2015). "'You Know, You Ain't Quite Right': Humanity and the Monstrous 'Other' in Joss Whedon's *Firefly*," in *Watcher Junior: The Undergraduate Journal of Whedon Studies* 8.2: 1–10.

Gensini, Gian Franco, Maghi H. Yacoub, and Andrea A. Conti. (2004). "The Concept of Quarantine in History: From Plague to SARS," in *The Journal of Infection* 49.4: 257–61.

Kahn, R.S., and I.E. Sommer. (2014). "The Neurobiology and Treatment of First-Episode Schizophrenia," in *Molecular Psychiatry* 20.1: 84–97.

Lingappa, Jairam R., L. Clifford McDonald, Patricia Simone, and Umesh D. Parashar. (2004). "Wresting SARS from Uncertainty," in *Emerging Infectious Diseases* 10.2: 167–70.

Marra, Christina M. (2015). "Neurosyphilis," in *CONTINUUM Lifelong Learning in Neurology* 21.6: 1714–28.

McNeil, Donald G., Jr. (2003). "Fight in Taiwan Is Impeded by Resistance to Isolation," in *The New York Times*. On-line. Available HTTP: www.nytimes.com/2003/05/12/world/fight-in-taiwan-is-impeded-by-resistance-to-isolation.html?mcubz=1 (September 9, 2017).

Nischal, Anil, Adarsh Tripathi, Anuradha Nischal, and J.K. Trivedi. (2012). "Suicide and Anti-depressants: What Current Evidence Indicates," in *Mens Sana Monographs* 10.1: 33–44.

Northington Gamble, Vanessa. (1997). "Under the Shadow of Tuskegee: African Americans and Health Care," in *American Journal of Public Health* 87.11: 1773–8.

Patrick, David. (2016). "The Real Public Health Science Behind the Zombie Apocalypse." Grand Rounds Lecture: School of Population and Public Health, University of British Columbia.

Perry, David. (2017). "Police Killings: The Price of Being Disabled and Black in America," in *The Guardian*. On-line. Available HTTP: //www.theguardian.com/us-news/2017/jun/22/police-killings-disabled-black-people-mental-illness (18 September 2017).

Rabb, J. Douglas, and J. Michael Richardson. (2008). "Reavers and Redskins: Creating the Frontier Savage," in Rhonda V. Wilcox and Tanya R. Cochran (eds.) *Investigating* Firefly *and* Serenity: *Science Fiction on the Frontier.* London: I.B. Tauris, 127–38.

Tandon, Rajiv, Wolfgang Gaebel, Deanna M. Barch, Juan Bustillo, Raquel E. Gur, Stephan Heckers, Dolores Malaspina, Michael J. Owen, Susan Schultz, Ming Tsuang, Jim Van Os, and William Carpenter. (2013). "Definition and Description of Schizophrenia in the DSM-5," in *Schizophrenia Research* 150.1: 3–10.

"She's a creature
of extraordinary grace"
*Resistance Through Dance
to the Myth of "Civilized Cultures"*

JOEL HAWKES

River: Introducing a Moving Figure

"She's a creature of extraordinary grace," comments a lab technician of River Tam (Summer Glau) at the beginning of *Serenity* (Joss Whedon, 2005). Her brother, Simon (Sean Maher), replies, "Yes, she always did love to dance." River's evolution, like that of *Firefly* (2002–03), cut short due to the show's cancellation, achieves a kind of completion in *Serenity*—a dance, if you will, finding its final form. River is defined by movement. Glau—a trained ballerina originally hired by Whedon to perform as Prima Ballerina in the *Angel* (1999–2004) episode "Waiting in the Wings" (4 February 2002)—appears to draw upon her dance training, performing a suitably embodied expression of a woman "displaced," in her own mind and body, who, having escaped Alliance control, must (like the rest of the Serenity crew) inhabit the margins of Alliance "civilization," always on the move to evade capture. In her seeming disorder, River embodies the victims of the Alliance's "civilizing" mission but also the resistance that refuses to conform, that "aim[s] to misbehave": a rebellious movement to be deliberately "out of place." Her movement, at times fragmented and uncertain, is at other moments graceful, dance-like in composure, finding full form in *Serenity*'s climatic battle, as she stands over dead Reavers, her pose reminiscent of the iconic image of the Indian god Shiva in his incarnation Nataraja, the cosmic dancer who can dance both the creation and destruction of the world.

I argue that in this moment, River manifests as a goddess figure in the completion of a "dance" that has lead the crew of Serenity in their resistance to the patriarchal structures of an Alliance-dictated universe. Dance is not just an acting technique or a metaphor for the show and film's structure, nor simply a symbolic event recurring through each (though it is all of these). It is also a suitably physical challenge from a voiceless victim to a regime that relies on language, dogma, and the rule of law in its ordering of the universe. And it is an act of bodily defiance that allows viewers to re-examine their understanding of their own (dominant) cultural narratives, which order society. Questioning the Alliance "school" storytelling in the opening moments of the film, River goes on to complete a dance of resistance, interrupted in episodes like "Safe" (8 November 2002) by her kidnapping, and distorted by the "civilized" ball of "Shindig" (1 November 2002). Her revelation of the crimes on Miranda exposes the lies of Alliance mythmaking that map and make the world a place devoid of movement—empty of freewill, creativity, and ultimately life itself. River reinvigorates space, leading a chaotically choreographed remaking of the world of "civilized cultures"—a dance of resistance and recreation.

Establishing Shot: The State of Control and Resistance Through Movement

River's dance is on display before *Serenity*, though we see her first steps in the film's opening sequence. River's dream of her childhood schoolroom establishes the Alliance as a hypermodern civilization that must be resisted. Conforming to Zygmunt Bauman's understanding of modernity as a state-controlled project, self-conscious in its attempts to order the world (1991: 5), the Alliance seeks absolute control as a self-proclaimed "beacon of civilization" that battled the "savage outer planets" to achieve a "safer universe" for all to "enjoy the enlightenment and comfort of true civilization." Jeffrey Bussolini compares the Alliance to the United States' twentieth century attempts "to pacify much of the world" (2008: 147). The Alliance rhetoric of empire enforced in the classroom, accompanied by hi-tech planetary maps, highlights the expansionist nature of the project, and its position as the dominant (and well-funded) cultural narrative—one that aspires to and self-justifies as myth, through its "in the beginning" storytelling.

The cut to a screaming adult River demonstrates just how far the Alliance will go to ensure their order, and begins to reveal the troubled complexity of this modern reality as we shift from childhood memory to River's rescue by her brother, Simon—an image that then collapses into a holographic video watched, and literally walked through, by the pursuing Operative (Chiwetel Ejiofor), who oversees its dissection and analysis in the further pursuit of order. Bauman identifies such "grand societal designs" in our own time and identifies their darker acts in Nazi concentration camps, the extremes of a modernity that treats "society as a virgin plot of land to be expertly designed and then cultivated and doctored to keep the design to form" (1989: 113). Experimentation on River and the sense of a layered reality echo these crimes as an extension of a system that experiments, categorizes and controls. However, like Bauman's vision of modernity, the Alliance's search for order in fact further fragments, pushing ever onward the search for control, while also inspiring resistance to itself (Bauman 1991: 1, 3). This fragmentation is again glimpsed in the scene's layered depictions of reality and in Simon's rescue (and, of course, in River's own psyche). Strapped into a laboratory chair, unable to move, River is the preeminent symbol of the Alliance's drive for order—everything in its place.

But she is also the preeminent symbol of resistance to this order. River is the "disadvantaged" and "vulnerable" body that Tarja Väyrynen et al. theorize in *Choreographies of Resistance*, suggesting that a body with an assumed lack of agency can still "obstruct" and "resist the smooth functioning of practices of governance," opening a "space of political resistance and action" (2017: 7). In *Serenity's* opening scene, River begins her "dance." She questions the Alliance myth: "We tell them what to do, what to think. Don't run. Don't walk. We're in their homes, and we're in their heads, and we haven't the right. We're meddlesome" (*Serenity*). The "we" of this speech aligns River with the Alliance (as school girl, citizen, and product of experiment), but the use of "we" is also a rejection of conformity, initiating her own origin story (her "In the beginning"), as rebellion and counter myth. She is a child, whose innocent words hold the dominant power to account, an angel questioning the creator, God the father, and his "divine" plan. She is prophet: her childhood words, "we're in their heads," anticipate the cut to a screaming River strapped down in an Alliance medical facility, a needle penetrating her forehead. Her scream breaks her childhood dream and the Alliance's dream of control—something primal pushes back against the modern, clinical (what Whedon calls "antiseptic" [2005]) Alliance method, and escapes through the words "she always did love to dance," which initiate Simon's freeing of River. The Operative's word's, "Where are you hiding, little girl?" soon follow, setting up the pursuit narrative of the film, begun in *Firefly*—a struggle of movement against the restrictions of order.

The scene that follows on Serenity, in the film, further establishes the idea of resistance through movement, introducing ship and crew with a four and half minute tracking shot. In his recent paper, Brent M. Smith-Casanueva notes the "resistance" of Serenity and crew through their "mobility," eluding—not confronting—the Alliance (2016: 178–79), and connects this long shot to Matthew Hill's observation that static shots define scenes set on core

(Alliance) planets in contrast to the use of handheld cameras on Serenity (2009: 493). The tracking shot as introduction brings Serenity to life: as theorist Michel de Certeau suggests, movement is a practice of set place, transforming it into space (1988: 16); this practice creates, for Whedon, a sense of "safety in space," a dwelling, a sense of home and the "homemade," half of a continuing dichotomy, positioned against the unmoving and professional spaces of the Alliance (2005). This movement is reminiscent of the final *Firefly* episode, "Objects in Space" (13 December 2002), with its opening shot moving from outside into the ship—in part a representation of River's psychic ability, which then tracks the different crew members, revealing their position on ship but also something of their minds and pasts. She brings the place alive as she moves, "touching the ship," and, psychically, the crew. As Glau explains, River "communicates" with her "face and body"—"physicality [is] important to her expression" (qtd. in Whedon 2007: 205). This is particularly true in this episode, as she figuratively and playfully becomes the ship.

Appropriately, on the viewer's return to Serenity in the film, the long tracking shot opens up the ship, inviting the viewer "back on board," and to the ultimate discovery of River, laying on the floor—still, in a sense, part of the ship, but also clinging to it, hiding, listening, lit, as Whedon explains, to show her "sense of alienation" (2005). She is alienated from the crew but also representative of them in their precarious position "on the raggedy *edge*" of space, where, as Malcolm "Mal" Reynolds (Nathan Fillion) points out, one day "there won't be room for naughty men like us to *ship about* at all" [emphasis added]. The language, here, draws attention to a sense of movement and limited freedom under an advancing civilization. The tracking shot and Mal find, then, what The Operative seeks, further complicating River's ever oscillating role: sought for, marginal, dangerous, rejected, protected, and essential—to both the Alliance and Serenity. In Mal's discovery, he has also found the film's "narrator" who will guide the viewer through the story of resistance to come: the leader of the "dance."

River: The Dancer vs. the Patriarchy

River's resistance through movement is developed through an explicit language and practice of dance, which further distinguishes River as a woman (as feminized and feminist figure) struggling against a patriarchal order. The introduction of River in *Firefly* and *Serenity* is partly achieved through a narrative of dance, with her brother introducing her to Serenity's crew in "Serenity" (20 December 2002), listing off her skills, which end with "*even* dance. There was nothing that did not come as naturally to her as breathing does to us" [emphasis added]. Simon's "Yes, she always did love to dance" in *Seren-

ity reestablishes that narrative at the beginning of the film. It is almost as if she is "birthed" twice through dance. This "birth" is a mystical experience, highlighted by her vulnerable female form emerging, with a rebellious birth cry from the laboratory in the film, and naked from an egg-like pod in the series premiere.

It is easy to identify patriarchal threat in the *Firefly* universe, especially in the Alliance: a hi-tech, wealthy, overly policed state, reliant on military might to enforce its doctrines. Such state control and modernity have very much been a patriarchal endeavor in our own cultures, often to the exclusion of women. In many ways, the Alliance is Whedon's critique of our own modern nation states. The Alliance mission is mostly "manned" by a male military, the blue-gloved men, with male scientists leading experimentation on River. Generally, smaller patriarchal figures and power structures organize the universe. Mal as captain of a military unit and Serenity's crew (tellingly referred to by River as "Daddy" in "Safe") is a benevolent paternal figure, and there is something of him reflected in Shepherd Book (Ron Glass) and the minor character of the honorable Sheriff Bourne (Gregg Henry) in "Train Job" (20 September 2002).

But other figures' control is aggressive and directed specifically towards women: nobleman Atherton Wing's (Edward Atterton) sense of sexual ownership of Inara Serra (Morena Baccarin) in "Shindig," suitably taking place on the planet Persephone (The name of the Greek fertility goddess abducted into the underworld by Hades); the Patron's (Gary Werntz) decision to burn River as a witch in "Safe"; Ranse Burge's claim to his unborn son, conceived with the prostitute Petaline (Tracy Ryan) in "Heart of Gold" (14 July 2002); and bounty hunter Jubal Early's (Richards Brooks), pursuit of River, which includes a threat of rape to Serenity's mechanic Kaylee Frye (Jewel Staite) in "Objects in Space." Control here is sexual, objectifying. Even River, who is the least sexualized woman (almost asexual or childlike) remains objectified, her body penetrated—a needle is forced into her head—in the opening of *Serenity*, and later pursued by the Hands of Blue, and by the Operative, wielding a rather phallic sword.

Dance further develops River as the threatened but also resistant feminine in the *Firefly* episode "Safe." Here, the first significant character development of River relies on dance to illuminate her when, in a flashback to childhood, Simon asks River, "Aren't you supposed to be practicing for your dance recital?" Her reply is, of course, precocious: "I learned it all." In the present, River's first trip off ship allows further character development, aligning her with the natural world in opposition to the manmade. Her position is reflected in the cows brought onto Serenity as cargo: "They weren't cows inside. They were waiting to be, but forgot. Now they see sky and remember what they are," she says. With River off ship, we see something of her nature too. From browsing in a store and discovering a "post holer" ("You dig holes … for posts," Kaylee explains to Simon), River wanders off through the interior of a dark building to emerge into a kind of village green bathed in light under a blue sky (a ritual/rebirth moment), where a community dance is taking place. For a moment, she is free of her "paranoid schizophrenia," "handcrafted by government scientists," lost in the unthinking movement and enjoyment of the dance. She dances by herself and with a partner around a tree—an older symbol of the sacred feminine (the oak), and reminiscent of the regenerative ritual of the maypole dance. This not-so-subtle aligning of River with the sacred feminine (also achieved through her connection to the sacred mother figure of the cow, as found in Hindu teachings), again positions her against patriarchal structures. The dance is interrupted when she and Simon are kidnapped by two men.

In the village they are taken to, she is accused of witchcraft for seeing into people's minds, and sentenced to death by the village patriarch, "Patron," a figure of death (having murdered his predecessor) contrasted to River as life giver. River is, of course, to be burnt at the stake (reflective of a historical persecution of women), and tied to a pole—significantly, this is to restrict her *movement*, just as her death is meant to stop her movement into people's minds. "Post holer: digging holes for posts," she smiles at the irony of the situation and narrative, not so subtly reminding the viewer of the early encounter with a post holer. But the unsubtle seems to be the point: the imagery of post and hole is sexual, and speaks to unsubtle phallic/patriarchal dominance that attacks a feminine it feels threatened by: oppression and brutality are never subtle in their effect, and here they reflect the Alliance's greater "civilizing" mission.

This mission, and resistance to it, is further illustrated through River's repurposing of written language in the show. The multiple narratives of the female body collide with dogma and the word of patriarchy (and perhaps the pen as phallus), to borrow Hélène Cixous's understanding and definition of the feminine and its language, as Alyson R. Buckman describes in her discussion of *Firefly*, as "multiplicity and fluidity" (2008: 45). Her cutting up of Shephard Book's Bible in "Jaynestown," (18 October 2002) is a renegotiation of the preeminent patriarchal narrative that orders the universe, similar to her childhood dismissal of her school texts ("The book is wrong") and her subversion of the Alliance narrative through coded letters home that function as a secret cry for help in "Safe." Her response comes through movement—the female body controlled, impinged upon by dogma, by words rebels. The feminine not allowed to speak, and refusing to use the oppressor's words, responds with the body, and with dance.

This sense of the sacred feminine in the *Firefly* universe, aligned with nature, and manifested through movement and dance, is also located in many other female characters. One need only look at character names to read the implications of what is sacred and vulnerable but also resistant (as nature and sexuality). Zoe (Gina Torres) is of Greek derivation and a form of the name Eve, the first woman—a figure of corrupted purity and mother to us all; Petaline means to resemble the petals of a flower; Saffron (Christina Hendricks), also a flower, as well as a spice; Nandi (Melinda Clarke) signifies growth and is the name of a gatekeeper (often represented as a sacred bull) to the Indian god Shiva; and, Inara might refer to the Hittite (bronze age Mesopotamian) daughter of a storm god, comparable to the Greek Artemis (goddess of hunt, virginity, wildness, and childbirth). River appears as the preeminent incarnation of these women, her name replete with implications: a powerful, moving, natural force of purity and strength, death and rebirth. Her name presents fewer sexual associations than the others (as does her character), but also, fittingly, holds more power and ambiguity—meaning in her is unstable, like the body of water, which, as an archetypal symbol, can mean many things. Even here there is resistance to the modernizing mission of the Alliance that wants to set meaning, creating one order. These names and characters inhabit a shifting, dynamic feminist narrative.

Another dance, the ball on Persephone in "Shindig," further illustrates the precarious position of the feminine in a patriarchal universe. Occurring immediately before the events of "Safe," River remains confined to Serenity. The ball is an excuse for Atherton Wing to show his power through "ownership" of Inara. Inara is victimized and objectified, handled like goods. While Mal's more honorable attempts to help Inara do little but demonstrate a more benevolent form of patriarchy (the duel with swords might be read as a "penis measuring" competition), it is in the unassuming Kaylee (her name signifies a Scottish dance) that we see a more successful (but still troubled) assertion of the feminine. She combines her knowledge and love of ship and mechanics (traditionally a masculine pursuit) with the desire to attend the ball wearing a pretty dress (her feminine aspect). Misunderstood and mocked by Mal, her femininity is denied, as it is again at the ball by rich young women who look down at her store-bought dress. A kind, older gentleman, recognizes Kaylee's worth, and she becomes the center of a group of men discussing ship mechanics. This scene is another kind of dance, Kaylee as spectacle in the middle of them.

However, again, she is not valued for her femininity (this aspect is dismissed by the older gentleman as vanity and promiscuity in the debutants: "I cannot abide useless people" he comments). Kaylee's usefulness seems to come from her mechanical knowledge—usefulness is then identified with masculinity. And, yet, she remains a feminized and indeed sexual figure, even in her little-girl prom dress. She manages to balance the two sides of her femininity—a position reestablished in the later episode "Out of Gas" (25 October

2002) in a flashback to her hiring. There, she is introduced having sex with the ship's then mechanic and is offered his job when her superior technical knowledge of the ship is revealed. Kaylee can be at once a figure of sexuality, an innocent, and an effective mechanic—the problem ultimately comes from how others observe her, and what value they place on these various aspects of her character. She is the freest female presence at the ball, yet still restricted by the male gaze.

River: Constructed by the Male Gaze

The gaze that troubles Kaylee in "Shindig" troubles the representations and understanding of women throughout the *Firefly* universe. The negotiation of woman as "dancer"—as sexual, nature-aligned, feminine, and feminist body—is greatly problematic. River as preeminent dancer, who represents opposition to the patriarchal order of Alliance modernity, is also the feminine desired and pursued by a male gaze, indeed, even constructed by it. Returning to the "birth" of River from lab and pod, we see creation partly engendered by the patriarchal Alliance. River is aesthetically and narratively a Frankenstein's creature—both a man-made and self-made being. She is introduced and constructed by the Alliance and then by Simon, who wakes her and explains her to the crew. And Whedon too, as the show's creator, is complicit in her creation. We appear to witness an exploration of the cultural construction of the female and feminine in relation to the male gaze, but also perhaps something of that very gaze under critique in its own operation.

River's development through dance in *Firefly* is, therefore, troubled because of the dance and dancer's simultaneous position as exoticized spectacle and feminist rebellion against patriarchal order—a dancer (and dance) not only at war with the Patriarchy but also with itself. We might see this battle and instability reflected in River's own mental disorder that results from Alliance experimentation (and creation). This is a problem of female identity, objectification, and arguably archetype, played out in other Whedon works. *Dollhouse* (2009–10) most notably examines the position of the female body and identity in society, and in the media, and the forces that act upon, create and destroy it. Elsewhere I have discussed, the role of an Ophelia archetype in Whedon's representation of women—an image based on the mad, wan, beautiful, victim of Shakespeare's *Hamlet* (Hawkes 2016). Drusilla (*Buffy* and *Angel*), Fred (*Angel*), Echo (*Dollhouse*), and indeed River all conform to this model: figures abused Damn exoticized by men, and driven to madness. Men in the shows want to rescue and bed them (Spike with Drusilla; Gunn and Wesley with Fred; Ballard with Echo). While only River avoids this sexualization, she remains an object that men desire to rescue (referring to Mal and Simon, primarily)—she is vulnerable, and in the tradition of Ophelia an "exquisite" figure (Lerer 2012: 14, 15), like Whedon's other "mad" women. She is an object and an art form, rather than a woman. River's position as a dancer of the sacred feminine, a mad earth-goddess/mother figure might be seen as being similarly reductive, playing to the traditional dichotomy of male as knowledge, science, civilization and order in opposition to woman as emotion ("She feels everything," Simon says in "Ariel"), art, nature and freedom. Rather than simply a trite creation, River seems to be an exploration of the problems of the show's (and our culture's) creation of the female and feminine, drawing attention to the traditional dichotomies of sex and gender—asking us what we, the viewers, see (as is asked of Kaylee at the ball in "Shindig").

Glau's dance background and technique nicely explores this problem, utilizing what Myron Howard Nadal has suggested every dancer struggles with: "constantly involved with the imperfections of [the] human form," attempting through the power of the "mind" to achieve understanding of [oneself]" (1970: 15). Becoming conscious of this, the viewers themselves are, in a sense invited into the dance in discovery of oneself and indeed one's own culture: the repeated language and action of dance, elevates the "exquisite" nature of the female subject, making us hyperaware of the female body, what is written upon it, and that we are, in fact (as we are in *Dollhouse*) watching a performance. In this way, the ritual qualities of dance are elevated also (unambiguously with the "maypole" dance of "Safe"), drawing on a past of dance and rites of the feminine. The anthropologist Mircea Eliade would see River's dance as a "reactualization of a sacred event that took place in a mythical past, 'in the beginning'" (1987: 69)—one that arguably draws upon older myths and rites of dance and the sacred feminine—an empowering tapping of older "powers," but one that might also be criticized for tapping a past, and indeed present, of reductive representations of the feminine. We must ask, then, how far Whedon frees or snares himself and us in this trap of representation.

Crime: A Figurative Dance of Resistance and Belonging

River (the "dancer") struggles to break free from certain traditional representations of the feminine, moving away from a figure of passivity (subdued victim) to activity and agency, and from isolated individual (and spectacle) to group or family member. As Lorna Jowett writes, "Sharing physical and tactile space experiences allows [Serenity's crew] to enjoy real communication and community, rather than Alliance alienation (2008: 109), which is in part a technologically disembodied experience. The proliferation of dance-related terms and acts again suggests a reading through dance. This development of community like and as choreography "articulates a body's capacity to communicate and integrate with other bodies" (2017: 11). Though River remains a minor protagonist in *Firefly*, her presence increases during the series so that she becomes more fully a member of the crew and participant in what might be termed their (figurative) dance of crime.

Many of the episodes revolve around a criminal undertaking led by Mal—each one something like a dance in its planning and execution. "The Train Job" relies on an elaborate plan, with Jayne lowered from the ship onto a moving train. "Shindig" sees Mal position himself at an actual dance to pick up business, and the following episode "Safe," follows the attempt to sell the merchandise on another world. "Jaynestown" sees a similar endeavor of moving goods without being caught. Each exploit is a series of movements that aim to beguile, persuade, and hide from, the Alliance or some other representative authority. Saffron perhaps represents this dance best—a (sparring) partner to Mal, she begins her long con, literally with a dance, to create a charade of marriage in "Our Mrs. Reynolds" (4 October 2002), then in a later encounter when the crew helps plan the elaborate theft of a gun in "Trash" (21 July 2003). Though River often stays on Serenity, not taking part in the crimes that help develop a sense of the other characters, she watches and learns the crew and its movements, just as we watch her. River's learning (despite her outsider status) is clear in her scrutiny of a ball game played on the ship in "Bushwhacked" (27 September 2002), which, as Simon points out, doesn't seem to be played "by any civilized rules that I know." But by the episode "Safe," flashbacks of her (and Simon's) past, and their rescue from kidnappers (initiated into crime as victims of it), develop her character, and simultaneously identify her as part of the crew. Accused of being a witch, River is defended by Mal, who replies, "Yeah, but she's our witch."

In "Ariel," River becomes more central to the "dance" of crime, in an elaborate scheme to raid an Alliance hospital for profitable medical supplies and to treat River. This is a *turning* point in River's development, a "time to wake up" into a resistance to the Alliance. The event might be read as a rite of passage, a transformative event for both River and crew, helping to further their sense of community, or what anthropologist Victor Turner has called *communitas*, in reference to a community's shared ritual and sense of the sacred, often through a rite of passage (1969: 96–7). River wants to end her own Alliance-enforced passivity, and indeed fears it from another male figure, her brother: "Is it time to go asleep again?" Ariel is a core planet, microcosm of the "antiseptic" and homogenous Alliance universe: as Zoe puts it, "All central planets are the same," referring to the "sensors" and the "feds." The heist is the crews' most elaborate, intricately planned by Simon, requiring a refitted medical ship, uniforms, and learned medical dialogue, so that they look like they "belong." River might be read like a ballet dancer carried, lifted and spun by the others, through security into an imaging lab and out again, but she also enables the theft to take place; without her there is no dance.

The name of the episode and planet further emphasize River's leading role—"Ariel," Shakespeare's powerful, dancing, water sprite from *The Tempest*, who is servant to Prospero, master of his island world, but also rebellious spirit seeking freedom. So, appropriately, the episode allows a more direct engagement with River's captors and "creators," the Alliance, at their most threateningly physical as the grasping "Hands of Blue." This threat helps foster River's acceptance into the Serenity crew, with Mal claiming that Jayne's betrayal of River and Simon to the Alliance is also a betrayal of him. This particular dance of crime might be compared in significance to Roy A. Rappaport's observation of a religious ceremony and its group's tendency as the event proceeds to become a more "coordinated," "unified whole" (2002: 224). This event secures the community of Serenity, and allows River to begin a transcendence, where she might lead a dance of resistance, which we see in "Objects in Space," planning and directing her fellow crew. Though even here, she remains the female partner to the dance, safe again only when Mal has pushed Early into space, and caught River as she floats gracefully towards him through that same space.

Dance: The Final (il)Logical "Hero Shot"

In *Serenity*'s director commentary, Whedon draws attention to what he calls the "hero shot": River with sword and axe in hand (reminiscent of the Slayer's Scythe in *Buffy*), standing over a mound of dead Reavers. He says that set and sequence are designed to lead to this one shot (2005). In a sense, *Firefly* and *Serenity* build to this moment, too, moving towards a shot that Whedon even elucidates through dance: Glau performs the final choreographed fight scene in a single long take, the cameraman like a dancer himself spinning around the fighting/dancing Glau, who was trained in dance, unlike your typical action hero. Here, action hero and ballet dancer combine to produce a figure that Whedon suggests "doesn't make logical sense" (2005). This commentary supports a reading of the "illogical" feminine pitted against the logic of the patriarchal Alliance—chaos to its order. But Whedon's comments seem to suggest more about the role of River as dancer: in dance and dancer we struggle to find meaning just as River does in herself. If the final "hero" shot does not give answers, then it at least makes us ask the question: what does she (it all) mean?

Simon approaches the question in the episode, "Objects in Space:" "So River's not a person?" in response to Kaylee's observation on River's impossible shooting skills. The answer, I suggest, is both yes and no—she *moves* between meanings—human, less than human, and more than human, in her "dance." What is real, when we see from River's perspective? Does she hold a stick or a gun in the episode? She is part Alliance technology, part human (but extraordinary human). Illogical in madness, and in movement against the cold logic of the Alliance, she is also their product—an attempt to make a weapon. Her name feeds the ambiguity—"River," described as a "Reader" in "Objects in Space" and *Serenity*, is also very close to "Reaver." This struggle for meaning fully manifests when she is triggered by the Alliance via an advertisement, and attacks everyone around her. But as Michael Marano points out, River's "activation, as a weapon is at least partly an actualization of herself" (2007: 46). It is as though she is given choreography and then as all dancers do, she interprets and adapts. The dance is, as previously discussed, problematized by recourse to the trite feminine in her definition. And if she is "illogical," this further problematizes her as the "illogical" female; but again, the "dance" seems to adapt—River is, after all, ballet dancer and action hero.

River also internalizes the logical—she is born of it, but the Alliance's cold logic is antithetical to her as well: on Miranda, the harsh clinical lighting, the empty streets, and the rooms filled with corpses are stillness to her movement, but they also produce movement, as the camera and world spin around River. The logical produces (in part) her dance—and of course it does (relying on repetition of movement and perhaps the mathematics of music). The use of a sacred, dancing, ritual feminism also gives way to this duality (or perhaps plurality?): we might position it as older ritual against modern technology, a sacred famine against patriarchy, epitomized in her out of body experience after her activation. We see her "ascend" to goddess status, disembodied, in space above the planet, with a mark on her head: third eye, bhindi, or bleeding wound from Alliance needle? But this is also a cliché of the feminine feeding into a female position of subordination—a patriarchally enforced binary (illogical/logical). But, then, such ritual can also be read as the beginning of logic, an earlier system of ordering and reading the universe (See Horkheimer and Adorno 2002: 6, 7). David Magill locates River's femininity in dance and her masculinity in death (2008: 78). River, in a sense, twirls through these possible meanings; "movement" itself is a process of "constant becoming and being-in-between" (Väyrynen 2017: 15). It is not liminal, nor feminine or masculine, ultimately, but rather a constant process, perhaps of the human condition. After all, a *river* can signify many different things.

It is not coincidence that Miranda again refers us to Shakespeare's *The Tempest*, the overly protected daughter of the magician Prospero. Prospero too is often read as a figure struggling with himself (and representing Shakespeare struggling with his art), torn between the base, instinctual Caliban (close to "cannibal") and the spiritual, airy heights of Ariel. River, and indeed the story and its director seem similarly torn, circling meaning, using far too many systems and referents of meaning for there to be any final logic. Rather, we are given an exploration of possible meanings—far better in the greater ambiguities of movement than in the particularities of words. If River becomes anything, then she is the force that inspires others to movement, to resistance: Mal and crew in *Serenity* finally take on the Alliance oppression, and its myth of civilization, to allow a world where one is free to move between meanings, where one is given the "right to be wrong." Ultimately, though, she transcends even this achievement, a "dancer" uniting many possibilities and disparate ideas, becoming a cosmic dancer in the "hero shot." Akin to Shiva (male but also with female incarnations), she is the cosmic dancer of life and death, creation and destruction.

Works Cited

Bauman, Zygmunt. (1991). *Modernity and Ambivalence*. Cambridge: Polity Press.
_____. (1989). *Modernity and the Holocaust*. Ithaca, NY: Cornell Press.
Buckman, Alyson R. (2008). "'Much Madness Is Divinest Sense': *Firefly*'s 'Big Damn Heroes and Little Witches,'" in Rhonda V. Wilcox and Tanya R. Cochran (eds.) *Investigating* Firefly *and* Serenity: *Science Fiction on the Frontier*. London: I.B. Tauris, 41–9.
Bussolini, Jeffrey. (2008). "A Geopolitical Interpretation of *Serenity*," in Rhonda V. Wilcox and Tanya R. Cochran (eds.) *Investigating* Firefly *and* Serenity: *Science Fiction on the Frontier*. London: I.B. Tauris, 139–52.
Cixous, Hélène, Keith Cohen, and Paula Cohen. (1976). "The Laugh of the Medusa," in *Signs* 1.4: 875–93.
De Certeau, Michel. (1988). *The Practice of Everyday Life*. Trans. Steven Rendall. Berkeley: University of California Press.
Eliade, Mircea. (1987). *The Sacred and the Profane: The Nature of Religion*. Trans. Willard R. Trask. London: Harcourt Brace.
Hawkes, Joel. (2015). "Joss Whedon's *Hamlet*: The Problems of Ophelia and Representation," in Valerie Estelle Frankel (ed.) *After the Avengers*. Chicago: PopMatters, 2015: 243–50.
Horkheimer, Max, and Theodor W. Adorno. (2002). *Dialectic of Enlightenment: Philosophical Fragments*. Gunzelin Schmid Noerr (ed.). Trans. Edmund Jephcott. Stanford: Stanford University Press.
Jowett, Lorna. (2008). "Back to the Future: Retrofuturism, Cyberpunk, and Humanity in *Firefly* and *Serenity*," in Rhonda V. Wilcox and Tanya R. Cochran (eds.) *Investigating* Firefly *and* Serenity: *Science Fiction on the Frontier*. London: I.B. Tauris, 101–13.
Lerer, Seth. (2012). "I've Got a Feeling for Ophelia: Childhood and Performance," in Kaara L. Peterson and Deanne Williams (eds.) *The Afterlife of Ophelia*. New York: Palgrave Macmillan, 11–28.
Magill, David. (2008). "'I Aim to Misbehave': Masculinities in the 'Verse," in Rhonda V. Wilcox and Tanya R. Cochran (eds.) *Investigating* Firefly *and* Serenity: *Science Fiction on the Frontier*. London: I.B. Tauris, 76–86.
Marano, Michael. (2007). "River Tam and the Weaponized Women of the Whedonverse," in Jane Espenson and Leah Wilson (eds.) Serenity *Found: More Unauthorized Essays on Joss Whedon's* Firefly *Universe*. Dallas: Benbella Books.
Nadel, Myron Howard. (1970). "The Spirit of the Dance," in Myron Howard Nadel and Constance Gwen Nadel (eds.) *The Dance Experience: Readings in Dance Appreciation*. New York: Praeger, 16–17.

Rappaport, Roy A. (2002). *Ritual and Religion in the Making of Humanity*. Cambridge: Cambridge University Press.

Smith-Casanueva, Brent M. (2016). "Race, Space and the (De)Construction of Neocolonial Difference in *Firefly/Serenity*," in Mary Ellen Iatropoulos and Lowery A. Woodall III (eds.) *Joss Whedon and Race: Critical Essays*. Jefferson, NC: McFarland, 169–83.

Turner, Victor (1969). *The Ritual Process: Structure and Anti-Structure*. New York: Aldine de Gruyter.

Väyrynen, Tarja, Eeva Puumala, Samu Pehkonen, Anitta Kynsilehto, and Tiina Vaittinen. (2017). *Choreographies of Resistance: Mobile Bodies and Relational Politics*. London: Rowman & Littlefield.

Whedon, Joss. (2007). Firefly: *The Official Companion*, Volume 2. London: Titan Books.

______. (2005). *Serenity*: Film Commentary. 20th Century FOX Home Entertainment. DVD.

"The Indians ride over the hill"[1]
Revisiting "On the Paradoxical Construction of the Reavers"

AGNES B. CURRY

> This show isn't about the people who made history; it's about the people history stepped on.—Joss Whedon on *Firefly* [qtd. in Armstrong 2001]

Introduction: Once More with Feeling

What follows is an updated version of my essay published in the *Slayage* 7.1 (Winter 2008, Issue 25) Special Issue on *Firefly* (2002–03) and *Serenity* (Joss Whedon, 2005). I am grateful for the opportunity to reflect anew on the way representational tropes can undermine one's best narratological intentions.

In the decade since the essay's original publication, viewers, commentators, and scholars have of course continued to discuss the Reavers from various angles. Interpretations range from Jennifer Garlen's (2011) look at how the centuries-old Indian captivity narratives deployed as settler-colonial propaganda continue to construct the Reavers as familiar presences in our collective imagination, to Gareth Hadyk-Delodder and Laura Chilcoat's (2015) emphasis on the Reavers' utter strangeness. For Hadyk-Delodder and Chilcoat, the Reavers function as floating signifiers of the posthuman monstrous, joining the likes of Adam from *Buffy the Vampire Slayer* (1997–2003) and the Cylons of *Battlestar Galactica* (2004–09) to spark reflection on the agency of rhizomatic bodies.

Likewise, attention given to depictions of race, racialization and neocolonialist impulses in the Whedonverse has continued, including the collection *Joss Whedon and Race: Critical Essays* (2017), which offers a rich array of differing perspectives on Whedon's oeuvre as of 2011. In that volume, Daoine Bachran probes the chronic absence of Mexicans from the entire Whedonverse and offers an illuminating reading of *Firefly/Serenity* as a space deeply structured by U.S./Mexico border anxieties. As such, the Reavers represent the immigrants of popular fear, while Jayne the vaquero functions as a container for such anxieties, allowing them to surface and be quelled by humor and Mal's strong hand. Brent M. Smith-Casanueva underscores the ways the sci-fi 'verse depicted in *Serenity* differs markedly from those of the *Star Trek* and *Stargate* franchises in foregrounding the difference between the Core and periphery as politically and economically constructed and avoiding essentialist understandings of race. In his argument that the Reavers allegorize the Otherness foisted on colonized populations, he aims to shift the discussion beyond questioning stereotypes to instead interrogating whether or not the series "reproduces or subverts the essentializing and depoliticizing operations of colonial and neocolonial discourse" (Smith Casanueva 2017: 182). This is, I suggest, a false dichotomy. It is entirely possible—indeed likely—that artistic depictions of complex alternative worlds would both reproduce *and* subvert multiple discourses, in multiple directions at multiple levels. This is especially the case with Whedon, a prolific artist-activist who has never shied away from positioning his work near the crossroads of entertainment and politics (Jencson 2008). I thus see no inconsistency between affirming the above analyses while also amplifying my earlier line of critique. At the same time, some of my own formulations in my earlier essay, strike me as overly stark or at least unnecessary. Rather than accuse Whedon of some veiled intention, it is more productive to describe the repeated patterns, offer possible multiple readings, and consider the evidence from cognitive science.

Regarding stereotypes—a notion that may strike some as old-fashioned and tiresomely basic—it would be lovely to be able to prescind from interrogating their operation. However, further work in the wake of psychology's turn to neuroscience suggests that we do so at our peril. And, as many living in the U.S. discovered in November 2016 to their surprise and chagrin, the most retrograde of stereotypes can exhibit uncanny capacities for resurrection.

Working in popular culture, it is no surprise that stereotypes are part of Whedon's stock in trade. As a pop culture venture partaking in the genre conventions of post–World War II televisual sci-fi and Hollywood Westerns, the narrative world of *Firefly* and *Serenity* depends on the lurking presence of frontier savages to create moral order as well as narrative pleasure. Whedon has always been explicit about the parallels between the Reavers and Western conventions, noting, "Every story needs a monster. In the stories of the old west it was the Apaches" (Arroyo 2005). Yet Whedon also claimed to have deracialized the Apache metaphor (Arroyo 2005), instead intending a portrayal of the Reavers to illustrate the darkness of human nature in general (McCaw 2008). At the very least, however, Whedon's affection for some cinematic tropes operates at cross-purposes with what we might call his philosophical-political didactic commitment. In their visual presentation in crucial moments in *Serenity*, the Reavers are racially coded—as mainly Native American but also, in an important moment, as black (more precisely, as Afro-Caribbean). While my discussion below focuses mainly on the use of the cues reinscribing the Hollywood Indian, I would be remiss if I did not consider the significance of the black Reaver as well.

J. Douglas Rabb and J. Michael Richardson argue in *Investigating Firefly and Serenity* (2008) that in presenting us with the Reavers, "Whedon is attacking and deconstructing the 'savage Indian' found in 1950's 'B Westerns' and some early contact accounts of the Native Peoples of the Americas. It is, of course, necessary to present such stereotypes in order to deconstruct them" (Rabb and Richardson 2008: 127). However, it is not so clear how the deconstructive strategy works psychologically—in our actual heads and hearts. And if this is Whedons's strategy, then what are we to make of his claim to have de-racialized the reference when there are still patterns of visible racial coding? I argue that rather than successfully deconstructing stereotypes, Whedon's work with the Reavers tends instead to reinforce them at more implicit levels. By the time possibly deconstructive narrative moves take place, previous scenes in the movie (not to mention the series) have inculcated the savage stereotype under the threshold of consciousness such that the late-occurring scenes hardly trouble it.

Rabb and Richardson point out, quite rightly, that as an artist Whedon understands himself, and is commonly understood, to be operating at the level of metaphor. And Whedon's viewers understand themselves to be savvy consumers, comprehending the distinction between representation and reality and finding pleasure in the play of multiple layers of allusion. Catching the references and seeing through the representational conventions can even lead to a sort of smugness, detectable in the response of reviewer Paul DeAngelis: "And the Reapers [sic], savages that strike fear into travelers and settlers alike, are stand-ins for Indians—not Native Americans per se, but Hollywood's version of Indians. Whedon is too progressive to confuse the two" (2005). And by implication, so are we, "gentle viewers."

However, I think confusion between metaphor and reality in the case of "Injuns" and Indians reigns, even—and perhaps especially[2]—for progressives. Racist imagery, much of it promulgated by Hollywood, remains a prevailing mode of constructing real Indians. Living Native Americans, to a peculiar degree, continue to have a social unreality that cannot be accounted for unless we understand the importance of cinema and the Hollywood Western in light of earlier framings of this hemisphere's indigenous peoples. Hollywood stereotypes are tropes of the discourses operative long before the nineteenth century events and figures depicted in Western movies and television shows. The Hollywood Western is a chapter in the long project of constructing U.S. identity as premised on the abjection and disappearance of the native. And it remains a powerful chapter in the ongoing project of solidifying and exporting a colonialist form of identity. I thus find the instances of coding of the Reavers as Hollywood Injuns to lead, more or less directly, to instances of racial coding that construct and constrain perceptions of living Indian people. Those Indians of old, those "pesky" metaphors, keep wandering into "settled" discursive and psychological territory.

In interviews, Whedon has stressed the place of popular media in social change: "The idea of changing culture is important to me, and it can only be done in a popular medium" (qtd. in Nussbaum 2002). And Whedon's interest in using *Firefly/Serenity* to meditate on daily life in the U.S. Civil War, the reach of tele-politics into current life, and "an American immigrant story" is well known (Kennedy 2012: 27–32, 41 and Anders 2014). Yet it is fair to say that images of both power and heroism across the Whedonverse to date tend in the end to uphold white supremacy; early scholarly work by Ono (2000), Edwards (2002), Alderman and Seidel-Arpaci (2003), Kirkland (2005) and Battis (2005) has been joined by pointed analyses by DeJesus (2015), Nadkarni (2015) and Iatropolous and Woodall (2017: 13–14) to name just a few. On the popular front, activist and Whedonite Mike Le discusses an instance when he asked Whedon whether, if he had another chance with *Firefly/Serenity,* he would consider casting Asian or Asian American performers (as more than just extras). In addition to telling a less-than-coherent story about "getting flack" from another Asian journalist, Whedon's response trailed tellingly into abstraction: "Yeah, absolutely; it's not a mission statement, in terms of who I'm casting for a particular thing. It was a mission statement of the show to say that cultures inevitably blend, even if that happens through conquest and violence" (qtd. in Le 2012). Whedon further characterized a Sino-Anglo blending as a "utopian idea" (qtd. in racebending 2012). As Le notes,

> it was clear that the *notion* of cultural integration was more important than the practice. That the grand vision of a mixed Asian/American tomorrow was more important than the inclusion of Asian faces and voices today [Le 2012].

While as a philosopher I too have an attraction to abstraction, as a person of mixed Xicana/Anglo heritage living in a MAGA world and mothering an American Indian son, I also care about the effects of narratives, images and voices on the here and now.

What Indians? Aren't They All Gone?

Writing in 2008, I noted that American Indians are peculiarly invisible, arguing that this invisibility is due not merely to their relatively low numbers compared to other racial and ethnic minorities, or even to patterns of poverty and the isolation of reservations situated predominantly in the less populous Midwest and West. While the numbers are indeed small and their distribution is uneven, points that no doubt explain some of their invisibility, it is also important to keep in mind that over three-quarters of American Indians live off reservations, in cities, suburbs, and small towns, with New York City being the urban area with the largest number of American Indian residents (U.S. Census 2010). More to the point, in daily life, I also know of the phenomenon of American Indian people clearly and repeatedly identifying themselves as Indian to friends, neighbors, workplace acquaintances, etc., yet finding that they are either perceived stereotypically no matter what pains they take to present themselves otherwise, or dismissed as not really Indian because they do not match the images that owe much to Hollywood. I suggest these patterns of misperception and dismissal must also be seen in light of the fact that American national self-identity *as American*, i.e., as the rightful residents of U.S. national territory, depends on the destruction (either through assimilation or extermination) of the peoples who were here first. The invisibility of Indians thus has also to do with many Americans' deep psychological investment in their vanishing. For if Indians have in fact vanished, through death or assimilation, then the moral complexity of Europeans possessing the territory can be rendered a historical problem rather than an ongoing challenge.[3]

While I would argue that my 2008 essay's emphasis on the overall invisibility of real Native communities and life remains for the most part accurate, developments in both the U.S. and Canada can also be seen to complicate that assessment. In the U.S., after four decades of research and activism, discussion about the deleterious effects of Native American sports team mascots has gone mainstream (see Angle 2016; Brady 2014; Friedman 2013; and Wulf 2014). Moreover, actions and responses surrounding the Standing Rock Sioux Tribe and #NoDAPL has in some respects heightened the visibility of American Indians. In June 2017, District Judge James Boasberg ruled that in its approval process for the Dakota Access Pipeline, the U.S. Army Corps of Engineers did "not adequately consider the impacts of an oil spill on fishing rights, hunting rights, or environmental justice, or the degree to which the pipeline's effects are likely to be highly controversial" (qtd. in Williams 2018), an acknowledgment of the fact that the pipeline protests have drawn mainstream attention and sympathy to Native issues in the U.S. in a way not seen since perhaps the 1970s. Yet while response to #NoDAPL actions included significant financial and physical support to the tribes involved, it is arguable that in the post-presidential election polarization, #NoDAPL serves largely as a proxy for a nest of concerns about environmental regulation and the Trump Administration. In a similar pattern, the significance of a 2015–16 *Washington Post* poll suggesting that many American Indians regard furor over the "Redskins" football team name as trivial compared to the other issues they face has generally been elided in favor of using non-Natives' attitudes about sports mascots as fodder for partisan salvos about non-Native attitudes (see Smith 2017).

In the meantime, *Parents* magazine still managed to let slip a December 2015 cover featuring a white mother admonishing her whooping and war-bonnet wearing child from jumping on the furniture (Manning 2016) while in June 2017, Snoop Dogg posted on Instagram a painting of himself wearing a similar headdress, claiming his identity as "Big chief knocanew. From the knocahoe tribe" (Schilling 2017). In Canada, the 2017 Sesquicentennial of Canadian Federation sparked reflection on whether the 2008–14 Truth and Reconciliation project flowing from the 2005 Indian Residential Schools Settlement Agreement accomplished its aims. Writing in April 2017 for the *Globe and Mail*, Tracy Bear and Chris Anderson note, "At possibly no other time in our history has so much discussion taken place, country wide, about issues relating to reconciliation and the calls for a renewed relationship between Canada and Indigenous peoples." Yet the range of responses to this call has also made manifest the long half-life of both strategic ignorance and violent racism.

About Stereotype—Can't Stop the Visual

Like many fans of Whedon whose personal "Caucasian persuasion" is divided or absent, I initially made excuses for the lack of beyond-token ethnic diversity across the Whedonverse. And with respect to the Reavers, I initially suppressed my concerns about their representation, especially since the first episode of *Firefly* aired by FOX ("The Train Job") had featured Native American actor Valerie Red Horse in a small but nice speaking role as the Deputy in a town wracked by illness. As the story progresses, it is easy both to recognize the references to classic Indian stereotypes and dismiss them as surface clutter or a sophisticated intellectual bait-and-switch, particularly given the origin story presented in *Serenity*. But the use and continued life of specific images from the movie, combined with a host of associations set up for many viewers of the preceding *Firefly* series, supports a reading of the Reavers in which racialized associations persist because they cohere with racist mental schemata.

The notion of a schema remains central in cognitive science. A schema is an organized cluster of knowledge or information about an object or event, built by abstraction from previous experience with the object or event (Weiten 2005: 213). In turn, a schema greatly influences perception, interpretation and memory of subsequent experiences and events (Gilboa and Marlotte 2017). While there is some variance in theorists' definitions of a schema, Perry Thorndyke and Barbara Hayes-Roth isolate the assumptions common to the notion. They include: first, that the information encompassed by a schema is organized and conceptually related so that the schema forms a prototype; second, that a schema is developed on the basis of experience; third, that an existing schema guides the organization of new experience (1979). As Steve Thoma notes, schemas are highly contextual, thus triggered by similarly structured situations, and often operate automatically and without the subject's explicit awareness (Thoma 2006: 72).

Schemas are basic elements in cognition and the creation of meaning. They facilitate the combination of information into meaningful units that speed up inferential processes and provide bases for interpretation, prediction, emotional response, decision-making and action. Top-down, schema-driven processing can prompt inaccuracies that are highly resistant to change. This resistance affects interpretation of reading material (Narvaez 2006: 17) as well as of visual information and memory of a person's behavior, a phenomenon that has been noted for decades (see Cohen 1981). With respect to visual information, burgeoning work in neuroimaging continues the project of correlating the overweening importance we place on cues inferred from faces to specific locations of the brain, particularly an area of the temporal lobe called the fusiform gyrus—though perception of "race" is highly complex and seems to link as well to sectors involved with semantic knowledge, evaluation and self-regulation of one's behavior (Ito and Barthalow 2010). With respect to faces, however, it is well known that people are more adept at remembering faces of their own race than those of other races, a phenomenon called The Other Race Effect. These tasks seem to engage different parts of the brain, with processing of "others" dispensed with quickly, whereas more effort is expended on interpreting individualizing nuances of those in one's in-group (Lucas et al. 2011 and Brown et al. 2017).

In turn, schemas guide emotional response. As Dan Stein (1992) notes, while work on schemas opens many challenges to classical Freudian understandings of the mind, schema theory nonetheless maintains the Freudian emphasis on insight and the modern analytic emphasis on empathy (1992). And Shaun Gallagher argues that while cognitive science has many things to offer to hermeneutics, the reverse is true as well (2004). Work relating schema theory to literary criticism is now starting to be done in an effort to expand racial literacy (see Moya 2016).

Schemas are learned not only through personal experience but also by initiation into social groups. Social stereotypes are a particular class of schema. As widely-held cognitive and evaluative schemas linking people to characteristics because of their membership in specific social groups, social stereotypes are results of normal, generally non-conscious cognitive process (Bargh 1999). Stereotypes speed up mental processing (Macrae, Milne, and Bodenhausen 1994), but prompt overgeneralization and can foster biased perception of individual cases (see Hilton and von Hippel 1996 and Weiten 2005).[4] And, as Scott Plous summarizes, the media is a major disseminator of stereotypes, with even fleeting re-activations of stereotypes cumulating and re-enforcing chronically stereotypical thinking (2002: 27).

Negative stereotypes are readily enacted in people who claim to renounce prejudice (Devine and Monteith 1999) such that, for example, experimental work showed that while darkening the skin tone in photos of Barak Obama resulted in increasingly negative judgments of him from white perceivers in general, the shift was even greater for those who had expressed adherence to liberal-egalitarian, "colorblind" attitudes (West et al. 2014). Even neutral visual information juxtaposed with unrelated textual information can activate stereotypical interpretation of the information (Abraham and Appiah 2006).

Stereotypes affect memory recall, with individuals tending to forget information that does not fit in with their pre-existing schemas (Shechory et al. 2008) and concerns (again, the Other Race Effect is relevant). When people encounter persons whose identity is visually ambiguous, they rely on contextual clues (Ito et al. 2015) and interpretation of emotional expressions (Tskhay and Rule 2015) to categorize. And, not surprisingly, they have more positive attitudes about people they categorize as belonging to higher status groups (Ito et al. 2011 and Willadsen-Jensen and Ito 2015).

Stereotypes are also multi-leveled, organized into subgroups, with trustworthiness and competence appearing to be broadly salient organizational factors (Fiske et al. 2002). Subgroups remain subsumed under the broader stereotypes but in their operation, they are not necessarily consistent with each other and can spark varying, even opposing attitudes (Richards and Hewstone 2001). The operation of subgrouping within stereotypes is particularly relevant for understanding the sharp dichotomy of the noble/savage stereotypes that still shape the clusters of subgrouped stereotypes for American Indians (Burkley et al. 2017). When people encounter evidence that truly disconfirms the stereotypes operating for them, they may remember it and categorize it as atypical, but nonetheless integrate it into the organized schema by creating a new subcategory of the exceptional case—for example the friends who are "not like the rest" of the stigmatized groups to which they belong.

This suggests some epistemological conundrums. How does one enrich one's schemas enough to get beyond stereotypes? Mere contact between people of different social groups is not enough, especially under conditions of social stratification (Plous 2002). As both Fiske (2008) and Pewewardy (2006) note, while the less powerful (whose survival depends on navigating a hostile social terrain), may have some motivation for careful perception, the powerful may have little motivation for moving beyond stereotypes, particularly those that support culturally promoted fantasies. Indeed, the disruption of stereotypes is often unpleasant for members of dominant groups, with their efforts to navigate racially diverse settings causing high levels of personal stress (Stevenson et al. 2017).

On the other hand, self-motivated acknowledgement of the operation of schemas within our perceptions, thoughts, and emotions can increase self-awareness and allow the prefrontal cortex to override subconscious operations so as to arrive at a fuller and more nuanced perspective. Such effects are far from guaranteed, however. Attempts to suppress the effects of racial stereotyping by calling them to mind in order to suppress them, or just telling oneself that the stereotypes are inaccurate and morally wrong, are largely unsuccessful (Kawakami et al. 2000 and Jones and Fazio 2010). Meaningful negation, involving extensive and intentional training in constructing explicitly counter-stereotypical mental claims for oneself, can help to some extent (Stewart and Payne 2008; Jones and Fazio 2010; and Johnson et al. 2016). Again, no guarantees. On the positive side, research showing the complexity of interaction between task orientation and social categorization, and more subtly distinguishing the neurological operations of some social categorizations from stereotyping (Kaul et al. 2014 and Ito and Tomelerri 2017) may offer new perspectives on more effectively intervening in daily and popular culture.

Insofar as popular media is a primary teacher of stereotypes, perhaps it is the case that presenting a character that *both* triggers a schema and presents a fully complex human character can help in combatting stereotypical perception. Working in popular media within the conventions, it is at least arguable that with his major characters, Whedon provides cognitive and affective motivations to look beyond one's initial assumptions. Multiple readings of Inara (Morena Baccarin), Kaylee (Jewel Staite), and Zoe (Gina Torres) are a case in point. (see Davidson 2005; Holder 2005; Velazquez 2006; Kreider 2015; and Jarnagin 2017). On the other hand, when stereotypical elements operate without foregrounding, at the edge of awareness, with no critical space opened up by sympathetic emotional investment in the characters being stereotyped, they run a greater risk of merely triggering pre-existing schemas. And I think this is the case with Reavers and stereotypical Indians.

The Indian: Not "Just" Another Stereotype.
The Western: Not "Just" Another Genre

The claim that identity is stabilized through exclusion is, I am assuming, a familiar one, argued from the perspective of both social psychology and psychoanalysis. The claim that American national self-identity is in important respects premised on the abjection and "extermination" of the Native in particular is likewise quite broadly argued. (By this claim I am not ruling out other important exclusions, such as of blackness, Mexican-ness, the feminine, etc.). Finally, the claim that the repressed returns and remains an object of desire is a familiar basic tenet of psychoanalytic theory. Thus, as Karen Gagne notes, while the first move, of Indian-hating, has been culturally dominant, it has always been dialectically related to Indian-loving—the fascination and appropriative romanticism that, in its guilt-ridden ambivalence about the perceived costs of civilization, identifies with Indians and with wild and free Nature (2003). Both elements are indicative of an American psyche that is haunted, and fails to actually take account of Indigenous peoples as real and surviving in their own right (Neale 1998).[5] In this respect, post-structuralist work by Renee Bergland (1999) on the Native as the undead, haunting and thereby at once constituting and destabilizing American national literature, reflects what Lakota theorist Vine Deloria said twenty years before:

> Indians, the original possessors of the land, seem to haunt the collective unconscious of the white man and to the degree that one can identify the conflicting images of the Indian which stalk the white man's waking perception of the world one can outline the deeper problems of identity and alienation that trouble him [1980: x].

What does this have to do with the Western genre? Five centuries of European writings of all sorts—scientific, philosophical, legal, religious and literary—built a rich store of images of Native Americans for eventual deployment in film. Here I am going to touch on some of the ones relevant for analyzing *Serenity*.

The fantastical dichotomy between the good, noble, peaceful Indian victim—"fluffy Indigenous kittens, 'til we came along," as described in the *Buffy the Vampire Slayer* episode "Pangs" (23 November 1999)—and the evil, ruthless marauder goes back as far as Columbus's encounters with the Tainos and Caribs (which became Canibs, then Cannibals, a development that, as Harry Salwall reminds, tells us more about European paranoia than about the Caribs [2004]). But Jacquelyn Kilpatrick credits James Fenimore Cooper's *Leatherstocking Tales* (for example, *The Last of the Mohicans*) with uniquely entrenching the dichotomy (1999: 2). In Cooper we find not only the dichotomy but also the figure of the "Indianized white intermediary," the new, post–

European, authentically American hero, who is a better Indian than the Indians—who are, of course, the last of their kind (Kilpatrick 1999: xv).

The Indianized white intermediary features in one of Whedon's inspirations, *Ulzana's Raid* (Robert Aldrich, 1972). The shadow accompaniment of the new American hero is the person who has actually "gone native," lost psychic balance and interiorized Native consciousness. The presence of this trope renders problematic Whedon's claim to be using the Reavers to represent the darkness of human nature in general; historically, the view that darkness is a part of human nature was entirely compatible with the view that Indians were particularly malign representatives of this general principle. Indeed, the fears of "going native" depend upon it.

The savage rapist is likewise a figure several centuries old, while the "dumb Indian" is a more recent reversal of earlier framings of the savage as intelligent (endowed with Reason) but ignorant. The dialectical tension between these codes lives on in filmic portrayals of Indians as both inarticulate and primitive in their beliefs *and* demonically crafty. This tension is exhibited in the portrayal of the Reavers, as snarling, self-mutilating and suicidally careless about the radiation their ships emit, yet sophisticated enough to run those ships and devise booby-traps for other ships—a tension examined with vigor on fansites.[6]

Kilpatrick notes that visual media strive for the status of authoritative discourse, implicitly and often quite explicitly (1999: xvii). And, precisely as visual, film has enormous epistemological privilege. Simply put, we naturally tend to believe what we see, and we are further trained into such habits by prevailing practices and institutions. This is particularly the case for visual representations important to navigating social life.

The Western is characterized by critic Tim Dirks as "the major defining genre of the American film industry," and the connection between the Western and film goes back to film's very roots (n.d.). Some of Thomas Alva Edison's first Kinoscope recordings were of what he took to be an *authentic* Sioux Ghost Dance (Kilpatrick 1999: 17), and the projects of silent film often centered around white directors trying to get the story of the Indians "right." In fact, it was the Indian and not the cowboy who was the first subject of silent Westerns (Halnon). The fact that initial filmic representations of Indians were relatively benign compared to later ones may be an accident of timing—a function of the fact that the birth of film also happened to coincide with a period of ascendency for the Noble Native (exemplified in the immense popularity at the time of Longfellow's hospitable and conveniently departing Hiawatha) as the country grappled with the assimilation of Eastern European immigrants (Trachtenberg 2005).

The taking up of Indians almost immediately into film and the circulation of endlessly repeated ideas about "Indian-ness" has had peculiarly powerful repercussions for Native Americans (Fryberg et al. 2008 and Leavitt et al. 2015). Blatant distortions have sedimented into phantasmagoric cultural orthodoxy. Living, breathing tribal persons are projected into a sort of hyper-reality, becoming, in Deloria's words, "a pale imitation of the real Indians of the American imagination" (Deloria 1980: xvi) forced to confront present institutions that remain invested in a fantasized past.

The Western as a film/television genre occupies a uniquely powerful place in the construction of American national identity (Prats 1993 and Buscombe and Pearson 1998). That this has also had global consequences is nicely underscored in a comment by Gary Johnson: "The iconography of the Western is the largest and richest of all the film genres, and Hollywood has burned it into the minds of moviegoers from Dodge City to Timbuktu" (2006: 1). In turn the narrative of cowboys and Indians has shaped the colonial narratives of self-justification and modern identity in other contexts of settler colonialism like Canada ("Common Portrayals of Aboriginal People") and Australia, where it replaced the more homegrown figure of the bushranger (McGrath 2001).

Yet scholars have noted that while images of Indians have been ubiquitous in Westerns, their subjectivity has been notably absent for much of the history of Westerns (Prats 1996; Tomkins 1992; and Worland and Countryman 1998). While I think Tomkins perhaps overstates the case when she reduces their role to that of "a particularly dangerous form of local wildlife" (8), she has a point, reinforced by Prats' analysis of more recent Revisionist Westerns as just a more subtle play on the theme of the vanishing Indian. On the logic of abjection, this should make sense.

A further explanation for the hollowness that Tomkins notes is the fact that the Western genre has proven itself to be rather flexible in providing a frame for working out other problems of national self-identity. As Neale notes, Indians have thus functioned as signifiers for some other concern, such as black-white race relations (9). I cannot develop this rich theme further here, except to point out that the link between Westerns and space epics should be clear; in the 1970s, when racial tension and white guilt become a fairly evident theme in mainstream culture, science fiction presents the trope of the frontier generally unmoored from its historical associations. This point is relevant because here is one place where I believe Whedon missteps in his construction of the world of *Firefly*. His combination of the Western genre and space story triggers quite specific historical associations with the Western genre and, indeed with American history. But the futuristic framing encourages the move to explain away the obvious deployment of specific images and codes as invocations of broader cultural concerns without much reflection on how they are continuing to structure perceptions of current persons.

Indian Coding in Firefly

By the end of the intended series premier, the two-part episode "Serenity" (20 December 2002), the Reavers have been described as men "gone savage," running in "packs"[7] and forming raiding parties. They have been musically introduced with throbbing drumbeats and visually associated with vessels wearing red war paint. Viewers have also been treated to shot sequences hearkening to classic Western depictions of impending battles with the Natives (cross-cutting between the threat advancing outside and the settlers waiting inside). Tropes of these men as rapists[8] and cannibals who wear portions of their victims' skins are activated by a clearly unsettled Zoe (Gina Torres) (wow, they terrify Zoe!), heightening our sympathy for her and the rest of the crew. While the first episode utilizes these devices lavishly and, I suggest, unequivocally, Episode 3, "Bushwhacked" (27 September 2003) which aired before "Serenity" in FOX's scrambled lineup, can be read in more ambiguous ways. On one hand, the European idea of existential void is employed as the Reavers described as men who are "nothing," having stared at the abyss that stared back in return (Nietzsche 2002: 146). On the other, Jayne (Adam Baldwin) and Book (Ron Glass) give us a little taste of the debate between Bartolomé de *las Casas and Juan* Gines *Sepulveda* on whether the inhabitants of the New World were in fact human, while the discovery of a booby trap gives evidence of their scheming craftiness.

Indian Coding in Serenity

In *Serenity*, the introduction to the Reavers is a bit different from that intended in the series; gone is the "tribal" drumbeat and first shot of painted ships. Instead, there is action music through the scene in the bank vault where Mal and crew are robbing the payroll. We cut to a flash of River's alarmed face and then cut to outside, where a boy of about eleven is talking with his mother about hearing something. In the background, there are only some very light strings and natural sounds of crickets and a dog. The mother says she will tell the "lawman" about the shots heard, placing us squarely in the Western, something that actually had not been all that strongly signaled before; the previous scene with the futuristic blue room feels more sci-fi. With the scene outside, we have some scrambling of the iconography with the little boy's hat, but the mother is dressed in simple prairie-style garb, with a noticeably old-timey upswept hairstyle. She straightens up to turn around, and there is a slight pause in the background sounds. Then we cut to the Reaver's face and his slashing action. Like Injuns of old, he is presented as having managed stealthily to sneak up on the hapless woman and child—(in full daylight on an open street, no less). This first visual of a Reaver is note-worthy, not because all Reavers look like him, but because he is presented *first*. He has brown skin and long, straight, black hair. Red radiation burns are not enough to dislodge the visual presentation of brown-ness. I suggest this glimpse is enough to activate the stereotype of the savage Injun. Further, viewers are placed into the position of the victims in this scene and we are thus invited to identify with them.

The second Reaver we see initially from the legs down. With heavy boots, spikes, and what look like shin guards, he looks futuristic; subsequent shots show that he seems also to have long hair, but lighter-colored, while the first shot sequence emphasizes his landing and his energetic run for the kill. The only color on his black clothing is red, which has racial coding but can admittedly also symbolize blood.

Moments later we have a sequence in which a trio of Reavers grab a young man who had tried to board the hovercraft "mule" Mal and crew are using to get away from the raid; Mal had thrown him off the mule because they did not have room for him. The Reaver shown first grabbing him has noticeably long, flowing dark hair. Mal shoots the young man as he is dragged off. As noted above, in the commentary accompanying the DVD, Whedon explains he was inspired here by a scene in *Ulzana's Raid* featuring a Cavalry officer escorting a woman and her son from their ranch to the fort for pro-tection; they are ambushed, and when the officer attempts to outrun the ambush, the woman begs him to return to her side. Knowing it will do no good, he shoots her between the eyes in order to spare her the fate of being "raped to death."

Following this scene of direct homage to a specific Western, we have fleeting glimpses of other Reavers in action. The first is a pair, one wearing fringe dragging off a woman (the angle of the shots highlighting her skirt and struggling legs suggests she will be raped). The second is of a Reaver with a "Mohawk" haircut diving after a fleeing victim under what seems to be an arbor. We then cut back to a scene showing the back of the fringe-coated Reaver dispatching a victim, shot through a row of umbrellas; what is highlighted in the shot is the movement of the fringe. Finally, we get another very brief—almost subliminal—full-face close-up of the first Reaver, with brown skin and long, dark hair, snarling directly at the viewers, and, by impli-cation, attacking us again. The placement of the audience in the position of being attacked or chased by Reavers continues with the start of the sequence where a Reaver ship gives chase to the crew's mule. The shot places our per-spective in front of the mule looking back to the looming ship, situating us with the terrified crew.

As noted, one Reaver in these scenes has long, lighter-colored hair, while the Reaver who makes it aboard Serenity in the course of the "barn swallow" maneuver seems shorn of hair and of generally lighter skin-tone (though so much has been mutilated or burned that the dominant color registered is red). Thus one could object to my placing so much significance on the first glimpse of the Reaver, the brief shots of Reavers wearing Indian-coded garb or hairstyles and the shots of the Reaver directly threatening the audience. Perhaps these subsequent shots are supposed to question our first association between Reavers and Hollywood Indians. However, the first sequence, of the boy and his mother seized upon by the Reaver, is structured so as to garner a particularly empathetic and strong emotional response. First, the viewer's sympathy for the victims is fostered by the brief moment of pause and quiet conversation between the boy and his mother. The relative lack of background music in this instance pulls us in further. Then we have the startling, even terrifying scene of the Reaver's face from the perspective of the victim. I suggest that the strength of both emotional responses, and their order, contributes to the power (and enjoyment) of the scene, and that this response is, in most instances of viewing, strong enough to subvert subsequent critical responses that may take place. We know consciously that in the story Reavers are not Redskins. But the socially significant association continues unabated, based on activation of both the cognitive association between savagery and stereotypical Indian physiognomy and garb and a set of accompanying real sympathies and fears. Indeed, it is the conscious overlay ("Of course the Reavers aren't Indians. Look at the shots where they're shown not to be.") that makes the activation of the stereotype even more insidious.

Mal Goes Native

As mentioned above, one of the fundamental tropes of the narrative of American identity is of the person (i.e., white man) who makes himself anew by surviving on the frontier. To find his own place in the world, he frequently has to pass through enemy territory. To survive and flourish in this new land, this new man, as mentioned above, has to adapt himself to the frontier conditions and take up enough of the native ways to ensure survival in what is essentially another's world. Cinematically, this is symbolized sartorially, by the character's taking up of costuming that combines white and Indian elements. This life is a risk, of course; the Native monstrous threatens to engulf the white hero, and he frequently risks misunderstanding by other whites. These dimensions of the representation of the American frontier hero have to be employed when thinking about a major plot point in the movie, when Mal orders the crew to dress up the tenth character, Serenity herself, in war paint. Mal is going to the edge, literally and figuratively, and the crew is horrified, because not only is he using the bodies of friends, he is desecrating

Serenity. Yet he must go this far, into this frontier, to becoming, as blogger Jon Sprunk characterizes him, "a bad-ass ^$#@ who will never quit" (2014)—a description veering into fitting the Reavers too—to redeem himself and find his heroic moral compass. In the crucial scene in which the "Indians ride over the hill" to surprise the Alliance ships, Serenity is positioned at the lead.

Some Late Deconstructive Moves

The build to the climax of *Serenity* involves learning the Reavers' true origins as the creation of the Alliance, an unintended consequence of the Alliance's meddlesome wielding of pharmaceutical power. With this move, Rabb and Richardson (2008), Garlan (2011) and Smith-Casanueva (2017) all argue, Whedon has taken a deconstructive and liberatory turn, affirming the by-now truism that colonial power projects its worst fears about itself onto an alien Other it must construct for that purpose. Garlan claims that Whedon's revision "liberates the imagery from its racist foundation and allows *Firefly* to exploit it in ways that would be absolutely unthinkable in a conventional modern Western."[9] Richardson and Rabb specify further that River (Summer Glau), as a product of the Alliance herself, is a stand-in for viewers—at least those of British and European heritage—who, with respect to the savage images of Native Americans, should be brought to the "uncomfortable realization that 'we made them'..." (138). In their reading, Rabb and Richardson emphasize River's exhibition of cultural guilt, symbolized by her vomiting, upon learning of the Alliance's role in creating the Reavers.

Nevertheless, it is striking that River's regret is fleeting; of even more significance is the fact that she can now pick herself up and fight. Indeed, her singlehanded slaughter of all the Reavers in the raiding is the climax of the story and of her particular arc—the sign that she, like Mal, has come into her own and regained her psychic equilibrium. (Given the absence of her amygdala, her cure verges on the downright miraculous.) In this respect, I suggest that the moment of recognition of cultural guilt exhibited by a sympathetic character who has herself been victimized actually functions insidiously, prompting even more pleasure as she dances her way into blood-drenched heroism.

And in spite of the anti-totalitarian thrust of the overt narrative, I suggest there is the reinforcement of the Alliance-type logic (all-too familiar in U.S. global ventures as well) that says, "Well, we made this mess, now we must 'stay the course' and clean it up," at the further expense of political transparency and mostly Others' lives.

River/Reaver

As Garlen demonstrates in her reading of the series episode "Bushwhacked," Indian captivity narratives and later Hollywood use of the idea of Indian captivity are also relevant for understanding the Reavers (2011). The captivity narratives give us descriptors of Indians as monstrously "inhuman," slaughtering settlers like livestock then wearing tokens of their flesh, while the fascination with female captives is replayed through the 1950s and 60s in such influential films as John Ford's *The Searchers* (1956). As depicted in both *The Searchers* and "Bushwhacked," the likely consequence of captivity is the contagion of the savage's insanity such that the captive, "gone native," is seen as no longer capable of inhabiting a recognizably human life.

River, too, has been captive, her sanity direly threatened, and in this respect she can be seen as prompting a different, perhaps more effective deconstructive turn. She and the Reavers are parallel, their similarities even marked by name—both captives of the Alliance, both victims of overweening State biopower. There is even a visual parallel, with crucial publicity shots in which River's long darkish hair is unkempt, hanging in strings in her haunted face.

In this respect, there is a possibility for more complex sympathy with the Reavers themselves—a recognition that they are not just a "percentage of the population" but thirty-thousand suffering individuals, people who, like River, had answered "calls" put out by the Alliance in hopes of securing productive lives. In feeling the tragedy of their parallel captivities, we might even expand on the narrative's underlying question of what to do with the violently insane—a question openly debated by the crew in the case of River and resolved compassionately. But that would be *too* complex for cinematic comfort, and would undercut the cool fight scene. Nope. In bad-ass fashion, River's self-overcoming has to be premised on violence. And with her reinstatement as an agent in her own right, there is also the narrative reinscription of white-savior womanhood.

Manifest Destiny on Miranda

In contrast to the other villain of the movie, the Alliance Operative (Chiwetel Ejiofor), who is given a free pass in the end, the only good Reaver is a dead Reaver. This is not surprising; while the Operative is evil and plausibly interpreted as subtextually reinforcing a narrative of black male brutality, irrationality, and subjugation to authority (De Jesus 2013), he also speaks and exhibits a range of recognizably human motives. In contrast, the Reavers only snarl and scream.

Like its namesake, the female mediator in Shakespeare's *The Tempest,* the planet Miranda is clearly coded as white, signified by the bleaching sunlight, the clean, modern white buildings, and the light-colored costuming, skin tones, and hair of the corpses. Yet the broader narrative of Miranda also situates us in another familiar trope—that of the noble savage who is too naïve to protect himself. Indeed, the narrative of the entire fate of Miranda subtextually replays the familiar trope of Manifest Destiny; in the face of Western intellectual, technological and immunological superiority, the peaceful ones laid down and died of their diseases while the remainder are fit only for slaughter.

The Reavers Beyond the Movie— A Toy Story

I hope I have made plausible that *Serenity*'s moments of deconstructing the initial visual associations between Reavers and Redskins are, like all deconstructive play, narratively ambivalent. Returning to the visual, it is noteworthy that the most commonly circulated online image of a Reaver in the post-movie world is the shot of the one with long, straight dark hair, facing the viewer. This is also the image used to mark Chapter 5 on the DVD.

Another image worth discussing, however, is an image from River's dream sequence (Chapter 11 on the DVD), in which a black, dreadlocked Reaver grabs her and prepares to eat her face. After the image, we have a quiet shot of River looking unsettled but reflective—a moment that seems designed to spark some sympathy for her sometimes jarring, even alienating character. This image has some internet presence, but much less than the first Reaver image. However, this image merits half of page 113 in Whedon's *Serenity: The Official Visual Companion.* With his bared and sharpened teeth in proximity to the terrified girl, he is a visual exemplification of the metaphor of "big black wolf" that De Jesus (2013) argues unites the two most noteworthy individual villains of the *Firefly/Serenity* story, Jubal Early in the *Firefly* episode "Objects in Space,"(13 December 2002) and the Operative. In addition, while his prominently visible dreadlocks have a long, global history, my bet is that that their most immediate association for most viewers is to the Afro-Caribbean culture of Jamaica and the political religion of Rastafarianism—again landing us into a New World colonialist positioning of the image.

Then there is the Reaver action figure licensed to Diamond Select Toys and Collectibles. The packaging for the separately sold version features a shot of the first Reaver, the one with long straight dark hair, while the figure itself looks like it might be a bit of a mash-up between the "Indian" Reaver and the "Afro-Caribbean" Reaver.[10] Whatever he is, he is not white and not Asian.

Shod in what seem intended to be punk boots that also register as surprisingly similar to nineteenth century wingtips, he wields an ax as one of his weapons. (One can be thankful, at least, that he's not wearing fringe.) He is included in the special edition four-piece set along with Mal and two versions of Jayne, with the contrast of skin tones noticeable. There is also a more recent statue, of River standing triumphant on a pile of Reaver corpses and now wielding the ax, also available from Diamond Collectibles. While it depicts dead Reavers as a multiracial lot, with its limited edition status and price in the hundreds of dollars, its reach is narrower than the cheaper action figure. Speaking of the ax, along with more expensive replicas popping up from various sources, an inflatable version of the "Reaver Ax" originally available from QMX still circulates via eBay.

Thus, in spite of possible cognitive complexities set in motion by *Serenity*'s overt narrative, commercial decisions sanctioned by the production team support the further circulation of the most culturally stereotypical and racialized of the Reaver images.

Conclusion

> A picture held us captive, and we could not get outside of
> it....—Ludwig Wittgenstein [1958: Section 115].

The ways the Reavers are visually represented at crucial moments in *Serenity*, regardless of intended function, tend to entrench rather than deconstruct racist associations. The first sets of images code as "savage Indian" in several ways, while the most powerful set are the facial shots of the brown skinned Reaver attacking the camera. Another powerful image codes the Reaver as Afro-Caribbean. Both are particularly powerful because they are images of faces, occurring quickly, at the margins of awareness, and accompanied by strong emotional responses of startle, fright and disgust. They are situated in narrative moments designed to make us identify and sympathize with their victims, sparking little motivation to raise the initial sets of associations to the level of conscious examination. I argue further that the deployment of the images at the start of the film is noteworthy because of the uniquely foundational role that discourses about Indians play in the formation of American identity and the important place cinema and television have had in exporting that identity to other relevant contexts. To this extent, *Firefly* and *Serenity* function to continue structuring viewers' pleasures, moral frameworks, and motivations in a way that paradoxically supports continued investment in colonialist mentalities, with their predictable geopolitical effects.

In his paper about the phenomenon of *Buffy* Studies and the question of theory (presented at the 2006 *Slayage* Conference), Greg Erickson noted that television studies must now reckon with the interactive nature of visual-textual media. He mentioned that Whedon has acknowledged being illuminated by some fans' interpretations of his work that he had not considered. To me, this signifies the legitimacy in *Buffy* Studies of questions about accountability in the production of these texts. I am not holding Whedon to some pre-defined model of political correctness. But it is undeniable that Whedon has authority; fandom, including academic fandom, is also at bottom a search for some guideposts in a world with precious few. While we are all caught up in the historical deployment of discourses, Whedon's agency is not negligible, nor is ours. Given our position as adults, at the very least, and often teachers and parents, this raises questions about our modes of complicity and responsibility.

I am certainly not arguing that it is Whedon's intent to promote racism or a colonialist mentality; indeed, I think the evidence regarding his explicit intentions is to the contrary. However, I do think that, in working with the Western genre, he was playing with fire of a peculiar sort. The Western is not just another story form. Whatever we might wish to say about its connections to other forms and archetypes, and whatever its transmutations and attempts at revision, the Western may be particularly tethered to its colonialist underpinnings in a way that challenges attempts to unmoor it.[11]

Iatropolous and Woodall introduce their collection of essays on Whedon and race with a quote from Whedon in which he acknowledges that there is plenty going on in his texts, and in himself, of which he is unaware (2017: 10). Whedon has also spoken quite beautifully of the rift within each of us that is the unstable ground of our identity. Addressing Wesleyan University graduates in 2013, he warned,

> … let me say when I talk about contradiction, I'm talking about something that is a constant in your life and in your identity, not just in your body but in your own mind, in ways that you may recognize or you may not…. And for your entire life, you will be doing, on some level, the opposite—not only of what you were doing—but of what you think you are. That is just going to go on. What you do with all your heart, you will do the opposite of. And what you need to do is to honor that, to understand it, to unearth it, to listen to this other voice [qtd. in Rubenstein 2013].

For anyone coming up in the tangle of looping contradictions that is colonialist history and contemporary culture, it would be entirely expectable that the other voice would tell stories in which these loops repeat, transpose, combine, and in the process also encrust perception. It would be entirely expectable that the other voice would tell stories of the creation of monsters in ways that continue to create them, as well as stories reflecting unthinking comfort with some of the stratifications characterizing the "Earth that is"—

stories propping up the fascist regimes lurking within all our heads and hearts (Foucault 1983). As seeing, speaking creatures built of contradictions, our stories create dangerous—and necessary—mirrors for all of us, storytellers and audience alike. Each needs the other to unearth and listen—and reflect back.

NOTES

1. Joss Whedon, describing the Reavers attacking in *Serenity* (2007).

2. In research on the relation between political identity and susceptibility to negative native mascot images, Angle et al., using implicit association tests, found that exposure to the brand images can reinforce bias and that the strengthening of association between Native Americans and negative attributes like "warlike" was actually larger for liberals than for conservatives (2016). Justin Angle also discusses this in his article in *The Conversation* (2016) and *The Washington Post* (2016). Critics of Implicit association tests argue that the link between evidence of patterns of implicit bias and specific behavior is shaky at best (Mitchell and Tetlock 2017). In the essay, I have tried to avoid such inferences.

3. In addition to the research cited further in the essay, part of my evidence for this claim is admittedly personal observation of a particular pattern of response manifested by non-Indian (usually white) U.S. Americans when they are faced with situations where Indians make reference to land claims or sovereignty, or even when they simply attempt to assume control of their own cultural narratives. I was initially surprised to see this response but have seen it often enough, among people of various ages and social positions, to suspect it is indeed a pattern. The first phase of the non-Indian person's response is often polite and framed in terms of regret about past history, often using moral language of right and wrong. But if the Indian claimant presses the case in the present or persists even in maintaining narrative control about the past, the attitude and attendant language abruptly shifts. Veneers of politeness and morality drop away, and the response is predictably some variant of, "We won the war; get over it." When the person feels pushed into saying this, it can be quite discomfiting to the speaker, because such discourses of raw force are antithetical to the strong sense of moral exceptionalism that is also part of U.S. political identity. It is easier to avoid the clash altogether by pretending, against all evidence, that Indians are extinct.

4. Weiten summarizes experiments that had white subjects evaluate various versions of a video of two people arguing where one person eventually shoves the other. Various versions were presented to the subjects. "The shove was coded as 'violent behavior' by 73 percent of the participants when the actor was black but by only 13 percent of the participants when the actor was white" (2005: 482).

5. Teaching environmental ethics in the Northeast U.S. has afforded some interesting experiences in this respect. In North America, the notion of the "environment" remains interwoven with assumptions that the land was originally a pristine wilderness, thus must come up for philosophical examination. Likewise, it is important to consider patterns of environmental racism, which leads to discussions of tribal moves for sovereignty, which can sometimes result in Indian communities' decisions in favor of nuclear waste dumps, oil pipelines, etc. Students often have an overt investment in the Noble Savage myth, dialectically wedded to an underlying resentment. For example, upon learning that American Indians have *various* opinions about controversial environmental issues, one non-Native student of roughly my age responded that I had "shattered" something precious to her, that she felt the exact same way she had when she learned that Betty Crocker was not a real woman, and that now she really *disliked* Indians. (That she felt comfortable enough, and entitled enough, to voice this dislike is worth noting.) Another reaction, more common among younger left-leaning students, is a posture of mourning and guilt, coupled with strong resentment of the U.S. government for its part in destroying native cultures; what is intriguing about this response is that students persist in this attitude in spite of any and all evidence supplied that Native people are still here and their cultures are not completely destroyed.

6. Googling "how do the Reavers fly spaceships" yields several sites with threads as late as December 2015.

7. The term "pack" is applied only to carnivorous mammals. The term "pack of wild Indians" has a long history, with written record of its widespread use stretching back at least as far as the U.S. Civil War (see Christ et al. 2014: 57 and Wittenberg et al. 2008: 64).

8. When I first viewed this scene, the phrase "rape us to death" seemed noteworthy as it reminded me of *Ulzana's Raid,* in which the Burt Lancaster character describes the Apaches as raping women to death. In the commentary on *Serenity,* Whedon specifically mentions *Ulzana's Raid* as an inspiration for the scene in which Mal shoots a young man (2007).

9. It is not clear if *Bone Tomahawk* (S. Craig Zahler, 2015) is too close to horror to qualify as a modern Western, but it does not shy away from playing with the cannibalism trope.

10. In efforts to view the figures up close, I visited several local stores specializing in games, comics and collectibles. In the process of inquiring whether they had *Serenity* action figures, I conducted a small and obviously unsystematic survey, asking store personnel who were familiar with the Reavers what their mental image of a Reaver was. Invariably, it was the image of the first Reaver shown in the film.

11. As a posthumanist sci-fi inquiry about memory, agency and identity that also employs many tropes from the Western, *Westworld* would be interesting to compare to strands of Whedon's work, perhaps particularly *Dollhouse.* In this respect, Aaron Brady's (2016) quite critical reading of the way *Westworld* reaffirms a white supremacist perspective is instructive.

WORKS CITED

Abraham, Linus and Osei Appiah. (2006). "Framing New Stories: The Role of Visual Imagery in Priming Racial Stereotypes," in *The Howard Journal of Communications* 17: 183–203.

Alderman, Naomi, and Annette Seidel-Arpaci. (2003). "Imaginary Para-Sites of the Soul: Vampires and Representations of 'Blackness' and 'Jewishness' in the *Buffy/Angel*verse," in *Slayage: The International Online Journal of Buffy Studies* 10.

Anders, Charlie Jane. (2014). "The Real Reason Why Joss Whedon Named His Space Western *Firefly,*" in *io9.* On-line. Available HTTP: http://io9.gizmodo.com/the-real-reason-why-joss-whedon-named-his-space-western-1614273050 (25 July 2017).

Angle, Justin. (2016). "New Research Shows How Native American Mascots Reinforce Stereotypes," in *The Conversation.* On-line. Available HTTP: https://theconversation.com/new-research-shows-how-native-american-mascots-reinforce-stereotypes-63861 (25 July 2017).

Angle, Justin. (2016). "Sorry, Redskins Fans: Native American Mascots Increase Racial Bias," in *The Washington Post.* On-line. Available HTTP: https://www.washingtonpost.com/news/speaking-of-science/wp/2016/09/15/sorry-redskins-fans-native-american-mascots-increase-your-racial-bias/?utm_term=.df7a0aedd287 (25 July 2017).

Angle, Justin W., Sokiente Dagogo-Jack, Mark R. Forehand, and Andrew Perkins. (2016). "Activating Stereotypes with Brand Imagery: The Role of Viewer Political Identity," in *Journal of Consumer Psychology* 1:27: 84–90.

Anon. (2010). "The American Indian and Alaska Native Population Brief." *U.S. 2010 Census.* On-line. Available HTTP: https://www.census.gov/prod/cen2010/briefs/c2010br-10.pdf (25 July 2017).

Anon. (2006). (n.d.). "Common Portrayals of Aboriginal People," *Media Smarts.* On-line. Available HTTP: http://mediasmarts.ca/diversity-media/aboriginal-people/common-portrayals-aboriginal-people (18 September 2017).

Armstrong, Mark. (2001). "Whedon Bites Off Another New Series," in *ENews.* On-line. Available HTTP: http://www.eonline.com/news/42612/whedon-bites-off-another-new-series (17 September 2017).

Arroyo, Sam. (2005). "Joss Whedon Panel @ Wondercon: Full Report," in *Comic Book Resources.* On-line. Available HTTP: http://www.cbr.com/joss-whedon-panel-wondercon-full-report/ (25 July 2017).

Bachran, Daoine S. (2017). "Mexicans in Space? Joss Whedon's *Firefly,* Reavers, and the Man They Call Jayne," in Mary Ellen Iatropolous and Lowry A. Woodall III (eds.) *Joss Whedon and Race: Critical Essays.* Jefferson, NC: McFarland, 184–199.

Bargh, John A. (1999). "The Cognitive Monster: The Case Against Controllability of Automatic Stereotype Effects," in S. Chaiken and Y. Trope (eds.) *Dual Process Theories in Social Psychology.* New York: Guilford, 1999.

Battis, Jes. (2005). *Blood Relations: Chosen Families in* Buffy *and* Angel. Jefferson, NC: McFarland.

Bear, Tracy, and Chris Anderson. (2017). "Three Years Later, Is Canada Keeping Its Truth and Reconciliation Promises?" in *The Globe and Mail.* On-line. Available HTTP: https://www.theglobeandmail.com/opinion/three-years-later-is-canada-keeping-its-truth-and-reconciliation-commission-promises/article34790925/ (25 July 2017).

Bergland, Renee. (1999). *The National Uncanny: Indian Ghosts and American Subjects.* London: University Press of New England.

Black, Jason Edward. (2002). "The 'Mascotting' of Native America: Construction, Commodity, and Assimilation," in *The American Indian Quarterly* 26:4: 605–622.

Brady, Aaron. (2016). "*Westworld,* Race, and the Western," in *The New Yorker.* On-line. Available HTTP: http://www.newyorker.com/culture/culture-desk/how-westworld-failed-the-western (25 July 2017).

Brady, Erik. (2014). "Report: Indian Mascots Hurt Native American Children," in *USA Today.* On-line. Available HTTP: https://www.usatoday.com/story/sports/nfl/2014/07/22/indian-mascots-report-washington-nfl-team/13006145/ (25 July 2017).

Brown, Thackery I., Melina R. Uncapher, Tiffany E. Chow, Jennifer L. Eberhardt, and Anthony D. Wagner. (2017). "Cognitive Control, Attention, and the Other Race Effect in Memory." *PLoSone* 12.3. On-line. Available HTTP: http://journals.plos.org/plosone/article?id=10.1371/journal.pone.0173579 (25 July 2017).

Burkely, Edward, Susan T. Fiske, Federica Durante, and Melissa Burkley. (2017). "Structure and Content of Native American Stereotypic Subgroups: Not Just (Ig)noble," in *Cultural Diversity and Ethnic Minority Psychology* 23:2: 209–19.

Buscombe, Edward and Roberta E. Pearson. (1998). "Introduction," in *Back in the Saddle Again: New Essays on the Western.* London: British Film Institute.

Cohen, Claudia. (1981). "Person Categories and Social Perception: Testing Some Boundaries of the Processing Effect of Prior Knowledge," in *Journal of Personality and Social Psychology* 40.3: 441–52.

Cox, John Woodrow, Scott Clement, and Theresa Vargas. (2016). "New Poll Finds 9 in 10 Native Americans Aren't Offended by Redskins Name," in *The Washington Post.* On-line. Available HTTP: https://www.washingtonpost.com/local/new-poll-finds-9-in-10-native-americans-arent-offended-by-redskins-name/2016/05/18/3ea11cfa-161a-11e6-924d-838753295f9a_story.html?utm_term=.66cbcda369b7 (25 July 2017).

Christ, Mark K., and Patrick B. Williams. (2014). *I Do Wish This Cruel War Was Over: First Person Accounts of Civil War Arkansas from the Arkansas Historical Quarterly.* Fayetteville: University of Arkansas Press.

Davidson, Joy. (2005) "Whores and Goddesses," in Jane Espenson and Glenn Yeffeth (eds.) *Finding Serenity: Anti-Heroes, Lost Shepherds and Space Hookers in Joss Whedon's* Firefly. Dallas: BenBella Books, 113–30.

De Angelis, Paul. (2005). "*Firefly,*" in *CultureVulture.* On-line. Available HTTP: https://culturevulture.net/television/firefly/ (18 September 2017).

Deloria, Vine. 1980. "Foreword: American Fantasy," in Gretchen M. Bataille, Charles L.P. Silet (eds.) *The Pretend Indians: Images of Native Americans in the Movies.* Ames: The Iowa State University Press.

Devine, Patricia G., and Monteith, M.J. (1999). "Automaticity and Control in Stereotyping," in S. Chaiken and Y. Trope (eds.) *Dual-Process Models and Themes in Social and Cognitive Psychology.* New York: Guilford Press, 339–60.

Dirks, Tim. (n.d.). "Western Films," in *The Greatest Films.* On-line. Available HTTP: http://www.filmsite.org/westernfilms.html (25 July 2017).

Edwards, Lynne. (2002). "Slaying in Black and White: Kendra as Tragic Mulatta in *Buffy,*" in

Rhonda V. Wilcox and David Lavery (eds.) *Fighting the Forces: What's at Stake in* Buffy the Vampire Slayer. Lanham, MD: Rowman & Littlefield, 85–97.

Erickson, Greg T. (2006). "21st Century Theory and Cultural Studies: A View from the Edge of the Hellmouth." Presentation at SC2 Conference on the Whedonverses. Gordon College, Barnesville, GA.

Fiske, Susan T., Amy J.C. Cuddy, Peter Glick, and Jun Xu. (2002). "A Model of (Often Mixed) Stereotype Content: Competence and Warmth Respectively Follow from Perceived Status and Competition," in *Journal of Personality and Social Psychology* 82:6: 878–902.

Foucault, Michel. (1983). "Preface," in Gilles Deleuze and Felix Guattari (eds.) *Anti-Oedipus: Capitalism and Schizophrenia.* Trans. Robert Hurley, Mark Seem, and Helen R. Lane. Minneapolis: University of Minnesota Press, xi–xiv.

Friedman, Michael A. (2013). "The Harmful Psychological Effects of the Washington Football Mascot," in A Report Commissioned by the Oneida Indian Nation. On-line. Available HTTP: http://www.changethemascot.org/wp-content/uploads/2013/10/DrFriedman Report.pdf (25 July 2017).

Fryberg, Stephanie A., Hazel Rose Markus, Daphna Oyserman, and Joseph M. Stone. (2008). "Of Warrior Chiefs and Indian Princesses: The Psychological Consequences of American Indian Mascots on American Indians," in *Basic and Applied Social Psychology* 30: 208–18.

Gagne, Karen M. (2003). "Falling in Love with Indians: The Metaphysics of Becoming America," in *CR: The New Centennial Review* 3.3: 205–33.

Gallagner, Shaun. (2004). "Hermeneutics and the Cognitive Sciences," in *Journal of Consciousness Studies* 11.

Garlan, Jennifer. (2011). "Bushwhacked by the Nightmare Native: The Western Roots of *Firefly's* Reavers," in *Virtual Virago*. On-line. Available HTTP: http://virtualvirago.blogspot.com/2011/12/bushwhacked-by-nightmare-native-western.html (25 July 2017).

Gilboa, Asaf, and Hanna Marlatte. (2017). "Neurobiology of Schemas and Schema-Mediated Memory," in *Trends in Cognitive Science* 21.8: 618–31.

Gilbert, Daniel T., Susan T. Fiske, and Gardner Lindzey (eds.). (1998). *The Handbook of Social Psychology.* 4th ed. New York: McGraw-Hill.

Hadyk-Delodder, Gareth, and Laura Chilcoat. (2015). "See What's Inside: Understanding the Reavers' Posthuman Identity and Role in *Firefly* and *Serenity*," in Michael Goodrum and Philip Smith (eds). Firefly *Revisited: Essays on Joss Whedon's Classic Series.* Lanham, MD: Rowman & Littlefield, 37–52.

Halnon, Mary. (n.d.). "Indians and Mexicans: Alternative Cultures in the Silent Western," in *The Silent Western: Early Movie Myths of the American West.* University of Virginia American Studies Department. On-line. Available HTTP: http://xroads.virginia.edu/~HYPER/hns/westfilm/west.html (25 July 2017).

Hight, Christopher. (2003). "Stereo Types: The Operation of Sound in the Production of Racial Identity," in *Leonardo* 36.1: 13–14.

Hilton, James L., and William von Hippel. (1996). "Stereotypes," in *Annual Review of Psychology* 47.

Holder, Nancy. 2005). "I Want Your Sex," in Jane Espenson and Glenn Yeffeth (eds.) *Finding Serenity: Anti-Heroes, Lost Shepherds and Space Hookers in Joss Whedon's* Firefly. Dallas: BenBella Books, 139–54.

Iatropolous, Mary Ellen, and Lowrey A. Woodall III. (2017). "Introduction. The Individual, the Institutional and the Unintentional: Exploring the Whedonverse Through Critical Race Theory," in Mary Ellen Iatropolous and Lowry A. Woodall III (eds.) *Joss Whedon and Race: Critical Essays.* Jefferson, NC: McFarland, 10–33.

Ito, Tiffany A., and Bruce D. Barthalow. (2009). "The Neural Correlates of Race," in *Trends in Cognitive Science* 13:12: 524–31.

Ito, Tiffany A., and Silvia Tomelleri. (2017). "Seeing Is Not Stereotyping: The Functional Independence of Categorization and Stereotype Activation," in *Social Cognitive and Affective Neuroscience* 12:5: 758–64.

Jarnagin, Mayam. (2017). "Zoe Washburne: Navigating the 'Verse as a Military Woman of Color," in Mary Ellen Iatropolous and Lowry A. Woodall III (eds.) *Joss Whedon and Race: Critical Essays.* Jefferson, NC: McFarland, 200–215.

Jencson, Linda Jean. (2008). "'Aiming to Misbehave': Role Modeling Political-Economic Conditions and Political Action in the *Serenity*verse," in *Slayage* 7.1.

Johnson, Gary. (2006). "The West: An Overview," in *Images: A Journal of Film and Popular Culture* 6.

Johnson, India R., Brandon M. Kopp, and Richard E. Petty. (2016). "Just Say No! (and Mean It): Meaningful Negation as a Tool to Modify Automatic Racial Attitudes," in *Group Processes and Intergroup Relations*.

Jones, Christopher R., and Russell H. Fazio. (2010). "Person Categorization and Automatic Racial Stereotyping Effects on Weapon Identification," in *Personality and Social Psychology Bulletin*. 36.8: 1073–85.

Kawakami, K., J.F. Dovidio, J. Moll, S. Hermsen, and A. Russian. (2000). "Just Say No (to Stereotyping): Effects of Training in the Negation of Stereotypic Associations on Stereotype Activation," in *Journal of Personality and Social Psychology* 78.5: 871–88.

Kennedy, Bruce. (2012). "*Firefly* 10th Anniversary: Browncoats Unite." Pangolin Pictures, Science Channel. On-line. Available HTTP: http://www.dailymotion.com/video/xvedx1 (25 July 2017).

Kilpatrick, Jacquelyn. (1999). *Celluloid Indians: Native Americans and Film*. Lincoln and London: University of Nebraska Press.

Kirkland, Ewan. (2015). "The Caucasian Persuasion of *Buffy the Vampire Slayer*," in *Slayage* 5.1.

Kreider, S. Evan. (2015). "To Live and Die in the 'Verse: A Re-Evaluation of Inara," in *Slayage* 13.2.

Le, Mike. (2012). "Frustrations of an Asian-American Whedonite," in *Racebending*. On-line. Available HTTP: http://www.racebending.com/v4/featured/frustrations-asian-ameri can-whedonite/ (25 July 2017).

Leavitt, Peter A., Rebecca Covarrubias, Yvonne A. Perez, and Stephanie A. Fryberg. (2015). "'Frozen in Time': The Impact of Native American Media Representations on Identity and Self-Understanding," in *Journal of Social Issues* 71.1: 39–53.

Lucas, Heather D., Joan Y. Chaio, and Ken A. Paller. (2011). "Why Some Faces Won't Be Remembered: Brain Potentials Illuminate Successful Versus Unsuccessful Encoding for Same-Race and Other-Race Faces," in *Frontiers in Human Neuroscience*.

Lusted, David. (2003). *The Western*. Harlow, UK: Pearson Longman.

Macrae, C. Neil, Alan B. Milne, and Galen V. Bodenhausen. (1994). "Stereotypes as Energy-Saving Devices: A Peek Inside the Cognitive Toolbox," in *Journal of Personality and Social Psychology* 66, 37–47.

Manning, Sarah Sunshine. (2016). "Manning: When Media Promotes Offensive Indian Stereotypes," in *Indian Country Today*. On-line. Available HTTP: https://indiancountrymedia network.com/news/native-news/manning-when-media-promotes-offensive-indian-stereotypes/ (25 July 2017).

McCaw, Derek. (2008). "WonderCon 2005: Finally, The Joss Whedon/*Serenity* Panel," in *Fanboy Planet*. On-line (Link no longer available).

McGrath, Ann. (2001). "Playing Colonial: Cowgirls, Cowboys, and Indians in Australia and North America," in *Journal of Colonialism and Colonial History*. 2.1.

Mitchell, Gregory, and Philip E. Tetlock. (2017). "Popularity as a Poor Proxy for Utility: The Case of Implicit Prejudice," in *Public Law and Legal Theory Research Paper Series 2017–32*. The University of Virginia School of Law.

Money, Mary Alice. (2006). "The Reavers' Origin in *Serenity*: Whedon's Mistake or Masterstroke?" Presentation at SC2 Conference on the Whedonverses. Gordon College, Barnesville, GA.

Moya, Paula M.L. (2016). *The Social Imperative: Race, Close Reading, and Contemporary Literary Criticism*. Stanford: Stanford University Press.

Narvez, Darcia. (2006). "The Neo-Kolbergian Tradition and Beyond: Schemas, Expertise and Character," in *Nebraska Symposium on Motivation* 51. Lincoln: University of Nebraska Press.

Neal, Christopher. (2008). "The Ballad of Jayne and Marching Out of Step: Music and Otherness in the *Firefly/Serenity* Saga," in Rhonda. V. Wilcox and Tanya. R. Cochrane (eds.)

Investigating Firefly *and* Serenity: *Science Fiction on the Frontier.* London: I.B. Tauris, 191–98.

Neale, Steve. (1998). "Vanishing Americans: Racial and Ethnic Issues in the Interpretation and Context of Post-War 'Pro-Indian' Westerns," in *Back in the Saddle Again: New Essays on the Western.* London: British Film Institute.

Nietzsche, Friedrich. (2002). *Beyond Good and Evil.* Rolf-Peter Horstmann (ed.). Trans. Judith Norman. Cambridge: Cambridge University Press.

Nussbaum, Emily. (2002). "Must-See Metaphysics," in *The New York Times.* On-line. Available HTTP: http://www.nytimes.com/2002/09/22/magazine/must-see-metaphysics.html?mcubz=0 (18 September 2017).

Ono, Kent A. (2000). "To Be a Vampire on *Buffy the Vampire Slayer*: Race and ('Other') Socially Marginalizing Positions on Horror TV," in Elyce Rae Helford (ed.) *Fantasy Girls: Gender in the New Universe of Science Fiction and Fantasy Television.* Lanham, MD: Rowman & Littlefield, 163–86.

Pewewardy, Cornel. (n.d.). "Why Educators Can't Ignore Indian Mascots," in *American Indian Sports Team Mascots.* On-line. Available HTTP: http://aistm.org/cornel.why.educators.htm (18 September 2017).

Plous, Scott. (2002). "The Psychology of Prejudice, Stereotyping, and Discrimination: An Overview," in *Understanding Prejudice and Discrimination.* McGraw-Hill, 3–42.

Prats, Armando Jose. (1996). "His Master's Voice(over): Revisionist Ethos and Narrative Dependence from *Broken Arrow* (1950) to *Geronimo: An American Legend* (1993)," in *ANQ* 3.3.

Rabb, J. Douglas and J. Michael Richardson. (2008). "Reavers and Redskins: Creating the Frontier Savage," in Rhonda. V. Wilcox and Tanya. R. Cochrane (eds.) *Investigating* Firefly *and* Serenity: *Science Fiction on the Frontier.* London: I.B. Tauris, 127–38.

racebending. (2012). "Joss Whedon on Asians in Firefly at San Diego Comic-Con 2012," in YouTube. On-line. Available HTTP: https://www.youtube.com/watch?v=7UcbuSN90Cs (25 July 2017).

Richards, Zoeë, and Miles Hewstone. (2001). "Subtyping and Subgrouping: Processes for the Prevention and Promotion of Stereotype Change," in *Personality and Social Psychology Review.*

Rubenstein, Lauren. (2013). "Whedon '87 Delivers 181st Commencement Address," in *News @ Wesleyan.* On-line. Available HTTP: http://newsletter.blogs.wesleyan.edu/2013/05/26/whedoncommencement/ (25 July 2017).

Salwall, Harry. (2004). "Cannibalism as a Trope in Colonial Discourse." *Proceedings of the 2004 Annual Conference.* Association of University English Teachers in Southern Africa.

Schilling, Vincent. (2017). "Snoop Dogg Headdress Pic Gets Heat on Social Media," in *Indian Country Today.* On-line. Available HTTP: https://indiancountrymedianetwork.com/culture/arts-entertainment/snoop-dogg-gets-heat-social-media-headdress-pic-knoca hoe-comment/ (25 July 2017).

Shechory, Mally, Israel Nachson, and Joseph Blicksohn. (2008). "Effects of Stereotypes and Suggestions on Memory," in *International Journal of Offender Therapy and Comparative Criminology* 54.1: 113–130.

Smith, Kyle. (2017). "The Left's 'Hamburger Problem' Is Not Going Away," in *National Review.* On-line. Available HTTP: http://www.nationalreview.com/article/449629/josh-barro-democrats-hamburger-problem-liberal-judgment-guarantees-political-failure (25 July 2017).

Smith-Casanueva, Brent M. (2017). "Race, Space, and the (De)Construction of Neocolonial Difference in *Firefly/Serenity*," in Mary Ellen Iatropolous and Lowry A. Woodall III (eds.) *Joss Whedon and Race: Critical Essays.* Jefferson, NC: McFarland, 169–84.

Sprunk, Jon. (2014). "Firefly: A Retrospective Part 8—A Look at *Serenity*," in *Black Gate: Adventures in Fantasy Literature.* On-line. Available HTTP: https://www.blackgate.com/2014/04/02/firefly-a-retrospective-part-8-a-look-at-serenity/ (25 July 2017).

Stein, Dan. (1992). "Schemas in the Cognitive and Clinical Sciences: An Integrative Construct," in *Cogprints Repository.* University of Southampton.

Stevenson, Margaret C., BreighAnna J. Baumholser, Brad L. Lytle, and Evan W. McCracken.

(2017). "Racially Diverse Juries Promote Self-Monitoring Efforts During Jury Deliberation," in *Translational Issues in Psychological Science* 3.2: 187–201.

Stewart, Brandon D., and B. Keith Payne. (2008). "Bringing Automatic Stereotyping Under Control: Implementation Intentions as Efficient Means of Thought Control," in *Personality and Social Psychology Bulletin* 34.10: 1332–45.

Thoma, Steve. (2006). "Research on the Defining Issues Test," in M. Killen and J. Smetana (eds.) *Handbook of Moral Development.* Mahweh, NJ: Lawrence Erlbaum Associates.

Thorndyke, Perry, and Barbara Hayes-Roth. (1979). "The Use of Schemata in the Acquisition and Transference of Knowledge," in *Cognitive Psychology* 11: 82–106.

Tomkins, Jane. (1992). *West of Everything: The Inner Life of Westerns.* Oxford: Oxford University Press.

Trachtenberg, Alan. (2005). *Shades of Hiawatha: Staging Indians, Making Americans, 1880–1930.* New York: Hill and Wang.

Tskhay, Konstantin O., and Nicholas O. Rule. (2015). "Emotions Facilitate the Communication of Ambiguous Group Memberships," in *Emotion* 15.6: 812–826.

Vargas, Theresa. (2016). "In Their Words: 12 Native Americans Talk About the Furor Over the Redskins Name," in *The Washington Post.* On-line. Available HTTP: https://www.washingtonpost.com/graphics/local/redskins-poll/ (25 July 2017).

Velazquez, Josef. (2006). "Dappled Things." Unpublished paper presented at the 2006 Conference on the Whedonverse.

Velazquez, Josef. (2005). "Dappled Things." Unpublished paper.

Weiten, Wayne. (2005). *Psychology: Themes and Variations.* 6th ed. Belmont, CA: Thomson Wadsworth.

West, Tess V., Adam R. Pearson, Dohn F. Dovidio, Blair T. Johnsons, and Curtis E. Phills. (2014). "Racial Attitudes and Visual Cues in Political Judgments: Support for Obama During the 2008 Presidential Elections," in *Cultural Diversity and Ethnic Minority Psychology* https://www.ncbi.nlm.nih.gov/pubmed/2509014020.4: 583–90.

Whedon, Joss. (2007). *Serenity*: Film Commentary. 20th Century FOX Home Entertainment. DVD.

_____. (2005). Serenity: *The Official Visual Companion.* London: Titan Books.

Wilcox, Rhonda V. (2008). "'I Don't Hold to That': Joss Whedon and Original Sin," in Rhonda. V. Wilcox and Tanya. R. Cochrane (eds.) *Investigating* Firefly *and* Serenity: *Science Fiction on the Frontier.* London: I.B. Tauris, 155–66.

Williams, Tamara. (2017). "NREL Amicus Brief Supports Tribes in Their First DAPL Victory," in the University of New Mexico School of Law. On-line. Available HTTP: http://lawschool.unm.edu/news/2017/06/nrel-amicus-brief.html (18 September 2017).

Wirth, Werner, and Holger Schramm. (2005). "Media and Emotions," in *Communication Research Trends* 24.3: 3–40.

Wittenberg, Eric J., J. David Petruzzi, and Michael F. Nugent. (2008). *One Continuous Fight: The Retreat from Gettysburg and the Pursuit of Lee's Army of Northern Virginia, July 4–14, 1863.* New York and California: Savis Beatie.

Wittgenstein, Ludwig. (1958). *Philosophical Investigations.* Trans. G.E.M. Anscombe. New York: Macmillan.

Wulf, Steve. (2014). "Why Use of Native American Nicknames Is an Obvious Affront," in *ESPN.* On-line. Available HTTP: http://www.espn.com/espn/otl/story/_/id/11426021/why-native-american-nicknames-stir-controversy-sports (25 July 2017).

Unspeakable Darkness
Truth, Power and the Taboo of Race

Renee St. Louis

In the preface to *Playing in the Dark: Whiteness and the Literary Imagination*, Nobel Prize winner Toni Morrison notes her abiding interest in "the way black people ignite critical moments of discovery or change or emphasis in literature not written by them" (1993: viii). In *Serenity* (Joss Whedon, 2005), a moral tension and struggle takes place within protagonist Malcolm Reynolds (Nathan Fillion), a conflict negotiated partially through oblique conversations with two black men, Shepherd Derrial Book (Ron Glass) and a nameless Alliance agent known as the Operative (Chiwetel Ejiofor). This essay aims to examine the film's complex relationships to autonomy and choice, informational privilege, authority and power as they rely upon the simultaneous visibility and disavowal of race. More precisely, it uses Toni Morrison's analysis of U.S. American literature and its reliance upon blacknesses both embodied and abstract to examine *Serenity*'s depiction of the hero's journey. The film's use of layered naming strategies, character mirroring, ontological and etiological dialogue, and references to competing depictions of the U.S. American frontier all rely upon a racialized literary imagination and encourage the audience to identify with the redeemed white male hero at the expense of other potential viewpoints. This redemption relies upon the labor, bodily mortification, and eventual destruction of two black men but also challenges some boundaries of similarly constructed dominant histories.

Serenity offers a wonderfully layered story, with elements of the U.S. Western film, dystopian science fiction using elements of steampunk and futurism, a traditional hero's tale, and several more. Each of these layers can be read, fruitfully, on their own. But, in order to unravel the complex depiction and disavowal of blackness, and of race more broadly, this essay will focus on three related but distinct knots or nexus points: the visual and story elements of post–Civil War Western as they engage with the unsettled conflicts of unification and civil war; the socio-political stakes of the central plot and its interest in autonomy, consent, and accountability as a reflection of immediate circumstances in the contemporary moment of the film; and, finally, the character depictions of Shepherd Book, Malcolm Reynolds, and the Operative as facets of an internal struggle for the future—a heroic attempt to create a functional ethical position in the absence of a coherent moral order.

Of Lost Causes and (Un)Civil Wars

> Through the simple expedient of demonizing and reifying the range of color on a palette, American Africanism makes it possible to say and not say, to inscribe and erase, to escape and engage, to act out and act on, to historicize and render timeless. It provides a way of contemplating chaos and civilization, desire and fear, and a mechanism for testing the problems and blessings of freedom.—Toni Morrison, *Playing in the Dark* [1993: 7]

Professor Morrison understands the heart of U.S. American literature as a story we tell ourselves, as a culture, about who we are. This story is an always-unfinished tale of becoming, and it relies on what she terms an American Africanism, a denotative and connotative blackness the assumptions and readings of which mark actual people and with which all must contend (1993: 4–7). As noted above, this use of color and race prove flexible, omnipresent, and inescapable; as such, it also offers an opportunity to read into the stories we tell for evidence of this structuring epistemology. Western genre films seem especially to invite this reading due to their frequent invocation of racial stereotype, broad stroke moralizing, and romantic notions of frontier heroism which act as idealized character types in the national consciousness (e.g., John Wayne).

Serenity, like *Firefly* (2002–03) before it, makes overt reference to the Hollywood West and unmistakable connections to the U.S. Civil War. The genre signifiers begin early and include costume, weaponry, and landscapes; the larger thematic concerns of lawlessness, land and property rights, and frontier hardship; and archetypal characters such as the warm-hearted prostitute, the hard-scrabble homesteader, and the local lawman. As Linda Jean Jencson notes in her insightful analysis of the political and economic world of *Serenity* and its parent show, "the space ship Serenity's crew of hungry outlaws travels the black reaches of space, landing on planets of exploited workers, forgotten colonists, trafficked slaves, and endangered prostitutes" (2008). This world of deep space is also recognizably the opening North American frontier, both literally (exteriors were shot in Southern California) and thematically.[1]

The genre brings with it a host of associations, particularly what Morrison terms "contemplating chaos and civilization" and the "problems and blessings of freedom." For *Serenity*, this is immediately apparent in the racial underpinnings of the colonial expansion narrative as it relates to the Reavers. In the context of the television show, the Reavers are constructed as "Hollywood Indians," conforming to a number of stereotypical elements of depiction such as war paint, raiding parties, and "savagery" typified by attack of innocents, mutilation of hostages, and rumors of cannibalism. That a Hollywood Western would also include some Hollywood Indians does not surprise; it is expected. Whedon himself remarks in the DVD commentary when the Reaver ships appear, "Indians ride over the hill and surprise the cavalry" (2005). In her influential and often-cited analysis of this depiction, Agnes B. Curry notes that "the Hollywood Western is a chapter in the long project of constructing U.S. identity as premised on the abjection and disappearance of the native," going on to note that the public invisibility of native peoples persists in contemporary life for an insidious reason: it is a crucial element of the culture's moral awareness (2008). As she states, "if Indians have in fact vanished, through death or assimilation, then the moral complexity of Europeans possessing the territory can be rendered a historical problem rather than an ongoing challenge" (2008). The physical and political presence of an oppressed native population undermines the claims of righteousness that underpin our preferred self-understanding.

Critics disagree as to whether the "Hollywood Indian" depiction of the Reavers contributes to racist depiction, challenges it, or instead functions as some uncomfortable combination. The film makes this more difficult to unpack by changing the story established in *Firefly* somewhat, explaining the creation of the Reavers as a side effect of the Alliance drugging colonists on Miranda. Initially, the film wrestles with the idea that "Reaver" is not an ethnic or political designation, but a manifestation of mental illness created by the frontier. Jayne (Adam Baldwin) and Kaylee (Jewel Staite) discuss the origins of the Reavers early in the film, with Kaylee relaying what Shepherd Book has suggested: "they was men that reached the edge of space, saw a vasty nothingness, and just went bibbledy over it." Interestingly, it is Jayne who notes that the "edge" of space is an arbitrary and false demarcation, saying "I been to the edge. Just looks like … more space."[2] Rabb and Richardson examine the ways in which the film's story of the Reavers' origins shifts the meanings away from a straightforwardly racist depiction, suggesting that "[i]f Whedon's Reavers are the Savage Redskins, then the origin of the Reavers is Whedon's metaphor for the creation of the savage in the imaginations of European explorers" (2008: 135).

Others seem inclined to sidestep entirely reading the racial implications of this depiction, as when Froese and Buzzard assert that because the Reavers aren't explicitly racialized, and are later revealed to have been created by Alliance technology, they should be understood more as an economic class than as racially marked (2015), a reading which seems to forget that the category of race is to a large extent an artifact of a legal system which naturalizes and legitimates its own terms of exclusion. The Reavers were created by the Alliance, but that doesn't undo their racialization; after all, the "Indians" aren't a natural grouping either but a racial category created by government, in a series of legal proceedings aimed at denying a vast and widely variable group of people rights.[3] The racialized depiction of the Reavers points to the difficulty of untangling racial constructions, government legal machinations, and depiction—a critical task further complicated by the film's explicit connections to the U.S. Civil War and thematic concerns with autonomy, information, and consent.

Serenity develops along a path distinct to cinema and following many tropes of a familiar sub-genre: that of the former Confederate who seeks freedom from the manipulations of the Reconstruction government or to perpetuate an experience of or belief in the ideals of the antebellum South. This puts the film in a lineage that includes *The Searchers* and *The Outlaw Josey Wales* as well as the oft-noted connection to *Stagecoach* (see, for instance, Wilcox and Cochran 2008: 5 and Money 2008: 116–7). This matters for a few reasons. The space Western as a genre mash-up takes on new and problematic resonances when that hybridity comes with a core of violent political conflict organized around multiple competing and mutually exclusive struggles for autonomy.

And, lest we should forget, the film (like the show) reminds the viewer that this is specifically the U.S. Civil War being signified. The battle in which Mal and Zoe (Gina Torres) lose most of their forces, face defeat and then realize that they are being left behind, the Battle of Serenity Valley, echoes through the series and the film. The signature battle of their war service and its ultimately lost cause contributes its name to the television show's feature-length intended pilot, the ship itself, and the film. And this battle reaches out to actual history in its connections to the Battle of Shenandoah Valley in the U.S. Civil War. As the National Parks Service (n.d.) notes, the Shenandoah Valley campaign came relatively late in the war, and represented the signature loss for the Confederacy, the one that turned the tide definitively. The out-numbered Confederates faced multiple losses, were divided, began to desert, retreated steadily and ultimately abandoned some of their own soldiers on the field as the retreat grew more desperate and the losses more overwhelming. While the same could be said of a few campaigns, the connections are not only broadly descriptive nor located in the similar names; to understand the depth of the connections here, note that the Confederate officer in charge was Lieutenant General Jubal Early, the name of the bounty hunter in the episode "Objects in Space" (13 December 2002). That this character has also been considered a forerunner of the film's antagonist The Operative only deepens this link (see Candra K. Gill 2017 and Wilcox 2008: 158).

The cognitive dissonance and discomfort of embracing the Browncoats as a force for some moral good should not be ignored; attempting to construct the former confederacy as positive all but demands that we unpack the racial implications of this move but the film steadfastly refuses to engage with this dimension of the story. As Samira Nadkarni succinctly states, "the thematic use of the American Civil War is one that focuses on the right to self-governance and secession, and seemingly strips it of the popular association with the issue of slavery, thereby encouraging the viewer to invest in the Independents' evocation of the Confederate army, its struggle and eventual loss" (2015). The decision not to address race slavery fits into a problematic trend Morrison spotted more than twenty years earlier. In discussing why there is not more, and more substantial, critical writing on race in U.S. American culture, she notes that in addition to evasion and silence, there is a problem of what we might call cultural manners:

> It is further complicated by the fact that the habit of ignoring race is understood to be a graceful, even generous, liberal gesture. To notice is to recognize an already discredited difference. To enforce its invisibility through silence is to allow the black body a shadowless participation in the dominant cultural body. According to this logic, every well bred instinct argues *against noticing* and forecloses adult discourse [Emphasis in original] [1993: 9–10].

Whedon's liberal sensibilities, both political and cultural, are well established. That he might fall into the trap of a broadly understood liberal gesture which unintentionally erases an important dimension of discussion is entirely possible, and not even necessarily a critique of his work so much as a note about the difficulties of the conversation.[4] That does not, however, negate the reality that the three black characters in the film—Book, Zoe, and the Operative—enjoy exactly what Morrison describes—a "shadowless" or insubstantial existence. Inside the story, Book lives as a "man with a mysterious past" on the little-inhabited moon of a frontier planet; Zoe lives as an outlaw on a falling-apart brigand ship; the Operative lives close to the center of the dominant culture, but does so as an entity without name, title, or apparent social world of his own. Whedon may wish to write a post-racial story, but there is no way to avoid the racialized past or present; at minimum, they haunt the story.

The unresolved tension created by the racial underpinnings of the story, while rarely addressed academically, features heavily in more audience-centered conversations. The blog *Compromise and Conceit* notes, "Joss Whedon is really latching onto a confederate lost cause symbolism in his story, and risking importing a very racist and particular political subtext to his movies [sic]." The author goes on to note elsewhere that through craft, casting and performances, Whedon clearly tries to "neutralize the toxic politics of modern Confederate Lost Cause-ism" but, in threaded conversation with their readers, addresses the missing element of race slavery, noting that "[b]y leaving out a clear story about what was going on before the war, but drawing on the confederate imagery, Whedon leaves us with the uncertain possibility that the analogy can be drawn all the way, and opens the possibility that the rebels wanted to own slaves" (faustusnotes 2011). It bears note that the debate goes on to discuss the legal definitions of personhood, rights, and citizenship as central to both the world of *Serenity* and to understanding the U.S. Civil War. Elsewhere, John Seavey notes that "the Browncoats are basically the Greybacks," connecting Mal and his crew to the Confederate veterans who migrated westward before noting that this "haunts" him specifically because Whedon does not specify why the war started, and the notion that the Alliance "meddled" replicates "the basic attitude of most slaveowners as well," leaving him wondering about Captain Mal: "What did he stand for? What made the Alliance say, 'No. This cannot be tolerated, not in a civilized culture?'" (Seavey 2010).

Others take this discomfort with the historical revisionism to its furthest reach by proclaiming that, while the show and film attempt to strip racism from its story of the post-Civil War frontier, it cannot be parsed separately, leaving them to conclude that the story's "bedrock is racist. *Firefly* is racist from its terraformed surface all the way down to its molten core" (lierdumoa 2016). I would not go nearly so far, but would agree with the author that the story does aim to "geekwash the confederacy," sweeping away the complex and uncomfortable racial dimensions of U.S. history for the purposes of a celebratory fantasy constructed as post-racial—a construct which is itself an implicitly white fantasy.

While it is fair to examine the film's engagement with ideas of freedom, resource control, and autonomy as worthy in their own right, doing so cannot come at the expense of recognizing race as a dimension. Doing so mimics the depiction of "states' rights" as the driving force behind the U.S. Civil War in discourses that aim to ignore the importance of race slavery to that debate. Marking a black man with the name of a Confederate general (in the series) has meaning, and cannot be read as mere play; the legacy of race slavery continues to inflect the present and requiring black actors to carry that weight also has meaning.[5] To suggest that the future *Serenity* represents functions without our contemporary understanding of race posits a "post-racial" future predicated upon erasure of an explicitly racialized past and present; that the film continually evokes that past and present without ever acknowledging the racial categories or struggles of those moments points to the film's anxiety about race. As Morrison notes, "[t]he world does not becomes raceless or will not become unracialized by assertion. The act of enforcing racelessness in literary discourse is itself a racial act" (1993: 46). Putting the struggles of the present in the form of a conflict with a black man demands that we look closer, particularly because race—and blackness in particular—also figure so heavily in the film's science-fiction lineage.

American science fiction films may not depend upon black men as monstrous threats (largely to white women) as overtly as fictions of the past, but as Adilifu Nama reminds us, such films still create "a representational space for repressed racial anxieties associated with black physicality" and black corporeality on screen acts as "a reminder of the way the black body is imagined and the real sociopolitical struggles associated with it" (2008: 95). These anxieties inflect the film, as well as the contemporary world in which it was created.

Miranda: Information Control, Accountability, Rights and Consent

> Autonomy is freedom and translates into the much championed and revered "individualism"; newness translates into "innocence"; distinctiveness becomes difference and the erection of strategies for maintaining it; authority and absolute power become a romantic, conquering "heroism," virility, and the problematics of wielding absolute power over the lives of others. All the rest are made possible by this last, it would seem—absolute power called forth and played against and within a natural and mental landscape conceived of as a "raw, half-savage world."—Toni Morrison [1993: 44–5]

If both the characters' pasts and the film's backstory are set against the historical backdrop of a civil war, the story's present conflict centers around a struggle for autonomy and self-determination set against a background of information control. From the first frames of the film, information and its containment or circulation drives the action. As frequently noted, the opening narration serves as both a contextual voice-over and as diegetic content of River's dream; both layers give a blandly whitewashed history of the Alliance consolidation as introduction to the story-world. More tellingly, when River (Summer Glau) contests this sanitized history by pointing out the Alliance's intervention upon people and curtailment of their autonomy, saying as a representative of the core planets that "we meddle" and "people don't like to be meddled with," she is immediately disciplined. Within the dream or hallucination, the teacher drives a stylus into her forehead, a forceful reminder that the state has won the war and controls the narrative (Sutherland and Swan, 2008: 92–3). On screen, the jarring moment of state violence against a child immediately cuts to a parallel image of an adolescent River strapped into a chair and suffering as she is acted upon by the technicians of the state; they perform brain surgery upon her as a means of remaking her into a weapon for Alliance use.

The story told in her childhood class acts on her mind, a memory or thought driven to the surface while the state operates on her brain directly; control of the story is equated with control of bodies even when those two forces do not act simultaneously or entirely in concert. River is also dually constructed in this moment: both as a person victimized by the consolidation of state power despite her position of relative privilege as a daughter of the core planets, and as an object of political struggle. She is, as Mal suggests shortly thereafter, both a girl and a weapon. The struggle to define, possess and wield the information power, which River both contains and represents, animates the rest of the film. The Operative would reclaim her as a tool of the state or, failing that, see her destroyed; Captain Reynolds would use her precognitive abilities to facilitate his labors or, failing that, use what she knows to resist and damage the state. What she knows but cannot fully understand or contain, the secret of Miranda, is both the plot's central story and the backdrop for a complicated engagement with the larger world inhabited by the film's audience.

That the world of *Serenity* invites some uncomfortable connections to the larger, real world outside of the film appears inescapable but resists a singular understanding. It would be impossible to consider them all here, but several deserve at least brief mention as they inform this reading. Lorna Jowett examines the show and film's uses of "retrofuturism"—a variant of science fiction combining elements of steampunk anachronism and cyberpunk concerns with technologies as undermining embodied humanity and notes the productive nature of the instability produced by this hybridity (2008: 101–2). Jeffrey Bussolini examines the story's engagement with geopolitical "blowback" or unintended consequences of colonial and neocolonial actions, explicitly linking them to neocolonial economic practices promulgated by the United States (2008: 144–9). Joceyln Sakal Froese and Laura Buzzard examine the ways in which the Alliance's terraforming of planets for human habitation constitutes a "biopower" which locates so much power over survival in the hands of the state that existence outside of it cannot be imagined (2015). Samira Nadkarni brilliantly extends this observation of the geopolitical stakes beyond the frame of the story and of the United States by observing that the viewer's life more closely resembles the Alliance/Core than the crew with whom we are encouraged to identify, implicitly asking us to reckon with our own position as complicit with the state even while we imagine ourselves as resistant to it (2015).

One of the most direct and troubling connections to the larger world at the moment of the film's release appears in Linda Jean Jencson's analysis connecting the economic conditions of *Serenity*'s depiction of a global economy, which serves the core while exploiting the resources of the periphery, to her own consumption of the televised human horrors in the wake of Hurricane Katrina (2008). In her moment of turning off the DVD to watch the news, the connection between state biopower—here in the form of levees which allow habitation of low-lying areas; disaster relief provided by agencies of government; and, most terribly, in the freedom of the state to select which of the lives threatened by the hurricane would be prioritized and which would be treated as expendable—and an escapist science fiction story threatens to escape both the realm of metaphor and the story's frame.

Miranda, both the planetary space and the secret of its state-created horror, provides arguably the greatest point of slippage between the level of story and that of factual reality. While previous scholars have focused, with some justification, on the Shakespearean allusion implied by the name Miranda (for example, Wilcox 2008: 161–2), little attention has been paid to another allusion which offers a less pleasing and exculpatory interpretation: the Supreme Court case of Miranda vs. Arizona. Perhaps best known today as the impetus behind the recitation of what are commonly called "Miranda Rights,"[6] the 1965 case resulted from a 1963 arrest of Ernesto Miranda. After two hours of interrogation, police officers obtained a signed confession; in court, his defense argued that, because he had not been informed of his rights to an attorney or to refuse to answer questions, the confession was inadmissible evidence. Miranda was convicted, and this conviction was upheld by the state supreme court. Ultimately, a 5:4 SCOTUS opinion issued in 1966 held that the Fifth Amendment right to avoid self-incrimination extends to police interrogation and that failure to inform a person of their rights could be seen to create state coercion that invalidates any evidence collected under such circumstances (Chicago-Kent College of Law at Illinois Tech, n.d.).[7] The case centers on issues of state coercion, individual rights, advocacy, and information control; that this name animates a central conflict centered on these same elements should not go unexamined.

River's first response to being subliminally manipulated by the Alliance is to whisper "Miranda" before enacting violence on all parties present in the Maidenhead bar. The vulnerable teenage girl utters the hint of knowledge she contains but does not want; the land she mentions both generates and conceals that which is unspeakable—the origin story of the Reavers. Escaped prisoner and victim of state coercion River makes oblique reference to the state-sponsored violence against unknown, disavowed others. The struggle over the girl is transformed by this moment into a contest for control of the information she contains. All of this happens in the Maidenhead, a direct if seemingly inexplicable reference to a hymen and therefore also to her status as an exemplary symbol of innocence. The events we observe are also watched by the state that would possess her and its inescapable, panoptical technologies (as shown in Mr. Universe's accessing of the security footage). The knowledge, peril, complicity, and struggle for control packed into this brief scene overwhelm a viewer with more than just the visceral enjoyment of Glau's athleticism.

This scene marks the weaponization of knowledge on multiple levels and in multiple ways simultaneously: River is a weapon made of information, both as a fighting machine programmed by the state and as the possessor of information crippling to her own well-being and detrimental to the authoritarian state. The film revisits and entrenches the potentially lethal power of information through such elements as the false signals of the nav-sats and pulse beacon used to throw the Operative off the trail of Serenity; the liminal rhetorical and physical space of Mr. Universe, who sees all and is destroyed for it even after he betrays Serenity's crew in an effort to retain his position of relative freedom; the Operative's use of the ship's flight history and crew's known associates to murder any potential allies; and, of course, the secret history of Miranda itself and its role in creating ongoing violence and instability for the frontier planets.

The struggle over Miranda culminates, of course, in direct confrontation with both the Operative and the ideological framework he represents and—until the final reel—advocates. The millions killed by the state's efforts to create peace without informing or seeking the cooperation of the public pose one portion of the horror; the Reavers created as blowback from that effort represent another. Just what the state's message is never quite coheres, though it is repeatedly referenced. While no singular message of state can be pointed to, by way of reading into this gap, it is worth considering that the drug responsible for both the genocide and the creation of the revenant tribe, Pax, carries complex potential readings. Bussolini notes the reference to pharmaceutical interventions like Paxil (2008: 144–6). I would add to his formulation the recognition that psychopharmaceuticals complicate questions of choice and consent by fundamentally altering the cognitive processes of those exposed to them; even if the colonists had survived, they would have been in an altered state of consciousness. Additionally, "Pax" not only references the Latin for "peace" but also carries two other important historical meanings that inflect the film. First, it references a ritual kissing of an object depicting the crucifixion, a form of genuflection to received knowledge delivered by a coercive authority. More subtextually, it sounds like "pacts"—the treaties between sovereign tribes and the growing U.S. government which commonly entrenched exploitative relations, refused rights, and even still were frequently violated or entirely ignored when the interests of the expanding state and retreating frontier came into conflict.

These layers encoded in the name draw back into the frame what has been steadily eroded: the lives lost, responsibility for the living conditions and destroyed mental health of the colonists-made-Reavers who are still alive, and the reality that exposure of the state's unintentional genocide does nothing at all to ameliorate it for the victims or their extended kinship networks. The survivors of the original genocide remain alive, coherent and cooperative enough to organize raiding parties, fly spaceships, and scavenge. They endure the hardest of frontier existences, written entirely out of the human story. If thirty million lived on Miranda, then approximately thirty thousand Reavers were made; despite their continual slaughter at the hands of Alliance, rebels, and colonists there are enough remaining to terrorize the colonies. How will they be dealt with? Will they be destroyed? Left alone? What, if anything, can be done to write them back into the human story?

In order to believe Mal's claim that exposing the genesis of Miranda will create a "world without sin," we must accept that this sinless world does nothing to capture or contain the Reavers, much less to treat or redeem them. Reynolds ramps up to a final stand with the claim that "somebody has to speak for these people" to prevent the Alliance's further efforts to intervene in human nature, "[m]aybe on another world, maybe on this very ground swept clean." Here, the Reavers act as the body marked by darkness, placing them in a position Morrison suggests acts as "the means of thinking about body, mind, chaos, kindness, and love; provid[ing] the occasion for exercises in the absence of restraint, the presence of restraint, the contemplation of freedom and of aggression; permit[ing] opportunities for the exploration of ethics and morality, for meeting the obligations of the social contract, for bearing the cross of religion and following out the ramifications of power" (1993: 47–8). One of the consequences of this, she notes, is a master narrative that speaks *of* people so marked, and speaks *for* them (1993: 50). So, Mal and the crew of Serenity speak for the Reavers, but nobody, it would seem, will ever speak to them. And, in order to speak for them, it is necessary not only to erase their agency and ignore their ongoing victimization but also to destroy and replace the two interlocutors who might disrupt the new story: Shepherd Book and the Operative.

The Word, the Deed and the Man
Among Men

> Romance, an exploration of anxiety imported from the
> shadows of European culture, made possible the sometimes

> safe and other times risky embrace of quite specific, under-
> standably human, fears: Americans' fear of being outcast,
> of failing, of powerlessness; their fear of boundarylessness,
> of Nature unbridled and crouched for attack; their fear of
> loneliness, of aggression both external and internal. In short,
> the terror of human freedom—the thing they coveted most
> of all.—Toni Morrison [1993: 36–7]

One of the consequences of the appropriation of Civil War imagery and its unusual marriage to retrofuturist technological manipulation is that it becomes difficult to identify the proper ethical conduct of a person in this world. The brigand is the hero, the virgin girl is a psychotic assassin, the mercenary is the first to sign up for an unpaid suicide mission, and the kindly preacher may have been a government agent: *Serenity* creates a world where roles fail to predict behaviors we would expect, engaging in world-building by complicating or subverting expectations. Additionally, this reflects a kind of behavioral liminality, one also attributable to space itself. The usually sunny Kaylee remarks early in the film "It can get awful lonely in the black. Like to get addlepated ourselves, we stay on this boat much longer," suggesting that the "vasty nothingness" of space has a deleterious effect on humanity. Out in the black, everything is up for grabs, even one's own character and moral compass. From the first strains of "The Ballad of Serenity" (Whedon 2002), we are reminded that this matters. The song mourns a loss but also stubbornly clings to "the black" and "the sky" inter-changeably as the last refuge. That blackness is coded as death but also as a stubborn claim to rights for one who will not surrender. It also reveals, in the unrecorded lyrics, that "the black" is active—it sings and reaches. In this, it is personified and imbued with the power to transform. Mal may have "lost [his] soul" (Whedon, 2002) but because he can "still hear" and "still see" he can also still be redeemed, or at least changed. It is this change, depicted as a revitalized heroism in Malcolm Reynolds, which is the final concern of this essay.

The conflict over River and Miranda animates Reynolds and supplies him with a mission, though it seems he takes some time to realize it. After deciding to eject her and her brother from the crew for insubordination on Simon's (Sean Maher) part, Mal witnesses her triggering and rapid dispatch of a bar full of hard cases. When Simon gives an emergency command to render her unconscious, Mal takes her and her brother back on board before fleeing, a seemingly nonsensical decision that even he does not profess to understand. His moral uncertainty appears repeatedly, from his shooting of a Reaver captive and its contextual questioning by Zoe to his assertion that despite having been a volunteer Independent he no longer identifies with that label: "We're all just folk now." It seems that he actively resists attempts to yoke him to a fixed belief system other than simple pragmatism, the "powerful urge to eat sometime this month." He insists he is a man without ideology. Yet, there remain hints of a more ethically code-bound and morally certain Reynolds. Perhaps the strongest of these hints is his enduring relationship with Shepherd Derrial Book.

Book's backstory remains a mystery to the crew, and to the original audience of the film.[8] He offers friendship even after leaving the crew and moving to Haven. Morally, his character is aligned with what Kowalski calls "a philosophical interpretive theory of religion known as religious non-realism" (2015), an understanding that the text of religion is less important than the effect that faith can have on the person who holds it. Within the series, this is supported by his conversation with River in which she asserts that his "Bible is broken" because it contains contradictions and illogical ideas. After a bit of banter, he explains, "It's not about making sense. It's about believing in something. And letting that belief be real enough to change your life. It's about faith. You don't fix faith. It fixes you" ("Jaynestown" [18 October 2002]).

This flexible but persistent model of faith as an end itself contrasts with the Operative's zealotry and Malcolm's apparent fall away from a more rigidly observant faith. Kowalski's analysis of Book uses K. Dale Koontz's work on faith in Whedon's work to suggest that doubt—of himself, of his faith's best application, of the right thing to do—actually works to make Book a more reliable and moral person (2015). His faith is about more than rules, about more than God, at least in a literal sense. Book challenges Malcolm to find his own faith by saying, "When I talk about belief, why do you always assume I'm talking about God?" The Book, as it were, is a way to get there. But it is not the only one. Within *Serenity*, Book's emphasis on belief without necessary religious trappings is depicted as a moral benefit to Mal and establishes him, ultimately, as the Shepherd who led Malcolm Reynolds back to the light.

This moral victory comes at great cost, however, and that peril is signaled during Book's first scene in the film. As they converse before the fire on Haven, Malcolm and Book share a moment of mutual affection and ongoing discussion. Reynolds notes Book's mysterious past and questions the sources of his Alliance knowledge, and they share a smile when Reynolds presses for information and Book refuses it; they share an understanding of what it is to be a man with a past better forgotten. In both this thematic content and the visual style, the scene mimics *Unforgiven* (Clint Eastwood, 1992) and in doing so foreshadows much of the developing internal conflict for Reynolds. Specifically, this scene echoes the discussion of a shared past and troubled present between Bill Munny (Eastwood) and Ned Logan (Morgan Freeman). Much like in Eastwood's film, two old friends come together somewhat reluctantly and facing great peril; they discuss their past and plans before the fire in compositions saturated in visual darkness from which the fire-lit men emanate. Soon after, Logan dies. As Patrick McGee analyzes this scene, "Ned will never be forgiven for the history he represents and for desiring beyond the dominant social system…" (2007: 198). In this, he and Book are aligned: Haven is a moon off a far-flung planet, a place of relative freedom and distance from both the Alliance and the loneliness of transience. He chooses a Haven and, like Logan, ultimately dies for it—and for having lost his taste for a world of killing. Like Munny, Reynolds comes to embrace "the world of the unforgiven, with the full realization that he can never repair the damage he has done or find forgiveness" (Ibid). While Eastwood places the two men across from each other, over the fire, Whedon positions his actors back-to-camera, facing the fire. They do not invite our scrutiny, but they stand together against the dark, facing the available light.

When next we see Book, he is dying. Having been the preferred place of refuge for Serenity's crew, Haven has been destroyed. When the ship's hull opens, the light is stark, the frame fleetingly whited out. The day is bright, unforgiving.[9] This brightness is immediately undercut by the smoking ruins, and Kaylee's discovery of a small boy's dead body. Mal locates the dying Book and they share their final exchange, a combination of banter about Book not taking orders from Mal and a dying exhortation from Book that Mal should believe in something, anything, suggesting that belief itself will ennoble Mal meaningfully enough that Book is willing to spend his dying breaths on the attempt. He also notes that he "killed the ship that killed us. Not very Christian," suggesting he sees this final act as being at odds with the morality of his religious order. When Mal tells him that he did the right thing, perhaps offering him a kind of absolution, Book responds "Coming from you, that means almost nothing," but he smiles. Forgiveness and redemption may not be easily found, but Book leads from his affections and the film valorizes him for doing so.

The Operative initially seems more an inhabitant of a science fiction world, a seemingly unstoppable and ruthlessly violent emissary of the dystopian state. Highly regimented and orderly, his crisp recitation of a chillingly emotionless pre-murder speech in the character's introductory scene exposes what Géraldine Crahay examines as the rigid identity of a person "strictly defined by the authority, the law, and the code that they serve" whose "strict framework gives them little or even no room to develop" (2017). While her concerns are tied to the development of masculinity, it fits in a larger sense as well: the Operative is reduced from human status to a function of the authoritarian order. If Book was the living embodiment of the non-literal religious faith symbolized by scripture and associated with the past, the Operative is state-sanctioned violence made flesh and projected into the future. That this position is a sacrifice of his own personhood and rights contributes to a reading of the Operative's assertion that he is a monster unfit to live in the better world he acts to help create. He immediately recognizes his connection to Mal as both of them are unfit to live in the new world coming into being: Malcolm because of his unwillingness to "see reason" or conform to the state despite repeated (if unreliable) invitation to do so, the Operative because his actions—which are his only definition beyond an abiding faith in the state—mark him as unfit. He commits the atrocities that allow others to retain their innocence. His connection to Mal also calls back to Book's warning that an Operative is someone who "believes hard" and Inara's depiction of the Operative as both "methodical and devout." In his steadfast refusal to comply with the state and certainty that its flaws outweigh its benefits, Mal is in fact as devout as the Operative is in his belief that the state offers a utopian possibility. The contest between them will be settled on the ground of methods.

The contrast between the person transformed by faith and the zealot blinded to all but their belief is not an easy one to draw, though it is essential to distinguishing Malcolm Reynolds as heroic and victorious in his confrontations with the Operative. This is complicated by the reality that the Alliance, and the effort to build a better world to which the Operative has sacrificed his identity and moral impetus, cannot be seen as always and only negative. As Crahay notes, the moral ambivalence of the Alliance and the Operative's devotion to its causes and rules demands that he not be read as a simple villain (2017). That there is an internal code, some variant of battle honor, is signaled when he willingly accepts Malcolm's point that Reynolds would never kill children in the service of a mission and responds with only, "I do." He follows this with a poetic line delivered as if it will be familiar to both: "If your quarry goes to ground, leave him no ground to go to." While the translation is not exact (and, given the show's history of questionable Chinese translations, we would expect no different), this mimics Sun Tzu's *Art of War* in Chapter 6, on positions weak and strong (1910, 2017). In this chapter, the war philosopher suggests that attacking undefended places is tactically necessary, and that position determines choice—not some external factor. In war, all is possible and much is necessary; desire is forfeit.

By accepting this designation for himself, the Operative also accepts that he will not be fit for the world he would create, a designation he shares with Reynolds. Thus both the Captain and the Operative also reflect a familiar figure from Westerns, men who "go on despite their self-doubts or the doubts of others around them, and who often leave society, die, or simply fall apart, in the process of redeeming society"[10] (McGee, 2007: 110). While Book's advice and death spur Mal to action, they do so in the form of the extended battle with another soldier; while he may not share the Operative's single-minded and therefore dangerous belief, Mal does share his fitness to purpose and potential for ruthlessness in seeing a mission to completion. In this sense, the Operative reawakens the battlefield Reynolds much as Book reawakened the man of faith.

The final act's heroic, Romantic redemption of Malcolm Reynolds relies upon both of these elements, fusing them into what Amanda Williamson names as a jeremiad. "Originally a religious text, the jeremiad has evolved to act primarily as a vehicle of criticism, particularly socially or politically. Mal acts as a Jeremiah: one who preaches of the moral bankruptcy in a community and traces its cause to specific societal ills" (2016). The "world without sin" that Reynolds works towards is not a religious one, though there are hints that it contains a moral order. He acts to enter into public knowledge the story of Miranda, suggesting information restores choice and allows change. Viewers get few hints of what these choices will mean for the future, other than the destruction of the Operative. Unlike Book, the Operative does not die in order to inspire Mal's jeremiad; it is his actions, not his words, that inspire. Now having had his zealous faith destroyed by revelation of its corrupt basis, the Operative loses all identity. Importantly, this moment is marked as one of freedom as well as loss; he tells Mal that he is "no longer their man" in reference to his break with the Alliance. To the degree that he was their nameless slave, he is free; on the level of his faith and hopes of creating identity and community, it is not at all clear that he even yet seeks them.

Reynolds' actions have more personal than societal resonance in the film; we are left to imagine what might come of this recent revelation with regards to the political struggles of the 'verse, but we are comforted that Mal chooses not to kill the Operative. Yet the ending reads as resolution, and reaches a new kind of serenity. In this, it enacts what Williamson calls "a personal jeremiad, as opposed to one focusing on the community." Reynolds regains his moral center in order to make a claim to a personal belief that hints he may yet find satisfaction and redemption of his earlier, lost cause. Nobody can take the sky from Malcolm Reynolds, but there is reason to hope that he may be coming back after all. Shepherd Derrial Book and the Operative, the two men who most directly shaped his thinking and spurred his actions, have no hope of doing the same.

NOTES

1. Even the brief note above signals multiple of Morrison's concerns: the literal black of space, the depredations of colonial projects, slavery, and the sexualized peril of (usually white) women all figure heavily in the structuring fictions of the U.S. literary imagination.

2. Discussing *Firefly* and *Serenity*, Daoine S. Bachran notes that the other side of the frontier into which (white) settlers moved was often Mexico, and that Mexico and its inhabitants occupy an important and complex role despite being frequently absent from the stories (2017). For a fascinating analysis of Jayne as the hidden Mexican of the narrative, see Bachran's "Mexicans in Space?: Joss Whedon's *Firefly*, Reavers and the Man They Call Jayne."

3. For more on this, see Ian F. Haney Lopez's *White by Law: The Legal Construction of Race*, especially pages 40–42 and 121–8.

4. For instance, despite personally avowed and intentionally constructed feminism in

his signature show *Buffy the Vampire Slayer*, Whedon and staff's writing decisions still leave behind some problematic traces of anti-feminism and unintentionally craft some distinct limitations into their version of female empowerment (See St. Louis and Riggs 2010).

5. While it is beyond the scope of this essay, Mayan Jarnagin offers a nuanced and helpful reading of Zoe as a character who must navigate the related but distinct tropes of black womanhood in "Zoe Washburne: Navigating the 'Verse as a Military Woman of Color" (2017).

6. Briefly summarized, these rights include the constitutional provisions for due process, adequate legal counsel, and the right to avoid self-incrimination.

7. Fruitful work remains to be done in examining the racial underpinnings of the case, at the peak of the Civil Rights era, in connection with this link. While it is beyond the scope of this essay to develop properly, I would simply note that Miranda, a Hispanic man, was retried by the state after SCOTUS set aside his conviction. He was sentenced to 20 to 30 years based on testimony from his estranged common-law wife, achieving parole in 1972. Less than four years after his eventual parole, he was stabbed during a fight in a Phoenix bar, dying at 35 years old in 1976. As it happened, Miranda remained spoken *for* more than speaking: while the man himself sometimes sold autographed "Miranda Rights" cards, he did not have audience or opportunity to tell his own story.

8. While there is a comic book detailing his backstory, which is treated as canon, for the purposes of this essay, Book's only story is that of the film and series.

9. This whiteness acts as a foil to the persistent dark, but also recalls another of Morrison's observations: "Because they appear almost always in conjunction with representations of black or Africanist people who are dead, impotent, or under complete control, these images of blinding whiteness seem to function both as antidote for and meditation on the shadow that is companion to this whiteness—a dark and abiding presence that moves the hearts and texts of American literature with fear and longing" (1993: 33).

10. It is interesting to note that McGee's analysis of this type also introduces the book's only extensive consideration of black men in Western film. On the very page cited above, the author notes the frequency with which this type in particular has been played by black actors, particularly in the 1990s.

Works Cited

Bussolini, Jeffrey. "A Geopolitical Interpretation of *Serenity*," in Rhonda V. Wilcox and Tanya R. Cochran (eds.) *Investigating* Firefly *and* Serenity: *Science Fiction on the Frontier*. London: I.B. Tauris, 139–152.

Chicago-Kent College of Law at Illinois Tech. "Miranda v. Arizona," in *Oyez*. Online. Available HTTP: https://www.oyez.org/cases/1965/759 (June 5, 2017).

Crahay, Géraldine. (2017). "*Serenity*'s Operative and *Les Misérables*'s Inspector Javert: The Masculinity of Scrupulous Civil Servants," in *Slayage* 15.1.

Curry, Agnes B. (2008). "'We Don't Say 'Indian'": On the Paradoxical Construction of the Reavers," in *Slayage* 7.1.

Faustusnotes. (2011). "*Firefly*, *Serenity* and Confederate Politics," in *Compromise and Conceit*. Online. Available HTTP: https://faustusnotes.wordpress.com/2011/01/16/firefly-serenity-and-confederate-politics/ (01 May 2017).

Froese, Jocelyn Sakal, and Laura Buzzard. (2015). "'I Mean for Us to Live. The Alliance Won't Have That': New Frontierism and Biopower in *Firefly/Serenity*," in *Slayage* 13.2.

Gill, Candra K. (2017). "On Soldiers and Sages: Problematizing the Roles of Black Men in the Whedonverses," in Mary Ellen Iatropoulis and Lowery A. Woodall III (eds.) *Joss Whedon and Race: Critical Essays* (Kindle Edition). Jefferson, NC: McFarland.

Jarnagin, Mayan. "Zoe Washburne: Navigating the 'Verse as a Military Woman of Color," in Mary Ellen Iatropoulis and Lowery A. Woodall III (eds.) *Joss Whedon and Race: Critical Essays* (Kindle Edition). Jefferson, NC: McFarland.

Jencson, Linda Jean. (2008). "'Aiming to Misbehave': Role Modeling Political-Economic Conditions and Political Action in the *Serenity*verse," in *Slayage* 7.1.

Jowett, Lorna. (2008) "Back to the Future: Retrofuturism, Cyberpunk, and Humanity in

Firefly and *Serenity*," in Rhonda V. Wilcox and Tanya R. Cochran (eds.) *Investigating* Firefly *and* Serenity: *Science Fiction on the Frontier*. London: I.B. Tauris, 101–113.

Kowalski, Dean A. (2015). "'Letting That Belief Be Real Enough': Shepherd Book as the Embodiment of Religious Non-Realism in the Whedonverse," in *Slayage* 13.2.

lierdumoa. (2016). "How Joss Whedon's *Firefly* Geekwashed the Confederacy," on *Tumblr*. Online. Available HTTP: http://lierdumoa.tumblr.com/post/129866383902/how-joss-whedons-firefly-geekwashed-the (9 March 2017).

Lopez, Ian F. Haney. (1996). *White by Law: The Legal Construction of Race*. New York: New York University Press.

McGee, Patrick. (2007). *From* Shane *to* Kill Bill: *Rethinking the Western*. Hoboken, NJ: Wiley-Blackwell.

Morrison, Toni. (1993). *Playing in the Dark: Whiteness and the Literary Imagination*. New York: Vintage Books.

Nadkarni, Samira. (2015). "'I Believe in Something Greater Than Myself': What Authority, Terrorism, and Resistance Have Come to Mean in the Whedonverses," in *Slayage* 13.2.

Nama, Adilifu. (2008). *Black Space: Imagining Race in Science Fiction Film*. Austin: University of Texas Press.

National Park Service, U.S.A. (n.d.). Showdown in the Shenandoah Valley: 1864 Valley Campaign, in *National Park Service*. Online. Available HTTP: https://www.nps.gov/cebe/learn/historyculture/showdown-in-the-shenandoah-valley-1864-valley-campaign.htm (20 May 2017).

Rabb, J. Douglas, and J. Michael Richardson. (2008). "Reavers and Redskins: Creating the Frontier Savage," in Rhonda V. Wilcox and Tanya R. Cochran (eds.) *Investigating* Firefly *and* Serenity: *Science Fiction on the Frontier*. London: I.B. Tauris, 127–138.

St. Louis, Renee, and Miriam Riggs. (2010). "'And Yet': The Limits of *Buffy* Feminism," in *Slayage* 8.1.

Seavey, John. (2010). "What Haunts Me About Firefly," in *Fraggmented*. Online. Available HTTP: http://fraggmented.blogspot.com/2010/12/what-haunts-me-about-firefly.html (1 May 2017).

Sun-tzu. (2017). "Chapter 6: Weak Points and Strong," in *Sun Tzu's Art of War*. Trans. Lionel Giles. John Watson, LLC. Available HTTP: https://suntzusaid.com/book/6 (5 May 2017).

Sutherland, Sharon, and Sarah Swan. (2008). "'The Alliance Isn't Some Evil Empire': Dystopia in Joss Whedon's *Firefly* and *Serenity*," in Rhonda V. Wilcox and Tanya R. Cochran (eds.) *Investigating* Firefly *and* Serenity: *Science Fiction on the Frontier*. London: I.B. Tauris, 89–100.

Whedon, Joss. (2002). "Ballad of Serenity," in *Firefly and Serenity Database*. Online. Available HTTP: http://firefly.wikia.com/wiki/Firefly (3 May 2017).

_____. (2005). *Serenity*: Film Commentary. 20th Century FOX Home Entertainment. DVD.

Wilcox, Rhonda V. (2008). "'I Do Not Hold to That': Joss Whedon and Original Sin," in Rhonda V. Wilcox and Tanya R. Cochran (eds.) *Investigating* Firefly *and* Serenity: *Science Fiction on the Frontier*. London: I.B. Tauris, 155–166.

Williamson, Amanda. (2016). "Aimin' to Misbehave: Jeremiads and Justice in Joss Whedon's *Firefly*," in *The Tunnels*, 1.1. Online. Available HTTP: https://www.thetunnelsmagazine.com/williamson-criticism-1-1 (1 May 2017).

Paint It Red
(and Black and Blue)
How Joss Whedon and Jack N. Green
Created the Bruised, Beautiful
Look of Serenity

K. Brenna Wardell

In one of the many tense moments in *Serenity* (2005), Joss Whedon's cinematic continuation of his TV series *Firefly* (2002–03), Captain Mal Reynolds (Nathan Fillion) barks orders at his crew, including a specific aesthetic choice that may help them survive a seemingly suicidal mission: "And we're gonna need paint. We're gonna need red paint." Smeared with this paint, paralleling the blood that stains its captain's face, the starship *Serenity* ventures into the film's heart of darkness—the mysterious planet Miranda—to discover a secret that will change the lives of the captain and crew, and the 'verse (universe) itself.

The success of Reynolds and his crew in this mission is based, in part, on a manipulation of aesthetics, from the look of their vessel to Reynolds's own appearance. Similarly, Whedon's ability to create in *Serenity* a work that is at once linked closely to its televised precursor and also decidedly stand-alone is based on his own understanding of aesthetics. This process of adaptation/continuation was facilitated, as Whedon acknowledges, by his collaboration with director of photography Jack N. Green (credited in *Serenity* as Jack Green), a film industry veteran famous for films ranging from *Unforgiven* (Clint Eastwood, 1992) to *The 40-Year-Old Virgin* (Judd Apatow, 2005).[1]

Analyzing select tools that Whedon and Green employ—from high-contrast lighting and saturated color to the long take—reveals the manner in which the men draw from and reimagine the iconography of diverse genres including film noir, science fiction, and the Western. It also showcases the bruised yet beautiful look of the film, its distinct place in Whedon's oeuvre, and its role in the development of science fiction on the silver screen. I'll begin with a short review of some notable aspects of the aesthetics of *Firefly* and then examine the distinctive elements of *Serenity*, focusing on the tools Whedon and Green employ to create a gritty and poetic, claustrophobic yet vast, decidedly cinematic world.

Inspired by Whedon's interest in the American Civil War, immigration, and frontiers (Earthly and otherwise), *Firefly* is a deliberately hybrid text combining genres (the Western and science fiction), tones (slapstick and chilling violence), and references (existential philosophy and the smallness of beagles).[2] In keeping with this mix, *Firefly*'s aesthetic is both homey and grand. Despite a tight budget, particularly for a series utilizing special effects, *Firefly*'s visual world is effective and often evocative, presenting a universe simultaneously authentically grubby and imposing.[3] The result is a speculative text whose sense of reality, despite its fantastic nature, creates high stakes, physically and emotionally, for its characters and for its viewers.

While the aesthetic of *Firefly* draws from genre traditions in Western and science fiction film and television, Whedon and his crew do not simply pay homage to this past; instead, they rework genre elements while combining them in often humorous, sometimes unsettling, ways. Part of the freshness in Whedon's approach to the TV Western relates to what the series does not do. For example, unlike Westerns such as *Gunsmoke* (1955–75) and *Bonanza* (1959–73), *Firefly* uses location shooting, not sets, for many exterior scenes, especially those set on the hardscrabble, low-tech outer planets. The expansive, often impressive, nature of these vistas—from lush greenery to vast, desolate deserts—provides physical reality coupled with visual spectacle while offering a stark contrast with the cramped spaceship Serenity.[4] Whedon's use of natural lighting and wide shots of these landscapes not only differentiates *Firefly* from many other TV series but echoes the aesthetics of classic film Westerns such as John Ford's *Stagecoach* (1939) and *The Searchers* (1956). Such citations foreground Whedon's knowledge of film history and his ambitions for *Firefly*, which include bringing film grammar to television. Similarly, Whedon's employment of science fiction iconography in *Firefly* is governed, at least in part, by what he avoids: eschewing the polished, high-tech environments and utopian ideals of some previous texts for gritty reality.[5] Discussing his desire to create a much less controlled and perfect world in an interview with Mike Russell for *CulturePulp*, Whedon contrasts *Serenity* with other spaceships, noting "…the textured reality is there. I want to *be* on that ship, and I never felt like I was *on* those other ships. They were big, giant Sheratons" (qtd. in Lavery and Burkhead 2011: 114).

The often-ambitious approach taken by Whedon and his crew to the aesthetics of *Firefly* foregrounds formal choices that not only advance the narrative and capture viewer attention but also demonstrate TV's expressive potential. For example, discussing the choice of a handheld effect for the photography with Russell, Whedon argues that this provides a sense of authenticity: "The template I was working from was *NYPD Blue*—it was 'you are there'" (qtd. in Lavery and Burkhead 2011: 109). By placing the viewer in close visual connection with the characters, Whedon also has the chance to emotionally link viewers to the characters and their goals, increasing investment in the unfolding drama. So too elements of *Firefly*'s mise-en-scène, such as the rich and varied colors and textures of the characters' costumes and environments, subtly advance viewer understanding of characters and the 'verse yet draw focus only when intended to achieve a certain effect.[6] For instance, as commentators have noted, the use of earth colors, particularly shades of brown, ties the series into the mise-en-scène of the Western with its dusty towns and sere deserts while keeping Mal and Zoe's (Gina Torres) backstory as Browncoats, soldiers for the Independent Planets during the Unification War, in mind.[7] Similarly, the drab khaki jumpsuits offset by colorful tops worn by Kaylee (Jewel Staite) reveal her mixture of practicality and imagination while the homemade charm of Jayne's (Adam Baldwin) knitted yellow and orange hat, a gift from his mother, has a warmth and eccentric wooliness, a homemade charm that contrasts with the character's seemingly amoral nature and hard-bodied masculinity. Together, these formal elements create dramatic effects, yet they rarely read as constructed with such effects in mind—their unobtrusive nature belying the care that went into them.

These formal elements are showcased in the presentation of the spaceship *Serenity* with its well-used, sometimes cluttered, spaces.[8] Described by Whedon in a *Firefly* DVD featurette as the tenth character, the ship is a lived in, homely, and, in places, homey space (in Anon. 2003). This hominess is particularly pronounced in *Serenity*'s dining area, featuring yellow walls decorated with a climbing vine and fruit design, a long wooden table, and mismatched chairs: the space's eclectic charm is enhanced by lighting choices such as the glowing candlelight on Simon's (Sean Maher) cake in *Firefly*'s eighth episode "Out of Gas" (25 October 2002). Barbara Maio even argues that the ship itself is watching, arguing: "But it is not in object and props alone that the spaceship acquires a personality: often the camera frames the protagonists in a false subjective point of view, giving the illusion that it is the spaceship itself that is watching" (2008: 209).

Like the genre mixing of the series, the ship itself is built on the tension and possibility of contrasts; the stripped down, functional space of the cargo bay, for instance, feels a world away from Inara's (Morena Baccarin) shuttle—an exotic fantasy space of draped red and deep bronze fabric and atmospheric lights that highlights her profession as a Companion—and Kaylee's room, with its colorful black, yellow, and green batik wall hanging and party lights.[9] Color plays a notable role in the presentation of the diverse locations and multiple tones found within the spaceship and in the series as a whole, with color quickly differentiating both characters and spaces, from the sunshine of the dining room and the rich, opulent reds of Inara's shuttle to the infirmary's blue, its cool, sterile mise-en-scène underscoring the shock of bright red when an injured crewmember is treated there.

The richness of *Firefly*'s visual world functioned, as Whedon acknowledges, as both a blessing and burden during the planning of *Serenity*: he had the advantage of a fully-conceived 'verse but had to balance it with the weight of building on and reinventing it in the challenging, high-stakes medium of film. To examine Whedon's choices in crafting a unique, distinctly cinematic text, I focus on select elements: the creation of a sense of narrative and visual scale/scope through precise, evocative use of cinematography and mise-en-scène; the addition of the genre of the noir Western with its shadowy visual world and emotionally, sometimes physically, wounded protagonists; and the collaboration between Whedon and DP Green, whose *Unforgiven*, with its meditation in form and content on violence anticipates *Serenity*'s bloodied beauty.

As Whedon notes in interviews, the move to the big screen required going big on multiple levels—from a narrative featuring high stakes that the characters might not survive to formal choices including expressive, experimental use of cinematography, lighting, and color.[10] Many of Whedon's choices in *Serenity* appear to derive from issues of genre, particularly from his wrestling with a problem connected to Mal and the traumatized psychic River (Summer Glau), the two characters who motivate many of the film's narrative and emotional threads. Whedon observes that "Mal is kinda a Western fellow and River is living in a kind of a noir" (2005). The solution lay, Whedon notes, in the suggestion by his mentor Jeanine Basinger that he consult the noir Western with its dramas of morally compromised, tormented protagonists played out in dark and unwelcoming physical and psychological frontiers. In addition to the noir Western, Whedon notes, in an interview with Thomas Leupp, the influence of revisionist Westerns, singling out *The Searchers* and *Ulzana's Raid* (Robert Aldrich, 1972) because, as he argues, "they're so uncompromising" (qtd. in Lavery and Burkhead: 2011 82).

"Uncompromising" is an apt word to describe *Serenity:* a film that dares the viewer to, like its heroes, dislike its antagonist, and move intellectually and emotionally through the narrative's twists and turns into and, possibly, out of its literal and figurative heart of darkness. To examine how Whedon and Green bring that "uncompromising" approach to character, narrative, and form, creating a 'verse full of vivid colors, dark shadows, and even more shadowy motives and desires, I will examine the film's prologue and introduction of the spaceship *Serenity* and its crew, then move to select scenes, including a discussion of the "paint it red" scene discussed in my opening.

The film's prologue—providing the backstory of the migration from "Earth-that-was" and the War of Unification between Independents and the Alliance, along with (re)introducing the cannibalistic Reavers—immediately announces Whedon's ambitions to take full advantage of cinema's toolkit. Consisting of multiple scenes that mix familiar and new characters while rapidly cycling through diverse genres, time periods, locations, and points of view, the prologue forcibly communicates to viewers both the film's connection to and departure from the TV series.[11] Through short scenes nestled together like nesting dolls—distinct, yet connected—the prologue presents multiple narratives false starts that are introduced only to be revealed to be just part of a series of expository breadcrumbs leading to the film's true beginning: a long take that reacquaints us with Serenity and its crew.

The prologue opens with the Universal logo, quickly transformed into an image of an Earth unable, as the modulated tones of a narrator note, to support an expanding population. As the narration continues, new terraformed worlds are shown: the contrast between the gleaming technology and lush environments of some of these worlds—the wealthy inner planets—and the crude buildings and barren environment of the outer planets alluding to the central conflict that would lead to war between the Alliance and the Independents. This epic history of migration is then revealed to be a lesson for children in a pastoral outdoor schoolroom. The children interrogate the reasons for the War of Unification and mention the Reavers, their lesson disrupted as, in a startling graphic match, the teacher plunges a stylus into the forehead of one of the children: River. The lesson scene is revealed to be River's nightmare, and the stylus transforms into a needle, jolting her awake in the Alliance facility where staff experiment on her. As this new scene continues, her brother Simon helps her to escape from the facility, but then the scene freezes as a man's voice yells "stop!" The scene is revealed to be a holographic recording, viewed by a new character, the Operative (Chiwetel Ejiofor), as he tracks River. Demanding information, he gazes into the holographic face of River as the prologue ends. The screen is then filled with darkness as the name "Serenity" appears, floating in the black, the letters moving away from the camera as a swirl of red and gold behind the letters resolves into a circular shape with Chinese characters that also read "Serenity." As the camera pulls back further, the shape is revealed to be a logo painted onto the hull of the spaceship Serenity.

With its series of richly colored widescreen images, disorienting moves through diverse genres, and introduction of old and new characters, the prologue sums up the *Firefly* 'verse while expanding the narrative and visual possibilities of the series. As Whedon notes on his DVD commentary, the fragmented narrative and genre mix of the prologue perfectly rhymes with, and takes the viewer into, River's disordered mental state and the roots of her trauma, wedding form and function (2005). Its disorientation and danger also provide, as Whedon notes, the perfect contrast with the introduction of Serenity and its crew, allowing him to create on the spaceship "a sense of safety in space" through tools such as a long take as Mal passes through its diverse areas, interacting with the crew. However, while the spaceship may indeed offer a sense of ease and comfort, particularly for viewers familiar with *Firefly*, Whedon and Green don't let the viewer relax. Instead, they subtly unsettle that safety through specific cinematography, lighting, and color choices that may foreground a sense of connection in the crew's relationships with each other within the unified space of their vessel but also highlight a sense of disorder: the fraying of the crew's psyches just as the spaceship itself threatens to come apart as it descends towards the planet below.

Our introduction to the ship and crew begins with a camera pass along the ship's flank and then a move to its front, focusing on the shapes of Mal and the pilot Wash (Alan Tudyk) on the bridge. The camera moves to the ship's interior for a conversation between Mal and Wash, then follows Mal as he moves from the bridge into the front hall, encountering Zoe, his second in command and Wash's spouse, and Jayne, the ship's muscle. Moving from the front hall through the empty dining area and into the back hall he arrives at the engine room to discuss the ship's problems with Kaylee, the ship's engineer, then turns to find his way blocked by Simon, the ship's doctor, who confronts Mal over his plan to involve River in a heist. The two men travel to the infirmary while arguing, have a final confrontation in the cargo bay, and a dissatisfied Simon is left behind as Mal moves out of frame.

Whedon argues that his main goals in the introduction were to reveal Serenity's space, to allow the viewer to meet the characters, and to provide a sense of safety after the quick and violent prologue (2005). And the tools he uses, particularly a long take and a gliding camera, emphasize a sense of homecoming while shedding a new light, literally and figuratively, on this home. First, there is the expansiveness of the long take, which extends for four and a half minutes as Mal interacts with the other characters and their spaces; second, there is the smooth, calming movement of the Steadicam, which glides along with Mal, seeming to pass through the cramped, even claustrophobic, spaces of Serenity with comforting ease.

Through these tools and others, Whedon and Green create a sense of a physically and emotionally balanced world. Gone are the quick cuts found in the prologue with its diverse locales; instead, there is a sense of welcome in the familiar spaces, dwelt on briefly but lovingly by the moving camera. As the camera travels with Mal, sometimes lagging behind him, at other times closer to him—peering over his shoulder and almost sharing, literally and figuratively, his point of view—a sense of emotional connection, verging on suture, is achieved.

At the same time, the length of the take and the camera's presence and movement work to complicate this same sense of safety and connection— both the link that the crew members have with each other and the bond the viewer may feel with them, especially with Mal. As Mal encounters character after character, questioning them with various degrees of forcefulness and encountering varying degrees of pushback, a more ambivalent portrait of the character emerges, and the long take starts to feel somewhat anxious, revealing the unsettled nature of both spaceship and crew: out in the black of space too long. So too the sharing provided by the closeness of the camera creates a certain doubt: the viewer may now feel a closeness with Mal, but given the prickly nature of his interactions with the other characters the viewer may feel unsure about this connection.[12]

A further formal tool that Whedon and Green use here and elsewhere in the film to draw attention to characters or objects while creating a sense of dramatic tension is high-contrast lighting—lighting that provides a strong distinction between light and shadow. In much of the introduction the light is severely limited, keeping a good deal of the characters' faces and the ship's spaces hidden. The lack of visible information provided creates both interest and unease. Perhaps the most notable use of limited light to create tension lies in Mal's interaction with Simon as they face each other in the cargo bay, their faces so faintly limned with blue light that their individual natures and relationship with each other seem mysterious. This sense of something hidden provides a visual counterpart to the mystery of the film's narrative as set out in the prologue: the fractured, potentially violent, nature of River's psyche and the question of how Mal will respond to the danger she may pose.

Drawing from the lighting tradition of German Expressionist cinema and film noir, the choice of high-contrast lighting creates a sense of hiddenness, even paranoia: of something literally and figuratively in the shadows. And the darkness is palpable, both externally in the frame and in the sense of Mal's barely-contained spiritual/emotional darkness. Green had used such lighting before, perhaps most memorably in his work on *Unforgiven*. And just as there are distinct emotional and visual parallels between *Unforgiven*'s protagonist William Munny (Clint Eastwood), the retired gunslinger haunted by his violent past, and Mal, the former soldier carrying internal and external scars, there are connections in the manner Green photographs the men and their environments.[13] Edward Buscombe's appraisal of Green's use of light for both literal and figurative purposes and its relation to characterization in *Unforgiven* may also illuminate Green's treatment of *Serenity*'s crew, particularly Mal: "*Unforgiven*, though, is dark even by the standards of previous Eastwood works.... One can read this as 'realism'; on the nineteenth-century frontier, bright lights were the exception. More symbolically, one may note that night is the time when we see into the darkness of Munny's soul" (78).[14] Whedon embraced Green's use of high-contrast lighting, noting on his commentary, "Jack's not afraid of his blacks, he's not afraid of negative space and dark colors and shadows, and I love that because neither am I. It brings your eye to what's important and it gives the skin such incredible texture" (2005). In going so far into the "blacks" in this way the film differentiates itself from the television series, in which lighting contrasts are often more muted and deep shadows, while used, are not necessarily utilized for such sustained periods.

Finally, in tandem with the film's lighting and cinematography Whedon and Green use color with precision for both practical purposes—defining and differentiating spaces and characters—and dramatic effect. As in the series, color signals the different areas of the ship—from the cool blues of the infirmary to the warm yellow of the dining area. However, Whedon and Green's use of color in the film is even more exaggerated. This occurs literally in the greater level of color saturation and the manner in which colors pop against contrasting backgrounds such as the harsh daylight of Haven, the new home of Book (Ron Glass), or the velvety blacks inside Serenity. There is also a metaphorical aspect to the use of color—the sense that the colors speak volumes about the characters' hidden psychological states. This is particularly so in the use of red, from the rusty red of Mal's shirt to the blood that flows from Mal and his crew in their confrontations with the Operative and the Reavers.

The introduction scene provides ample illustration of the manner in which Whedon and Green use color, particularly in tandem with lighting, to quickly differentiate the ship's distinct sections and their purposes while conveying crucial information about the characters associated with those spaces. Mal first appears in the cool gray-blue of the bridge, a place of relative serenity, although the lick of flames outside from the ship's descent and the sight of a piece of the ship flying off complicate this. Mal then moves from the bridge through the dark front hall, where he encounters Zoe and Jayne: the horizontal lines of blue light in the space providing illumination yet lending a coldness to the space and an anxiety about the interchanges held within it. Mal then passes through the dining room, the soft light on its yellow walls offering a break from the gloom and a reminder for *Firefly* viewers of the emotional warmth of past gatherings in that space. He then proceeds through the back hall with its few gray/blue lights, even more shadowed than the front hall, and stops at the door of the engine room. Flashes of red-gold sparks illuminate the space, along with lines of thin red lights overhead; these highlight Kaylee as she tends to her equipment, the red color emphasizing a sense of danger and chaos even as the relative brightness provides a further break from the gloom. Finally, there is a return to dim blue lights and shadows as Mal turns to encounter an angry Simon in the back hall. Simon follows Mal as he moves down to Serenity's lower level and into the sterile blue of the infirmary, and then the men face each other in the cargo bay, a faint blue light outlining their faces. The colors in the introduction scene are diverse, providing a sense of multiple separate spaces; however, the colors are also united by the use of a consistent background of velvety blacks, along with the amalgamation created by the uninterrupted long take and the camera's smooth glide through that space: the result is an eclectic wholeness.

An example of this precise use of color for dramatic effect, in tandem with lighting and cinematography, occurs in a seemingly insignificant moment in which Jayne moves through Serenity trying to locate River after the crew has determined she might be a danger to them. As Jayne passes through a doorway and into a dark corridor, he assures the unseen River "No trouble, little crazy person—we're going on a nice little shuttle ride." As he does, the viewer's eye is drawn to the yellow shirt he wears—the brightest element in the darkened frame. The camera then moves away and tilts up to reveal what is above him: River in a dark dress spread-eagled against the ceiling, her dress and hair blending into the darkness while her exposed limbs and face glow palely in the small amount of light. With its high contrast of dark and light, coupled with River's appearance and the mood of psychological peril, this moment could be a still from a German Expressionist film. In particular, River's expressionless face and eerie stillness make her look like a dreamer or puppet, echoing characters from films such as the surrealist masterpiece *The Cabinet of Dr. Caligari* (Robert Wiene, 1920), a text that has had a significant influence on screen horror.[15] Heightening the suspense of the moment, Whedon does not show the moment when River drops down onto Jayne. Instead we hear gunfire and witness the crew as they react before moving through the corridors to find Jayne unconscious.

The result of the care with which Whedon and Green use formal elements here, particularly high-contrast lighting, is that a sense of suspense builds as the viewer, like Jayne, tries to penetrate the space's darkness and locate River. Highlighting the contrast between the saturated yellow of Jayne's shirt and the black around him makes the seemingly powerful Jayne appear, for a moment, like the proverbial canary in a coal mine: his vulnerability to potential injury or death the first sign of true threat. This use of color and lighting puts forward a visual argument that enhances the narrative's sense of an impending danger from which no one will be safe: a danger that could come from the inhumanly still and powerful River who, in this moment, looks more like a vampire or wraith than a flesh and blood woman.

Similarly, the short scene in which Inara first encounters the Operative demonstrates the specific aesthetic choices that allow Whedon and Green to quickly convey narrative and character information. The scene begins with a shot of Inara in a long deep red dress, her hair flowing down her back, standing in front of the Companion training house. The dress' color makes her stand out against the background and anticipates the crimson cloak Mal will wear when he attempts to slip into the training house to find her. Inara's back is to the viewer, and she is framed by a portico of thin columns, the angular lines of this structure softened by the flowing movement of near-transparent draperies. Beyond her is the expanse of a green-forested valley, while below her, seemingly emerging from the woods, is the Operative. He is clad in light, cool blue, his hands placed behind his back, his face calm and serene. The image is peaceful, almost timeless: an Arcadian space that recalls a moment from an ancient epic, such as an imagining of the welcome home offered by Penelope to her far-traveling husband in Homer's *The Odyssey*. Yet given that the viewer knows the Operative's villainy, the fantasy cannot hold, and Whedon's cut from this image to a medium shot of Inara's face quickly transforming from a smile of welcome to a recognition of danger verging on horror upturns the scene's peace.

Effective in both advancing the narrative and providing a note of beauty in its classical allusions, attention to this Inara/Operative scene is also helpful in understanding Whedon's approach to *Serenity*'s aesthetics: reflecting not only Whedon's desire to differentiate his film from his TV series, but also serving as a reminder that this scene and the film itself are a rejoinder to the aesthetics of other science fiction films. Discussing his choices for the scene on his commentary, Whedon notes that he had this particular shot in his mind for some time, and that "I wanted something that was very, very different from what I was seeing, which was a lot of everything is monochromatic *Matrix* movies and obviously *Star Wars*, you know there's lots of deep reds and heavy coloring and I didn't want to go there, but I did want something that would make a bold statement of many, many worlds, and that this isn't just a simple … you know, everything is slightly green kind of world." While Whedon's statement primarily focuses on this scene, it may also speak to his aesthetic goals for the film as a whole: his desire to build on both genre conventions and specific film texts but to also innovate beyond them, creating a unique aesthetic for his 'verse.

This leads me to the final formal choices that I will discuss: the use of red paint mentioned earlier and further use of red in the penultimate scene of Mal's confrontation with the Operative in his attempt to send the recording detailing the true origin of the Reavers into the 'verse. In examining these scenes I want to not only foreground the formal elements upon which I have focused and their literal meaning and effects, such as red's association with blood and violence, but also to address the figurative levels of this formal choice. The first scene I will discuss is the crew's return to Haven, a scene that marks a turning point in Mal's arc within the film and propels the spaceship and its crew towards the unknown frontier of Miranda.

When the crew returns to Haven to see Book they discover desolation—the sight of the scattered bodies of Haven's inhabitants and a downed Alliance spaceship spewing dark smoke. The cruel loss of the scene is highlighted by the planet's too-bright daylight, the bodies standing out against the white of the ground and the desert environment and forming a stark contrast to the crew's previous visit, in which Green used Rembrandt lighting to enhance the warmth of the crew's welcome, the visual lushness of the nighttime scene's deep black and gleams of red and gold reflecting the joy of their reunion with Book. Mal locates the dying Book and holds Book's hand and head as he confesses his responsibility for the Alliance's actions against the planet's inhabitants.

As Mal tries to comfort Book, Whedon and Green emphasize the scene's horror: the camera dwelling on the red wound in Book's abdomen and the blood in his mouth and on his hand, blood transferred to Mal's ear, cheek, and neck as Book's hand slides down his face as he dies. This trail of red remains moments later, as Mal confronts the crew with his decision to go to Miranda and oppose the Alliance. The crimson of this blood is echoed by the rusty red shirt Mal wears, the red standing out against the shades of blue, purple, yellow, and brown worn by the other characters and the pale, almost colorless, background, isolating Mal from them. That Mal desires to cover the spaceship—their home—with the same red stain provides a further element of contention and separation, yet this protective cloaking is indeed the best solution. Just as Mal earlier manipulated aesthetics to try to enter the training house on Inara's world undetected by the Operative, sneaking in under the improbable cover of a bejeweled crimson cloak, so Mal's aesthetic choice of the red paint, along with other adjustments to Serenity's appearance, allows the crew to pass the Reaver fleet outside Miranda and learn the colonists' fate.

Emphasizing the sense of anger, passion, and alienation evoked by the color of Mal's red shirt and blood-streaked face, Whedon and Green compose the frame to further highlight Mal's separation from the crew and their initial opposition to his plan. As he stands facing them, his single body opposed to the group, the presence of all of their bodies within the same frame showcases a potential for unity. However, Mal's position on the opposite side of the frame from his crew creates a sense of dissociation. This is further emphasized when, rather than showing all the characters within the frame, Whedon moves to a shot/reverse shot, focusing first on Mal and then on the crew's reaction to him, an editing pattern that separates the characters, if only briefly. This bloody, fierce version of Mal is repeated, with some important variations, in his final battle with the Operative.

In this confrontation Mal is again clad in red, although the shirt he wears is not red, but brown; instead, it is the red of the blood that flows from his nose, his mouth, his damaged eye, and his wounded side that mark Mal, contrasting him with the cool calm of the Operative in his blue, unstained shirt. After he has defeated the Operative and left him to watch the recording the crew collected on Miranda, detailing the Alliance experiments that led to the Reavers, Mal leaves to find his crew. The moment speaks to celebration, but Mal does not pause to savor his victory; instead, he limps off, obviously damaged, holding his bleeding side. And as he comes out of the elevator to find his crew, Whedon and Green show him at first in darkness: just an unknown, possibly menacing, shadow against the wall—seemingly very much like the Mal of the introduction. River is similarly initially cast in darkness— only a shadowy outline with a weapon in hand, bodies piled around her—as the doors opposite Mal open to reveal her. Two damaged characters, wounded externally and emotionally, stare across the bodies of the similarly wounded crew: their baptism in blood a sign of the horror they have wrought and endured.

The broken, bruised face of Mal and his wounded body, photographed in intimate detail, is both a triumphant moment of endurance beyond pain and of doubt resolved and a critique of traditional representations of the hero, for rather than the morally upright and physically perfect hero glorying in his success, Whedon presents a visibly broken man who has just stepped out of the shadows into an uncertain light. And while the film's final scenes— the funeral ceremony and the final interaction between Mal and River on the bridge as Serenity breaks atmosphere and heads towards the stars—offer a certain benediction, the powerful, unsettling sight of the bloody, uncompromising face of Mal remains in the mind, an indelible image of the ambitious, even unsettling, nature of Whedon and Green's narrative and aesthetic experiments.

Notes

1. For instance, in a 2005 interview with Mike Russell for the website *The CulturePulp*, Whedon notes of Green, "He's the reason we got to make a movie that looks—I think—a good deal more expensive than it was. He moves *so* fast, and he makes frames that I think are just as gorgeous as anything" (qtd. in Lavery and Burkhead 2011: 114).

2. In a discussion of *Firefly* in "Must-See Metaphysics" from *The New York Times*, Emily Nussbaum notes the film's origin in Whedon's consumption of Michael Shaara's *The Killer Angels*, about the Battle of Gettysburg. She quotes Whedon on the origins for the series: "I wanted to play with that classic notion of the frontier: not the people who made history, but the people history stepped on—the people for whom every act is the creation of civilization" (qtd. in Lavery and Burkhead 2011: 67).

3. As David Lavery notes in *Joss Whedon: A Creative Portrait*, "The budget for *Firefly* was even smaller than *Buffy*'s or *Angel*'s" (2014: 112). Despite this, one of the reasons given by Fox executives for cancelling the show was its expense, coupled with its low viewership.

4. Addressing the setting for Western films in a discussion of Clint Eastwood's film

Unforgiven, Edward Buscombe notes, "From the early days of the last century, Westerns have used landscape to ensure authority.... Deserts particularly were favoured. Europe too had mountains ... but it had no deserts and canyons to rival the spectacular sights of Arizona and Utah" (2004: 45).

5. In the gritty, lived in look of the spaceship Serenity, Whedon recalls the messy communal spaces and well-worn industrial look of *Alien* (Scott, 1979), an important influence he has mentioned a number of times, including in his discussion with Mike Russell for *CulturePulp* (see Lavery and Burkhead 2011: 114).

6. For example, Barbara Maio notes the hybrid nature of the costumes in the series: Costumes are a mixed version of science fiction, Western, East and West. Influences can be identified with the Wild West in the use of denim and leather in hot colors, while a futuristic effect is given by the use of grey or dark colors—for example, Alliance uniforms that recall Nazi Germany (or *Star Wars* Imperial officers). Asian influence—from the Middle East to Japan—also pervades the series, with extensive use of rich and colorful fabrics (2008: 206).

7. Mal's costume, for example, references a number of the film characters played by John Wayne, especially Wayne's dress in films such as *Stagecoach* and *The Searchers*.

8. Describing the spaceship in "Must-See Metaphysics" in the *New York Times*, Emily Nussbaum notes, "At once majestic and junky, the Serenity resembles a blown-up kid's toy, and its interior had been filled with oddball details. A tiny plastic bobble-headed dog sits on the dashboard, and the ship's low-tech engine is reminiscent of an overgrown eggbeater" (qtd. in Lavery and Burkhead 2011: 65).

9. This space is made even more colorful by Kaylee's addition of her fluffy pink party dress in the sixth episode "Shindig" (1 November 2002).

10. Discussing the reflexive nature of the film, J.P. Telotte argues that Whedon's awareness of the medium and its demands may be a crucial element in the success of *Firefly*'s film adaption:
Yet what is arguably most interesting about the film version is something that hardly surfaces in *Firefly*'s relatively brief existence. For *Serenity* seems pointedly mindful of its medium, after a fashion that we do not typically see in most television series, but has always marked some of the best cinematic sf (2008: 68).

11. Whedon notes that he found the question of how to open the film particularly difficult, especially as he had "a lot of explaining to do" and he needed to do so while keeping the film dynamic; the solution was the prologue:
Part of that became the idea of constantly shifting our expectations of where we were, so what seemed like [the] typical beginning of a science fiction movie narration turns out to be a simple classroom scene ... all of this is done to keep feeding information to the viewer while still unsettling and keeping them interested (2005).

12. In an interview with Mike Russell, Whedon focuses on the shift in size on all levels needed to adapt *Firefly* for film, facilitating both emotional and visual impact: "It would really get into their lives and tell the big, epic story—with the big chases and the big trouble and the fights and all the glory that we go to the movies for. But at the same time, it would be about the people in it—as opposed to the things you can accomplish with CGI" (qtd. in Lavery and Burkhead 2011: 109).

13. In his discussion of *Unforgiven*, Edward Buscombe argues that this use of darkness was absorbed by Green through his work with Eastwood and with Eastwood's long-time DP Bruce Surtees (2004: 77).

14. Describing Eastwood's approach, Buscombe argues, "As a director Eastwood has always had a liking for the crepuscular, for scenes shot in semi-darkness with just one or two sources of light" (2004: 77).

15. River's appearance rhymes with that of several characters in that film, such as Jane, the dark-haired, pale-faced heroine who turns out to be an inmate of an insane asylum, as well as the ashen-faced, dark-clad somnambulist Cesare, who appears to be being used as an instrument to enact a series of killings planned by the mysterious Dr. Caligari, a hypnotist.

Works Cited

Anon. (2003). "Serenity: The Tenth Character." *Firefly*. 20th Century FOX Home Entertainment. DVD.

Buscombe, Edward. (2004). *Unforgiven*. London: British Film Institute.

Lavery, David. (2014). *Joss Whedon, A Creative Portrait: From* Buffy the Vampire Slayer *to Marvel's* The Avengers. London: I.B. Tauris.

Lavery, David, and Cynthia Burkhead (eds.). (2011). *Joss Whedon: Conversations*. Jackson: University Press of Mississippi.

Maio, Barbara. (2008). "Between Past and Future: Hybrid Design Style in *Firefly* and *Serenity*," in Rhonda. V. Wilcox and Tanya. R. Cochrane (eds.) *Investigating* Firefly and Serenity: *Science Fiction on the Frontier*. London: I.B. Tauris, 201–201.

Telotte, J.P. (2008) "*Serenity*, Cinematisation and the Perils of Adaptation," in *Science Fiction Film and Television* 1.1: 67–80.

Whedon, Joss. (2005). *Serenity*: Film Commentary. 20th Century FOX Home Entertainment. DVD.

Spaceships as Soundscapes in *Serenity*

HOLLY RANDELL-MOON *and*
ARTHUR J. RANDELL

Introduction: The Semiotics of Sound

This essay examines the use of sound in Joss Whedon's *Serenity* (2005) by contextualizing its semiotic and discursive meanings through the construction of soundscapes at various points in the film. We show how these soundscapes contribute to an understanding of the ship Serenity and its crew as a relational vehicle for transgression, escape, and empowerment from the homogenizing political-military mechanisms of the Alliance. In disclosing the semiotic and discursive construction of sound, we draw from sound, media, and cultural studies scholarship that emphasizes the constitutive nature of sound in visual media. Rather than treating sound as an element that simply reflects visuality, we approach sound as helping to normalize particular kinds of generic and visual associations between film score, sound effects, and voice that help to dramatize *Serenity*'s narrative politics about the need to resist, collaborate, and listen.

Just as visual style can be understood through mise-en-scène and genre as representing particular motifs and cultural themes, sound also functions with semiotic and intertextual meanings. Anne Cranny-Francis argues that "specific sonic elements" of visual texts such as film, convey meanings to audiences through "a kind of acoustic grammar" she terms, "cultural auracy" (2007: 88). Sonic elements such as a genre of music or choice of instrument convey a "semiotic code," borrowing from Anna Kasabian (95), that reflects "social and cultural assumptions" (87) about the meanings of sound and how we hear it. As Jonathan Sterne notes, citing Veit Erlmann, aurality comprises both the act of hearing itself and "the conditions that must be given for something to become recognized, labeled and valorized as audible in the first place" (2012: 8). Thus, what constitutes "sound" is culturally conditioned and learned through the semiotic codes of media consumption. Following Cranny-Francis, our aim in this essay is to analyze both the function of sound and how it is semiotically constructed in the soundscapes of *Serenity*.

Understood as both expressive of narrative meaning and created through learned cultural auracy, sonic elements are ways of incorporating "the viewer into the narrative and its assumptions" (Cranny-Francis 2007: 88). For this reason, Cranny-Francis proposes an analysis of sound in media that "encompass[es] not only music, but all sonic elements" (87). To this end, our essay examines the use of sound in *Serenity* by contextualizing the cultural auracy of its soundscapes. While work has been written on the film and television score for *Serenity* and *Firefly* (2002–03) respectively (Goltz 2004, Leonard 2010, Hung 2011), and within this treatment there is some discussion of the diegetic sounds used to create an exotic and futuristic setting (Granade 2015, Neal 2008, Pelkey II 2011), our essay examines the main elements of sound in *Serenity* in terms of its overall soundscape as a contribution to the film's narrative politics. These sound elements include the film score, special effects, and voice, which are analyzed as a coherent "sonic politics" (Cranny-Francis 2007: 92) that reflect the film's narrative and thematic focus on the spontaneous and unpredictable collaborations of the film's protagonist heroes in opposition to the authoritarian homogeneity of the Alliance.

The first section of this essay explains how the ship Serenity establishes the soundscape of the film and is used to relay the central conflict and narrative themes of *Serenity*. The remaining sections examine the role of the film score, special effects, and voice as markers of genres, visual culture, and character relationships used to create a sonic politics that is both problematic in its colonial nostalgia and critical in the film's appeal to collaboration and discord as effecting resistance.

Serenity *as Soundscape*

Serenity's soundscapes are intimately linked to the central narrative conflict between the Alliance and those who struggle against it, as well as to how the audience is encouraged to interpret this conflict. One of the defining spaces of *Serenity* is in its namesake, the ship Serenity, and the soundscape it occupies establishes the diegetic world the characters inhabit as well as their characterizations and relationships. Serenity is named after the Battle of Serenity Valley, where a military loss for the Independents was a decisive factor in the Alliance winning the war, and the ship itself therefore serves an important function in anchoring the narrative.

In R. Murray Schafer's theories of sound, the notion of soundscapes and spatiality are identified as an important tool for understanding the way in which hearing positions the listener in the world. For him, the most basic of noises can be analyzed to discover how sounds are infused with meaning. The "rich symbolism" of noise can be broadly defined along a scale from pervasiveness to uniqueness with a concurrent progression of conscious influence on the listener (1977). In this hierarchy, even sounds that can be crudely defined as constituting the background noise of a soundtrack belie their importance to the spaces depicted by the very fact that they are accepted unquestioningly in their verisimilitude. Schafer conceptualizes background noises as "keynotes," proffering that though "sounds may not always be heard consciously the fact that they are ubiquitously there suggests the possibility of a deep and pervasive influence on our behaviour and moods" (1977: 9). Similarly, when we are first introduced to the external and internal soundscapes of the spaceship Serenity, the relationship of the characters to the noise of the space is integral to efficiently communicating the central characters' relationships to each other and their surrounding world.

The scene opens with an exterior shot of Serenity gently gliding through space, accompanied by the film's score but with diegetic sound effects entirely absent. This score is then abruptly interrupted by a growing roar of wind as the ship enters a planet's atmosphere. The camera swings around to the cockpit of the ship where we glimpse some of the film's protagonists for the first time, while the surrounding entry noise becomes louder and louder. With a harsh metallic screech, a piece of the ship breaks loose and we cut inside to the cockpit to see Captain Malcolm Reynolds (Nathan Fillion) and the pilot Wash (Alan Tudyk). As a heated exchange unfolds over what the implications of the detached piece means for the crew's safety, the outside noise continues unabated but is now joined by intermittent jolts of short rumbling explosions that rock the characters and the ship.

Despite these sounds, Mal appears more annoyed than afraid. He even has time to quip over the ship's loudspeaker, "We have a little problem with our entry sequence, so we may experience some slight turbulence, and then explode," before exiting the cockpit and being tracked by the camera walking through the ship, which introduces the audience to Serenity's interior. On his way he meets the members of the crew who, despite his earlier warning of eminent destruction and the noisy evidence of it surrounding them, proceed to talk about anything other than their dangerous landing (excepting Kaylee [Jewel Staite], the ship's put-upon engineer). It's important to note that besides the cockpit, there are no windows in the ship that we see, so the only information the audience and the characters have of what is transpiring outside is through the noise of the ship.

The whole scene lasts for approximately five minutes and, subverting expectations, it becomes increasingly obvious that the entry and landing are not at all concerning for the characters—in fact these potentially distressing noises are communicated as being commonplace. Although this scene represents a point of dramatic exaggeration for the soundscape, it remains generally reflective of the sound whenever the ship exits or enters a planet's atmosphere. Even when the ship is in deep space, the sounds of its hull gently creaking can still be heard from within. Thus through this soundscape, the film is able to convey that the characters have all lived on the ship for long enough to become comfortable with the noises it makes and that they are accustomed to the dangerous circumstances that are part and parcel of being the crew of this particular ship. However, while the characters accept the soundscape around them as normal, we must examine how this normalcy is constructed, coded, and how in some circumstances it problematizes traditional soundscape definitions.

Framing Schafer's discussions of sound is a general concern with what he sees as modern society's progression towards environments that produce soundscapes defined by a lack of clarity. He categorizes this loss in terms of fidelity, with natural environments of "quiet ambience" that allow "the listener to hear farther into the distance" described as hi-fi soundscapes, compared against urban spaces with "an overdense population of sounds" where "perspective is lost," and which are labeled lo-fi soundscapes (1977: 43). Recalling hierarchies of low and high culture, where clarity is prized aesthetically, this categorization automatically inscribes noisy, urban spaces with negative values (as they are not considered aurally 'natural'). The relative abundance of noise in Serenity and the comfort the heroes have in this space is evident in its introduction in the film suggesting a positive connotation to lo-fi soundscapes.

Overlaying the ship's sounds is the sound of many voices, more often than not yelling, which adds to the reading of this space, at least in Schafer's terms, as being decidedly lo-fi. This aurality is in direct contrast to the soundscapes of scenes where the Alliance is in control. For example, the lab where River (Summer Glau) is undergoing experiments and the archive room where the Operative (Chiwetel Ejiofor) begins his investigation have almost no background noise. Rather than providing comfort, as per Schafer's scale, these soundscapes work to unsettle the audience and mark the spaces, and the character of the Operative, as lacking in emotion. Even more disturbing is the soundscape of the planet Miranda, discussed in more detail below, which when the heroes arrive, contains only the sound of wind. In this scene it is precisely the lack of urban noises and the normal noises of people, which trouble the characters and the audience, working to further denote the Alliance as inhuman. Therefore the film flips the dichotomy suggested by Schafer, to reinscribe noisy, urban, lo-fi soundscapes as being places of comfort. It is these spaces, where difference and plurality are valued, that the Alliance seeks to sublimate with their ideals of clarity and homogeneity. But what are the specific sonic elements that are used to realize this narrative? In the following, we will unpack how score, effects, and voice are used to establish the film's sonic politics.

The Sonic Politics of Serenity

Film Score

As much of the work on sound in *Firefly* and *Serenity* suggests, Whedon uses a score with conventions signifying the Western genre in order to realize the central conflict between the Independents and the Alliance. This generic use conveys a particular set of musical styles as well as the spaces with which these styles are associated. For instance, in *Firefly*, Kendra Preston Leonard argues "the show's 'space Western' feel" is based on generic approximations of folk songs from "New World colonists and Westward expansionists" (2010: 174), ethnically associated with Irish and Scottish settlers. These musical stylings are also reflected in the score of *Serenity*, with some key differences, and work to conjure a particular sonic politics about American colonial history and government control that are aligned with the film's framing of the Alliance.

The generic conventions of a Western are musically realized through the use of fast-paced acoustic guitar, banjo, and percussion. This musical style is first heard in the film when the Serenity crew rob a bank on a remote planet. The reference to the small transport spaceship the crew rides on as a "mule," their weapons (revolvers holstered on belts), and sparse landscape evoke a visual composite of outlaws and isolated settlements reinforced by the musical accompaniment. The choice of portable instruments in the soundtrack parallels how Westerns often feature characters who, as with Serenity's crew, undertake dangerous and unpredictable work that necessitates a readiness to pack up and change locations relatively quickly (Goltz 2004: 210).

The generic and semiotic coding of score and instrumentation is used to visualize the Alliance in opposition to Serenity's crew. Whereas the acoustic score and cues sonically frame the latter as spontaneous and reliant on improvisation, the Alliance by contrast is associated with more formal orchestration. As Christopher Neal notes, "The large, organized musical forces under the centralized and relatively inflexible direction of a single conductor evoke a significantly different aesthetic" (2008: 193). These sonic aesthetics correspond with the Alliance, which is positioned as wanting to control populations, to the point of rendering them immobile, as in the final revelation of the Reavers' origins. On the planet Miranda, the crew discovers that the Alliance experimented with a bio-chemical called Pax intended to calm and make docile the population. The Pax was highly effective in that the population simply stopped working, eating, and breathing, dying en masse. The use of piano and instruments associated with classical orchestration during the scenes on Miranda reaffirm the danger of a political system based on centralized and hierarchical forms of control.

The other significant geographical landscape invoked by the future of *Serenity* is the Anglo-Sino fusion of cultural and political power. Whedon centered an American-Chinese amalgamation of language, dress, and architecture in the 'verse on the basis that these two contemporary world powers would likely merge (Sullivan 2004). The Alliance flag is "a modified Chinese flag superimposed over American stripes" (Wright 2004: 29). In conveying the sonic politics of this Anglo-Sino hyperpower, a semiotics of "Asian-ness" is mobilized to signal the former power's presence in the 'verse. As with the use of Irish and Scottish musical elements associated with the American West, Chinese power is represented through a broad combination of Asian ethnicities. In *Serenity*, the main musical site of Sino influence is a Japanese anime-style cartoon jingle that advertises Fruity Oaty Bars but has a hidden aural code used to brain-wash River. The jingle begins with a slow-paced sitar chord before breaking into a high-energy electro-pop song, with the vocals doubled, that is reminiscent of Japanese dance-pop. While this brief sonic reference indicates the Sino influence in the 'verse, it is spatially distant from the Serenity crew, and the Fruity Oaty Bars jingle serves to distract them narratively, leaving the Anglo portion of the Chinese-American fusion prominent.

For Leonard, the association of the Western genre with the Serenity crew creates a sonic politics whereby the television show, and by extension film, "portrays American colonialism through a nostalgic and thus uncritical soundscape that emphatically preserves the divisions between cultures" and reinforce Anglo-settlers "as 'native' to North American culture" (2010: 186). Moreover, the musical stylings of *Firefly* and *Serenity* convey the importance of an anti-authoritarian and improvisational mode of living as a heroic challenge to Alliance governance. This semiotic coding of the Western musical genre reinforces a normative view of American history that evacuates histories of Native American communities, who were very much under violent governmental control and fought valiantly to resist it (see Rand 2008, Miller 2010).

The nostalgic sonic politics associated with colonial-era America are muted somewhat in the film by David Newman's score which overwrites the acoustic cues with more orchestration and electronic music. The aural framing of Serenity in the introductory scene discussed above, through classical orchestral cues (which are a variation of the *Firefly* theme song), indicates that the sonic and thematic binary established in the television series between the Independents and the Alliance is more complicated in the film. The generic sonic elements of *Serenity* are used to teach viewers that the film's resolution hinges on the collaboration between its two lead characters, Mal and River. These characters each bring to Serenity their personal histories associated with the two opposing political forces in the 'verse. As a former Independent solider, Mal is framed by the guitar, fiddle, and banjo musical cues associated with the Western. The presence of River in the opening scenes is sprinkled with a delicate piano sound that connotes her previous upper class status and emphasizes the difficulty her brother Simon (Sean Maher) faces trying to move River and keep her away from the Alliance.

In comparison to Mal, River's musical accompaniment and the instruments used to score it are much less improvisational. Her cues suggest a characterization that has been forced into a set pattern which can only be modified through the reverb and distortion added to her sonic framing. River is also framed and isolated through visual and sonic cues associated with the science fiction variation on film noir's femme fatale. In several close-ups, when the audience is privy to dialogue spoken by River that the other characters cannot hear, piano notes refracted through reverb evoke mystery and danger. This signals to the audience that they should pay attention to River and highlights her importance to the narrative even when the other characters ignore her or walk out of her earshot.

If the musical score then creates a sonic politics where the Alliance and the Serenity crew are representative of the broader conflict between the Independents and the central government, Reavers, a roving band of exceptionally violent raiders, occupy an even more disruptive and ambiguous sonic space than River since they are hostile to both sides. Leonard describes the music that accompanies the Reavers in *Firefly* as "mechanical and barbaric—music without melody or harmony" (2010: 185). This indicates their inability to be assimilated into the sonic politics of either the Independents or the Alliance. Leonard suggests that the music score for the Reavers has an Orientalizing function that works to semiotically invoke "[t]he image of the violent Eastern Other" (185). Here she is drawing on the work of Edward Said, who in *Orientalism*, detailed how Euro-Western literature and art constituted a discursive formation of the Orient as a space of barbarity, regression, and sexual licentiousness (1979).

The film score is less Orientalizing than that of the television series partly because the Reavers have much less screen time and partly because of the final revelation that they are the product of an Alliance population management experiment gone awry. Through a beacon sent by one of the surviving scientists, the Serenity crew discover that Pax made the population so docile that they died. It had the opposite effect on a small subset of the population who became psychotic and are now known as Reavers. In the show, Leonard notes that the Reavers' exoticism is reflected in their sonic isolation: "There is little interaction between these spheres of musical representation" (2010: 185). However due to the narrative exigencies of *Serenity*, the Reavers are integrated into a plan to attack the Alliance which combines their musical score with both the Serenity crew and the Alliance. This gestures towards a more complex sonic politics than in the television show, as hearing the Reavers, Serenity's crew, and the Alliance together reduces the narrative, spatial, and ontological distance between them.

Despite its problematic colonial nostalgia and stereotypical treatment of Sino culture, the film's sonic politics are an attempt to situate improvisation as an embodied challenge to hierarchical control, which is sonically associated with atrophy and immobility. The film suggests that listening to a sonic politics of blended and collaborative interpretation means being exposed to disruption as a way of life.

Special Effects

The sound effects in *Serenity* are also used to convey the sonic politics of the central conflict in the film through the interplay of onscreen and offscreen diegetic sounds and generic stylings. Sound scholar Michael Chion theorized that one of the possibilities of film sound was the creation of "a special kind of character ... who exists in the diegetic space but is placed consistently offscreen" (qtd. in Buhler, Neumeyer, and Deemer 2010: 88). He called this character the acousmetre (meaning acoustical being), and it is inscribed with a certain power in the narrative, due to its ability to be heard and not seen. In the soundscape of the film, Serenity the ship acts as an acousmetre because despite our ability to see some parts of it, the consistent use of offscreen sound suggests a much larger space which the audience can conceive without fully seeing. This onscreen/offscreen sonic relationship emphasizes the power of the ship as a whole—as opposed to any individual part—which is also reflected in the film's themes that value camaraderie over singularity or individualism.

While power is ascribed to objects and people that are heard and not seen when we are positioned inside the ship, an inversion of this principle holds when we view the exterior of the ship in deep space because the ship does not produce any sound. As discussed earlier, when viewed for the first time, the ship slowly and silently floating across the screen is uncomfortable to watch, due to our expectations surrounding the interactions of sounds and objects to create filmic verisimilitude. Commentary from the filmmakers confirms the lack of aurality as a deliberate choice and attempt to represent an authentic diegetic space, as without air, sound cannot exist in outer space. Cranny-Francis notes in her reading of Chion that the mute "challenges the notions of boundaries ... and can appear omniscient because his/ her voice-lessness does not allow her/ him to be located" (2007: 99). Moreover, just as the mute "elicits doubt regarding what he knows and can do" and produces an "uncertainty about boundaries" (Chion 1999: 97–98), so too does the ship and the characters within it exemplify and benefit from the power of silence. For the crew of Serenity, the ability to remain literally un-locatable is immensely beneficial in keeping them out of the reach of the Alliance, and in the narrative of the film, its silence as invisibility allows them to hide from the Operative for the majority of the story. So depending on whether we are inside or outside the ship, Serenity can be read as both an acousmetre or as a mute—both boundary-less sonic figures which exist at the tension between being seen and heard, off-screen and onscreen. In both cases the notion of indefinability is inscribed with a positive sonic politics in opposition to the strict rules concerning visibility and conformity upheld by the Alliance.

The importance of sound effects in anchoring the audience to Serenity is further highlighted by the choice to place the final spaceship battle in between outer space and a planet's atmosphere, thus allowing sounds of the battle to be diegetically justified. Whedon says of this decision, "So we sort of—I don't want to say 'cheated,' because that would sound too true—but since we're not looking at the stars, since we're close to atmosphere, let's just turn this into a big loud scary battle so that we can experience what they're experiencing" (Kozak 2005). In order to let the audience experience the full sonic action of the battle and its affect on the characters, the location had to be a kind of pseudo-space (both a liminal space and not quite outer space) where the sounds of the aerial fighting could be heard. Whereas the choice to leave the spaceship sounds in the silence of deep space opens up different spatial and creative interpretations, locating the major battle scene in a part of space where sound can be heard both inside and outside the ship represents the filmmakers' recognition of the necessity for a strong connection between diegetic spaces and sound to facilitate the audience's understanding of the stakes in such a dramatic moment.

In his writing on sound and science fiction, William Whittington notes that genre interplay in science fiction makes it particularly adept at "medi-ating changes in reading codes and meaning production, while also redefining audience expectations and subjectivity" (2007: 4). As has been shown with the film's score, the filmmakers use the interplay of the sonic genre elements to emphasize the narrative tension between the characters. Mal and the crew of Serenity embody characteristics of the noble gunslingers from the Western genre, pitting their sporadic authenticity against the oppressive homogeneity of the Alliance that, made of advanced worlds and technology, is more closely aligned with the science fiction genre. The weapons the characters use are a key extension of this ideological opposition and the sound effects used to represent these weapons highlight how the filmmakers employ genre to position audiences in this confrontation.

For instance, Mal uses what looks like a mid-nineteenth century revolver that shoots with a traditional bang, with bullets that whiz by the characters and then ricochet with a "ping" off the metal surroundings of buildings and ships. These elements are recognizable as belonging to a library of sounds traditionally used in the Western genre. These effects are stereotypes of the genre and as such "serve the purpose of efficient communication whilst activating a rich network of inter-textual associations" (Flueckiger 2009: 160). In this way Mal can be viewed positively in association with the gunslingers of past Westerns, from John Wayne to Clint Eastwood, who were all adept at shooting the same types of guns quickly, efficiently, and heroically. So although these sounds ostensibly represent acts of violence, they are intertextually associated with nostalgia for the tropes of old Westerns, and the violence Mal enacts can be coded as acceptable and even heroic—despite his tendency to shoot several unarmed people throughout the film.

While Mal and the heroes of Westerns specialize in firing guns from a distance, by contrast, the weapon of choice deployed by the Operative is considerably more personal. We are first introduced to it in one of the opening scenes of the film when the Operative suggests that an Alliance scientist (Michael Hitchcock) should throw himself on a figurative sword, to which the scientist responds glibly, "Well unfortunately I forgot to bring a sword." In the next shot, the tip of the Operative's very real sword becomes visible and the scientist's words are cut off by the metallic "sound" of the weapon.

Even though the sword is inanimate and hasn't actually touched anything, it makes a high pitched metallic noise, as if it is being sharpened or perhaps drawn from an unseen sheath, giving a sense of not just the sword itself but also its sharp edge. The sword also makes similar (disassociated) noises when it swishes through the air and when someone is stabbed. As Barbara Flueckiger notes, "sound is essentially related to movement" and "must be adapted to the optical representation" (153).

In this example, the optical representation is a sharp metallic object, but its position within the space is represented by something more, in this case the sound of sharpening steel. The combination of the visual and the sonic creates what Chion refers to as "added value" which he explains as "the informative value" creating an impression that a sound "'naturally' comes from what is seen" (1990: 5). Although the sound of the sword is semiotically stereotypical, these elements are representative of a more complex use of sound that became increasingly common after the studio era soundtracks that dominated Westerns. The combined effect of seeming to bring an inanimate object to life with the contemporaneous sound/vision synchrony both futurizes the object of the sword and invokes an unsettling affect, coding the violence that the Operative enacts as negative, and in turn, reinforcing the narrative tension between the between the new (science fiction) and old (Western) ideals of the film.

It is worth noting that sonic representations of swords in general use similar elements in a variety of genres, but the way the Operative's blade is emphasized both visually and aurally specifically calls to mind genres which fetishize blades, namely the Samurai genre (see Silver 2005). This connection with the Samurai genre is further supported by the consistent reference to the Operative as an "assassin" as well as through the use of Sino culture as part of the *Serenity* 'verse. This association has the effect of Orientalizing the Operative, creating a problematic hierarchy whereby sonically not only is the Operative coded as negatively futuristic but also as a dangerous Other, who opposes both the Western genre itself and the Western genre values of Mal and the crew of Serenity.

It is not just what constitutes the sound effects of the weapons but also where the sound positions the audience in the space that reveals important thematic differences defining the characters in the film. These differences are emphasized by the sound effects associated with the characters' weapons and where the audience is spatially positioned in relation to their usage. For example, when Mal shoots his revolver, the audience is positioned aurally within his vicinity, meaning that although we clearly hear the sound of the gun being shot and sometimes see the person he shoots, we do not hear the sound of the person that was shot. Being aurally divorced from the impact of the violence Mal enacts makes it easier for the audience to view his actions as heroic. This is juxtaposed with the violence of the Operative, exercised through his sword, which is a close combat weapon. In distinction to Mal, the audience is positioned close enough to hear the sound of the sword plunging into the Operative's opponents/victims and also the disturbing noises they make as they die. These sounds are obviously horrifying and work to frame the Operative as ruthless and cold-blooded. Thus it is precisely the inter-personal zones constructed through aural spatiality that position the audience not only in the diegetic space of the film but also communicate the interpretive values attached to acts of violence as being acceptable or not.

Voice

The sonic landscapes evoked by the film's score, effects, and its generic associations with the Western are also reinforced through the use of voice. Like the generic associations of music score, voices in film and the way they are performed by actors and recorded by sound technology "make meaning by reference to a 'semiotic code' that viewers learn through their hours of film viewing" (Cranny-Francis 2007: 96). The tonal quality and accents of the characters' voices place their language in the Western genre with dialogue such as: "how come none of us knowed that?," "Conjure it's the reason they're after us," "I won't get 'et," and "You've got some storytelling to do." Grammatically incorrect use of present tense and colloquialisms invoke a pioneer lifestyle where working and surviving take priority over education and appropriate language. The cultivation of refined language and speech requires the luxury of study, which is why it is semiotically coded with upper class-ness. The Tam siblings, River and Simon, are differentiated from the rest of the Serenity crew through their Anglicized accents and avoidance of colloquialisms and invective. Including both types of voices within the opening soundscape of Serenity suggests that it is collaboration and being able to listen to different kinds of aurality that will enable contestation of the controlling homogeneity of the Alliance. As noted above, Mal's ability to hear River and work with her is important to the resolution of the narrative.

In the broader Sino-Anglo geopolitical landscape imagined in *Firefly* and *Serenity*, Alliance controlled spaces often feature elements of the former, and "Chinese" slang is sprinkled through everyday speech, even that of the Serenity crew. For instance, Mal threatens Simon after he punches him, saying: "Ni3 zhao3si3 ma5? Ni3 yao4 wo3 kailqiangl?"[1] While this use of Mandarin is intended to demonstrate the cultural permeation of Sino economic power throughout the 'verse (even the uneducated Serenity crew apparently understands Mandarin), as Kevin M. Sullivan points out, there is no universal Chinese dialect and making Mandarin (which is sometimes drawn from a Taiwanese dialect in the show and film) the spoken language invites a (possibly unintentional) political reading of Mandarin as the authoritative cultural-linguistic marker of Chinese-ness that removes Cantonese entirely from humanity's future. Moreover, the performance of this language by non-native speakers is conspicuous and often incorrect. The lack of attention to accurate pronunciation and fluency is reflective of an attempt to sonically connote "Chinese-ness" rather than seriously represent the language, which would be evident to Mandarin speakers in the audience. This is particularly problematic when, as Sullivan observes, fans of the 'verse mimic the characters in their bastardized Mandarin expressions (2004: 205). As a result, fans who are non–Mandarin speakers are performing "yellow-face" or "yellow-voice" (see Moon 2005), mimicking a foreign language in a way that could be construed as mocking because of its inaccuracy.

As the discussion of sound effects and weapons illustrates, space and a sense of spatiality are central to the ways sound operates and is heard. Arnt Maasø writes that "The ability of speech to signify a communicative relationship between a speaker and listener" depends on "the spatial relationship between speakers" (2008: 37). The establishment of "proxemic zones" (39) between speakers or objects are used similarly to shot ranges in order to demonstrate relationships between characters. For instance, the close visual distance between Mal and Zoe (Gina Torres) is reflected in the volume of their dialogue delivery, which can only be heard within a short proxemic zone, indicating their close relationship. The close proxemic zones established between the Operative and his victims are unnerving precisely because such zones are normally associated with intimacy rather than violence. River is often framed in sonic close-ups that establish her isolation from the rest of the characters. Indeed, she often speaks directly to the audience in the absence of proxemic zones with other characters.

Proxemic zones not only serve to establish the spatial dimensions of voice and the relationships between characters and within space but also carry semiotic codes about appropriate bodily behavior. The audience is made aware of River's deteriorating mental health through the presence of multiple voices associated with her body. Within ableist conceptions of embodiment (see Mitchell and Synder 2015), a unified subjectivity is signified by a coherent identity and voice. Because voice in the singular is associated with normative conceptions of subjectivity, an excess of voices signifies multiple subjectivities existing in the same body—an ontological impossibility within Western liberal humanism. Where an excess of voice is read as a bodily disorder, the absence of voice is read as an absence of subjectivity. Thus the lack of voice can be associated with a lack of humanity in film mediations as with the case of the Reavers in *Serenity*. Their monstrosity is reflected in their lack of ability to speak clearly or be intelligently heard. As noted above, the mute challenges boundaries not only because of their silence but also because normal modes of cognition are associated with speech. There are political implications to the normalized association of voice with embodiment, as Sterne notes: "Voice has long been conflated with ideas of agency in political theory" and many political movements (2012: 9), such as feminism or black civil rights—indeed, the lack of any Native American accents or words completely evacuates this community from the American history alluded to in *Firefly* and *Serenity*. River's return to "normalcy" and political efficacy is signified by her unified voice and adoption of appropriate proxemic zones when speaking to other characters.

While the sonic portrayal of the Reavers is problematic in the context of their depiction in *Firefly*, where they are Othered as monstrous and separate from humanity, *Serenity* is able to complicate their portrayal by virtue of being able to contextualize their origins. As noted, we discover in *Serenity* that the Reavers are the product of a bio-engineering experiment gone awry, rendering their ontological distance to the humans in the show much more proximate than originally thought. Further, through River's association with the Reavers, in terms of the narrative and her crossing of multiple borders of class, gender, embodiment, and subjectivity, the film gestures towards a sonic politics that stresses the importance of listening to the voices of others, particularly the voices of suffering women. The Anglo-American pronunciation of "River" has an aural similarity to that of "Reaver," suggesting a tonal collapsing of the outcomes of the Alliance's imprisonment of and experimentation on River and their biopolitical intervention into the population of Miranda, some of whom later become Reavers.

The film's final resolution hinges on the Serenity crew's willingness to sacrifice their lives to play a recording of the final surviving scientist from Miranda (Sarah Paulson). Interestingly, despite the recording being audio-visual, Whedon chooses to focus on the voice of the character and what she is saying rather than the violence inflicted on her by the Reavers as her message ends. Ultimately, the crew are hopeful that the proliferation of this message and maximizing the amount of people who will hear it can enable political resistance and change to the existing forms of governance in the 'verse. This most visually daring of genres, science fiction, boasts an entry in *Serenity* that places the utmost faith on the aural power of voice to affect the future.

Conclusion

Our analysis of *Serenity* seeks to demonstrate the importance of soundscapes and sonic elements in positioning the audience in spaces within the narrative of the film. As with visual language, these sonic spaces are laden with semiotic constructions that produce meaning and reinforce the politics of the film. In this way, the Alliance's battle for control of space and agency that is disrupted by the actions of the crew of Serenity is echoed in the tension between interior and exterior soundscapes, Western and science fiction genre aesthetics, off-screen and onscreen sounds, normal and abnormal proxemic zones, and speaking and voicelessness. By investigating these sites of tension we can more thoroughly understand how sound is used to elicit specific intertextual and semiotic responses from the audience. However, while many films present clear spaces and monolithic subject positions to reach visual/aural synchrony, *Serenity* is able to achieve a critical sonic politics involving complex narrative, thematic, and spatial representations through which the audience is invited to view noise as a site for collaboration, listening, and resistance.

NOTE

1. This is taken from Kevin Sullivan's website (2014) which provides translations of the Mandarin used in *Serenity* (as well as *Firefly*). The language appears to be Taiwan Mandarin. The English subtitles on my DVD copy of *Serenity* (region 2, 4) simply say, "[Chinese speaking]," and there are no Mandarin options for subtitles. As noted in the essay, such production and distribution practices indicate a lack of attention to accurate Mandarin and Mandarin-speaking audiences, reinforcing the Orientalized and aural stereotypes of Asian-ness present in the film.

WORKS CITED

Adams Wright, Leigh. (2004). "Asian Objects in Space," in Jane Espenson (ed.) *Finding Serenity: Anti-Heroes, Lost Shepherds and Space Hookers in Joss Whedon's* Firefly. Dallas: BenBella Books, 29–35.

Buhler James, David Neumeyer, and Rob Deemer. (2010). *Hearing the Movies: Music and Sound in Film History*. New York: Oxford University Press.

Chion, Michael. (1990). *Audio-Vision*. Claudia Gorbman (ed.). Trans. Claudia Gorbman. New York: Columbia University Press.

_____. (1999). *The Voice in Cinema*. New York: Columbia University Press.

Cranny-Francis, Anne. (2007). "Mapping Cultural Auracy: The Sonic Politics of *The Day the Earth Stood Still*," in *Social Semiotics* 17.1: 87–110.

Flueckiger, Barbara. (2009). "Sound Effects: Strategies for Sound Effects in Film," in Graeme Harper, Ruth Doughty and Jochen Eisentraut (eds.) *Sound and Music in Film and Visual Media: A Critical Overview*. New York: Continuum, 151–179.

Goltz, Jennifer. (2004). "Listening to *Firefly*," in Jane Espenson (ed.) *Finding Serenity: Anti-Heroes, Lost Shepherds and Space Hookers in Joss Whedon's* Firefly. Dallas: BenBella Books, 209–215.

Granade, S. Andrew. (2011). "'So Here's Us, On the Raggedy Edge': Exoticism and Identification in Joss Whedon's *Firefly*," in *Popular Music and Society* 34.5: 621–637.

Hung, Eric. (2011). "The Meaning of 'World Music' in *Firefly*," in Kendra Preston Leonard (ed.) *Buffy, Ballads, and Bad Guys Who Sing: Music in the Worlds of Joss Whedon*. Lanham, MD: Scarecrow Press, 255–73.

Kozak, Jim. (2005). "Serenity Now!," in *Focus Magazine*, August/September.

Leonard, Kendra Preston. (2010). "'The Future Is the Past': Music and History in *Firefly*," in David C. Wright, Jr., and Allan W. Austin (eds.) *Space and Time: Essays on Visions of History in Science Fiction and Fantasy Television*. Jefferson: McFarland, 174–188.

Maasø, Arnt. (2008). "The Proxemics of the Mediated Voice," in Jay Beck and Tony Grajeda (eds.) *Lowering the Boom: Critical Studies in Film Sound*. Urbana: University of Illinois Press, 36–50.

Miller, Robert J. (2010). "The Doctrine of Discovery," in Robert J. Miller, Jacinta Ruru, Larissa Behrendt and Tracey Lindberg (eds.) *Discovering Indigenous Lands: The Doctrine of Discovery in the English Colonies*. Oxford: Oxford University Press, 1–25.

Mitchell, David T., and Sharon L. Synder. (2015). *The Biopolitics of Disability: Neoliberalism, Ablenationalism, and Peripheral Embodiment*. Ann Arbor: University of Michigan Press.

Moon, Krystyn. (2005). *Yellowface: Creating the Chinese in American Popular Music and Performance, 1850s–1920s*. London: Rutgers University Press.

Neal, Christopher. (2008). "Marching Out of Step: Music and Otherness in the *Firefly/Serenity* Saga," in Rhonda. V. Wilcox and Tanya R. Cochran (eds.) *Investigating* Firefly and Serenity: *Science Fiction on the Frontier*. London: I.B. Tauris, 191–200.

Pelkey, Stanley C. II (2011). "'Still Flyin'?: Conventions, Reversals, and Musical Meaning in

Firefly," in Kendra Preston Leonard (ed.) *Buffy, Ballads, and Bad Guys Who Sing: Music in the Worlds of Joss Whedon*. Lanham, MD: Scarecrow Press, 209–242.

Rand, Jacki Thompson. (2008). *Kiowa Humanity and the Invasion of the State*. Lincoln: University of Nebraska Press.

Said, Edward W. (1979). *Orientalism*. New York: Penguin.

Schafer, M.R. (1977). *The Soundscape: Our Sonic Environment and the Tuning of the World*. Rochester, VT: Destiny Books.

Silver, Alain. (2005). *The Samurai Film*. New York: Overlook Press.

Sterne, Jonathan. (2012). "Sonic Imaginations," in Jonathan Sterne (ed.) *The Sound Studies Reader*. Abingdon: Routledge, 1–18.

Sullivan, Kevin M. (2004). "Chinese Words in the 'Verse," in Jane Espenson (ed.) *Finding Serenity: Anti-Heroes, Lost Shepherds and Space Hookers in Joss Whedon's* Firefly. Dallas: BenBella Books, 197–207.

_____. (2014). "*Serenity* (Movie)," in *Firefly-Serenity Chinese Pinyinary*. On-line. Available HTTP: http://fireflychinese.kevinsullivansite.net/title/serenitymovie.html (10 September 2017).

Whedon, Joss. (2005). *Serenity*: Film Commentary. 20th Century FOX Home Entertainment. DVD.

About the Contributors

Eric **Benson** is an associate professor and chair of graphic design at the University of Illinois at Urbana-Champaign. He is cofounder of Re-nourish, LTD, and his design work has been seen at the Walker Art Center and the Smithsonian Cooper Hewitt National Design Museum, among others. He is the author of *Design to Renourish.*

Frederick **Blichert** is an independent scholar, journalist and film critic. His writing has appeared in *VICE, Paste Magazine, CBC, Senses of Cinema,* and *Bright Lights Film Journal.* He is the author of a monograph on *Serenity* from Columbia University Press.

London **Brickley** is an instructor in the University of Missouri–Columbia's English Department. Her research interests include depictions of science, sexuality, and monstrosity across media. She has worked as a script editor supervisor, production consultant, assistant director, and special effects artist.

Agnes B. **Curry** is a professor of philosophy at the University of Saint Joseph in Connecticut. Her research interests include how art conveys meaning and the intersections of philosophy and pop culture. She has published articles on *Buffy the Vampire Slayer, Firefly,* and fairy tales.

Aviva **Dove-Viebahn** is an associate professor at Arizona State University. She is web content manager for the Society for Cinema and Media Studies and a contributing editor to the Scholar Writing Program for *Ms.* magazine. She has published on Ridley Scott, *CSI, Mad Men,* and *The L Word* and is the coeditor of *Gender, Race and Class.*

Max **Ferguson** is a registered nurse and student in the dual master of public heath/ master of science in nursing program at the University of British Columbia in Vancouver. They have worked as a street nurse and in various youth mental health programs. Their research interests include health equity, gender, and homelessness.

Erin **Giannini** is an independent scholar who specializes in television studies. Her research focuses on portrayals of corporate culture on television, particularly in the works of Joss Whedon. She has also published on *Supernatural, Dollhouse, Heroes,* and *Mystery Science Theater 3000.* She is a TV editor at PopMatters Media.

Ina Rae **Hark** is a distinguished professor emerita of English and film and media studies at the University of South Carolina. She is the author of numerous scholarly articles and books, including *Deadwood* and *Star Trek*, and editor or coeditor of collections *American Cinema of the 1930s*, *Exhibition*, *The Road Movie Book* and *Screening the Male*.

Joel **Hawkes** is a lecturer in English literature at the University of Victoria in Canada. His work focuses on the physical and literary spaces we inhabit. He has published on the works of Joss Whedon, including contributions to *Joss Whedon's Dollhouse*, *The Comics of Joss Whedon* and *Joss Whedon and Race*.

H.S. **Hobma** is an independent scholar whose research focuses on death positivity and medieval feminism. She has researched site interpretation and visitor experience at rural cultural heritage sites in southern Scotland. Her interests include *Firefly*, augmented reality, pornographic medieval literature, and the *Star Trek* universe.

Andrew **Howe** is a professor of history at La Sierra University in California. He has published numerous articles and book chapters on film and popular culture, including on cultural artifacts in *Game of Thrones*, the role of cemeteries and burial rites in the Western genre, and the transformation of the Mohican myth in *Avatar*.

S. Evan **Kreider** is an associate professor of philosophy at the University of Wisconsin, Fox Valley. He is the author of numerous scholarly articles on pop culture and philosophy, including essays on *Firefly*, *Dollhouse*, *The X-Files*, and *Mr. Robot*. He also coedited *The Philosophy of Joss Whedon*.

Arthur J. **Randell** is an independent scholar whose research and writing interests include film and television analysis in visual representation and culture as well as audience reception studies. He has published on these topics in the edited collection *Television Aesthetics and Style*.

Holly **Randell-Moon** is a senior lecturer in communication and media at the University of Otago in New Zealand. She has published on popular culture, biopower, gender and sexuality and race, religion, and secularism. She is the coeditor of *Security, Race, Biopower*.

Renee **St. Louis** teaches critical thinking and research writing at Southwestern College, City College of San Diego, and National University. She has authored essays on film and television for *Slayage* and other journals, and written a chapter on *Dollhouse* in the upcoming anthology *War in the Whedonverse*.

K. Brenna **Wardell** is an assistant professor of film and literature at the University of North Alabama. Her research focuses on gender and sexuality, aesthetics, and place and space in media and literary texts. Her publications include articles on Joss Whedon and a piece on Alfred Hitchcock's film *Frenzy*.

Index